Please renew/return this item by the last date shown.

From Area codes 01923 or 020:	From Area codes of Herts:
Renewals: 01923 471373	01438 737373
Enquiries: 01923 471333	01438 737333
Textphone: 01923 471599	01438 737599

www.hertsdirect.org/librarycatalogue

STE

Great Hoaxers,
Artful Fakers and
CHEATING
CHARLATANS

Great Hoaxers, Artful Fakers and
CHEATING CHARLATANS

Nigel Blundell
& Sue Blackhall

True Crime

First Published in Great Britain in 2009
Wharncliffe Books
an imprint of
Pen and Sword Books Limited,
47 Church Street, Barnsley,
South Yorkshire. S70 2AS

Copyright © Nigel Blundell & Sue Blackhall, 2009

ISBN: 978 1 844680 63 4

Typeset in Plantin and Benguiat by
Pen and Sword Books Ltd

Printed in the United Kingdom by
CPI Antony Rowe, Chippenham, Wiltshire

Pen & Sword Books Ltd incorporates the imprints of
Pen & Sword Aviation, Pen & Sword Maritime,
Pen & Sword Military, Wharncliffe Local History, Pen & Sword Select,
Pen & Sword Military Classics, Leo Cooper, Remember When, Seaforth Publishing
and Frontline Publishing

For a complete list of Pen & Sword titles please contact:
PEN & SWORD BOOKS LIMITED
47 Church Street, Barnsley, South Yorkshire, S70 2AS, England.
E-mail: enquiries@pen-and-sword.co.uk
Website: www.pen-and-sword.co.uk

Contents

Introduction

A famous fraudster once averred: 'There's a sucker born every minute.' The quotation is generally attributed to one of the greatest tricksters of all time, Phineas T. Barnum, but was in fact stolen from one of his competitors. Which just goes to prove the point.

And in Barnum's case, as with all the other hoaxers, hucksters, fakes and fraudsters who followed him down the ages, no phrase better describes the art of deception.

Gathered in this book are a diverse assembly of them: some suave and charming, others with far less appealing characteristics. But what they have in common is a single-minded determination to get one over on the unwary and the unsuspecting.

Among the phoneys who had a field day at the expense of others were television quiz show contestants caught out cheating before audiences of millions.

More tragic was the case of yachtsman Donald Crowhurst, whose dreams of glory ended with the sad sailor paying the ultimate price for his pride.

Then there was Anna Anderson, the fake royal who falsely assumed an illustrious lineage. And Joyce Hatto was the phantom pianist whose magical music was the work of others.

There were also art forgers who delighted in conning the cognoscenti. And there were those with more mundane ambitions: to be loved, to be rich or simply to be respected.

Together they make up our astonishingly varied gallery of fakers, forgers, charlatans and cheats, with a few hoaxers and pranksters practising their tricks along the way.

Eventually most of them were exposed and sometimes caught, but not before they succeeded in making a fool of someone, and often gaining from their downfall. And, of course, the richer or more self-important the victims, the more satisfying the sting.

There are other powerful motives apart from greed that lure the unwary. Lust is a strong one, laziness is another, ambition often plays a part.

But they are all fair game for the hoaxers, whose traps are often set for no other reason than to satisfy a driving sense of adventure.

Various motives may link the disparate bunch of characters you'll meet in this book but they have one thing in common... the astonishingly brazen way in which they have pulled off their fantastic fakery while pulling the wool over the eyes of the rest of us!

Chapter 1

The 9/11 Liar Who Fell to Earth

N o one will forget the chilling images of September 11, 2001: New York's World Trade Center blown to pieces by airplanes hijacked by terrorists. The flames, the terror, the falling bodies.

The dead were many, the survivors dazed by their escape. It was no wonder that what was to be known forever as simply '9/11' spawned incredible stories of selflessness, courage, heroism and conquest of adversity at its extreme.

The tales of survival were vivid and heartbreaking. So many horrors witnessed. So many memories raw. But all made compulsive listening.

One of these tales came from Tania Head, her account making her one of only nineteen survivors who had been at or above the point of impact when the two planes hit. The story she told deeply moved audiences and the groups she led around 'Ground Zero' in tours for the Tribute World Trade Center Visitor Center.

Her tour would always start with the same words: 'My name is Tania and I'm going to be your tour guide today. I was there at the Towers. I'm a survivor. I'm going to tell you about that.'

Head would then go on to tell her story in great detail. 'We heard very loud sounds coming from outside our meeting room in the South Tower. I saw a plane about 113 feet away. It hit the North Tower. The fire was so intense that the windows of my tower were too hot to touch. I saw people begin to jump from the North Tower. It wasn't just one. It wasn't just two…

'This woman started saying, 'There's another plane coming! There's another plane coming!' We didn't believe her at first. The tip of the wing tore through the crowded lobby. The first thing you feel is a tremendous increase in pressure, all the air being sucked out of you lungs. The next thing you feel is flying through the air.'

Burned, bleeding, nearly blinded by dust, she struggled towards the stairway. 'Blood. Body parts. I crawled through all that. I realised that everybody around me was dying.'

Of seeing a member of the New York Fire Department, Head said: 'I always like to say that, for me, it was like seeing God. It was like, 'Okay, we're going to make it.''

The firefighter continued up towards Head's stranded co-workers and she managed to reach the street. 'That was it for me. I woke up in a hospital five days later. Those of us who were here always talk about how blue the sky was. What I witnessed there I will never forget. It was a lot of death and destruction, but I also saw hope.'

As one who witnessed a Head tour said: 'One way that Head has learned to cope with her own loss and horror is to tell her story to those who come to the Tribute Center. She stood by the entrance with a beautiful smile that is her ultimate message to everyone these five years later.

'To behold Head's smile is to know the terrorists did not come even close to winning. To see that smile is also to be challenged to be as decent and positive as this true survivor. She will tell you, 'If I get sad and cry, then everybody cries. You have to keep that smile coming.''

Tania Head's story was indeed, like that of all the survivors, a dramatic one. An employee of investment company Merrill Lynch, she was helping to close a merger on the 96th floor of the South Tower when the first plane struck at 8.46am. Reaching an express elevator, she was thrown to the floor when the second plane struck. Badly burned, Head crawled along the floor. At one point, she came across a dying man who handed her his wedding ring. She kept her promise to him and returned it to his widow some months later.

The last memories Head has of that dreadful day is recovering consciousness to find a young man, Welles Crowther, patting out the flames on her clothes. She later learned that, tragically, her fiancé working in the North Tower had not survived.

Head's story hit the headlines across the world. It made her an obvious choice for Chairman of the 9/11 Living Memorial

Survivors' Committee, to serve on the board of a foundation set up in her fiancé's memory and the board of the WTC Widows Social Group. She also co-founded the World Trade Center Survivors Network, at one time serving as its President. With so much knowledge and personal experience, Head became a tireless worker for survivors and family members of other disasters including the tsunami in Thailand and Hurricane Katrina in Louisiana.

Or, quite simply, *did she*?

Six years after the World Trade Center atrocity, with emotion levelling out and the dust settling on many people's lives, someone dared to suggest that perhaps the story Tania Head had told was not true.

Looking back now, it seems incredible that every aspect of her story was accepted without question; but that all those Head said she knew did not know *her*...

Merrill Lynch, the company she said she worked for, had no record of her. The family of her fiancé, a man called 'Dave' – his full name was always kept secret – had never heard him talk about her, even though the couple's courtship had supposedly been a particularly romantic one.

According to Head, they had met when they were fighting over a taxi and Head had torn up Dave's business card in a fury. They then bumped into each other again at a business meeting and started dating. The couple had 'committed' themselves to each other in Hawaii but their official wedding was to be held in New York in October 2001.

Head later related that it was the thought of this day and the dress she would wear that kept her going during the 9/11 horror. Subsequently, she attended three 9/11 anniversaries with a miniature yellow cab and flowers to commemorate her lover and how they had met. Yet Dave's parents and flatmate said they were unaware of any such relationship and said he had never even been to Hawaii.

The doubts about Head's story came after the *New York Times* reported that it had tried to interview her three times about her experience to mark the sixth anniversary of the attack in 2007. She had cancelled each time saying she needed to protect her privacy and that she was suffering from 'emotional turmoil'. She also refused to provide more details to validate her account of her 9/11 experience.

This in turn prompted the newspaper to approach all those Head had dealings with to request that they also ask her for more information. Head either refused to answer their questions or gave information that contradicted any she had given earlier. This included the reason that she was in the World Trade Center that fateful day. She told the family of Welles Crowther that she was working on the mergers team at Merrill Lynch, yet told others she was in the building to apply for an internship.

Involving Mr Crowther in her dubious tale was particularly cruel. He had become a hero of 9/11, credited with rescuing a number of people from the South Tower before losing his own life. While saving others, he wore a red bandana his father had given him to filter smoke should he ever get caught in a fire.

His mother, Alison Crowther, said of Head's story: 'She never shared those details and it was nothing we wanted to probe. I felt it was too private and painful for her.' The young man's father, Jefferson Crowther told the pitiful story of how he and his wife had arranged to have dinner with Head in a private dining room at a club because she said she was uneasy about meeting in public.

'During that dinner she said she still had her burned clothing and was going to send us a piece of it on a plaque since it was the last thing our son had touched,' recalled Mr Crowther. 'She explained that her clothes were on fire and that our son took a jacket and put out the flames. She told us she said, 'Don't leave me', and he replied, 'I won't. Don't worry, I'll get you down.' She seemed so heartfelt and genuine about what she said to us.'

Few people had previously even thought to ask who the man was who gave Head his wedding ring, or the name of his family. The name of the hospital where Head was treated was never given either, or the identities of any of the people with her in the South Tower. And 'Dave's Children Foundation', which Ms Head said she had established in his memory, did not seem to exist.

Janice Cilento, a social worker on the board of the Survivors' Network came forward to say that Head's stories seemed to change.

She said Head had told a different version of her life with Dave, relating now that they had only known each other for a few months and that their relationship had been kept secret from his family. Previously, Ms Cilento said, Head had told her that she knew Dave's family well and that the couple had been living together for some time. And most recently, Head had admitted to her in a phone conversation that her relationship with Dave had been a fantasy.

Said Ms Cilento: 'I've heard her story over and over and I've been there anytime she needed someone to listen, even if it was at three in the morning. She has stolen my time and my soul. We have members who thought Tania's trauma was so extreme they did not want to discuss their own. They gave their time to help her and she didn't even need it. Many of the network members feel very upset and betrayed.'

Even Head's life before 9/11 was a mystery. Her claims of having degrees from Harvard and Stanford were challenged when neither institute could find any record of her. Her other credentials looked in doubt too – that she had worked in Britain, Argentina, France, Singapore and the Netherlands, that she was the daughter of a diplomat and that she was a 'senior vice president for strategic alliances for an investment think tank'. And there was only Head's word that she had gone to Thailand and Louisiana to help the disaster victims.

Initially, Head's supporters were quick to say she had given a 'gentle face and passionate voice' to the survivors of the tragedy. They said they had seen the scars and marks on her arm that Head said she had sustained in the terrorist attack. But they did confess that they knew nothing about her before September 2001.

Head's work with the Survivors' Network, of which she became a board member then president, had begun in 2002 when one of its founders, Gerry Bogacz, said he had heard about her creating an Internet group for survivors. He had no reason to doubt any of what Head had to say.

'We had a long e-mail conversation over a two-month period before we met and shared our experiences,' said Mr Bogacz, who, quite genuinely, did escape the turmoil of the North Tower. 'The constellation of her experiencing the plane crashing into the 78th floor and her fiancé being in the other Tower and getting killed was just amazing.'

Such certainties began to crumble when the *New York Times* began unearthing inconsistencies and 'falsehoods' in Head's stories. No one on the newspaper was surprised when Head found herself an attorney, Stephanie Furgana Adwar, who told them: 'With regard to the veracity of my client's story, neither my client nor I have any comment.' More tellingly, Head went to great pains to add that she had not acted illegally or gained financially from anything she had done.

One of the difficulties for investigative journalists in finding any information about Head was, quite simply, because that was not her real name.

During the revelations about her dishonesty, a Barcelona newspaper, *La Vanguardia*, reported that Head had been known there as Alicia Esteve Head. Her father was not a diplomat. Her family was well known in another way, however. Her father and brother had served prison terms for their roles in a financial scandal in Catalonia in 1992.

This information apparently came from a wealthy family in Barcelona for whom Head had worked as a secretary. They said the scars on her arm had been there long before the Twin Towers horror. Head had told them that they had been caused in a high-speed crash in a Ferrari, adding: 'After the accident they had to look for my arm and re-attach it.'

Eventually, the board of the Survivors' Network voted to remove Head as president and as director of the group. Richard Zimbler, who took over her post, declared: 'The sense of betrayal is profound. We were, I thought, close friends and what she has done is not just betrayed our friendship but also the whole September 11 community. There was no reason to doubt her story. She looked the part. She had a badly injured arm that appeared to have scars and her story was very, very realistic. And why would I question the veracity of the chairperson of the organisation?'

Officials of the Tribute Center said she would no longer be doing volunteer work for them as a Ground Zero tour guide. The reason given was that 'at this time we are unable to confirm the veracity of her connection to the events of September 11'.

Many people were let down by Head's life of fantasy. Jefferson Crowther, the father of real hero Welles Crowther, found it hard to hide his hurt. 'The lady appeared to be truthful and honest. We had no reason to disbelieve what she was saying. We are mystified by the inconsistencies and feel badly for the survivors, the Network where she was a president and the Tribute Center where she worked.' He added: 'None of this detracts from what Welles did. If anything, it again brings light to the bravery and selflessness he displayed.'

The big question then became: if Head did not benefit financially from her web of lies, just why did she do it? Was it all simply to gain attention for herself? Robert Feldman, a psychology professor at the University of Massachusetts, said: 'This woman got a lot of attention and sympathy. Very often when people lie, they embellish more and more and can't walk away from it. They back themselves into a corner and become increasingly trapped by the lie.'

Bella DePaulo, Professor of Psychology at the University of California, offered her theories: 'The first thing that jumped out at me was that this is someone who was not in it for the money. So often, people think of liars as crass and materialistic, and lots of them are. But this woman is someone who is into it for something much deeper. She was someone who cared about the emotional rewards; the psychological rewards; the impersonal rewards. She wanted what most liars want when they tell their lies, which is to change the way other people look at them. To have them be loved and respected, and valued and cared for.'

New York Mayor Rudy Giuliani put it more simply: 'Never in my wildest dreams would I have ever thought any part of her story wasn't true.'

It says something of the enormity of the September 11 trauma and how it affected the people of America that Head's stories were believed without the need to verify them. For a country already reeling from their worst terrorist attack in history, her taking advantage of that horror, and all those so deeply wounded by it, will leave bitter memories for all time.

Chapter 2

Tragedy of 'the Marvellous Boy'

It is rare that the exploits of a fraudster or forger should have a tragic ending. The most their victims may suffer is financial loss and great embarrassment, while the tricksters themselves know the risks they run and often even revel in the scandal that follows when they are exposed. This was not the case, however, for poor Thomas Chatterton, perhaps the saddest of history's forgers. He was just seventeen years of age when he died, driven to suicide by a series of events brought on by his deceptions and feelings of worthlessness. It was therefore tragically ironic that Chatterton was immortalised by the poet William Wordsworth as 'the Marvellous Boy'.

Thomas Chatterton was born in Bristol on November 20, 1752, his schoolmaster father having died three months before his son's birth. Thomas's mother, left in poverty with two children to support, was forced to turn her hand to needlework to earn a living. From an early age, Thomas was difficult, moody and a bit of a bully – but a child prodigy. He was a bookworm, from the age of seven devouring works on such subjects as heraldry, music and astronomy. When he was eight, Thomas won a place a Colston's Hospital, a charity school for boys who were destined to become apprentices. This institution, housed in a former priory, first provided Thomas with his curiosity about the Middle Ages, for the boys had to have partly shaved heads and their uniform was a long coat and yellow stockings, styled very much on mediaeval fashions.

Thomas was not happy at the school. He found it boring, became the school rebel and made it clear his mind needed more stimulation than that his tutors offered. He began to spend time alone and, at the age of eleven, was writing serious poetry. There was only one teacher he had any time for: a young apprentice called Thomas Phillips, whom the young Chatterton was forever trying to impress, and it was this that led to his first poetic forgery.

Chatterton's free time was spent at the ancient church of St Mary Redcliffe, where his uncle was sexton. He could happily spend hours there, gazing at the mediaeval tombs and carvings, and running his fingers over their intricate forms. With his fascination for the Middle Ages, Chatterton began to believe he had been born into the wrong era. He felt more comfortable sitting in the quiet solitude of the church's graveyard, casting his mind back to the Fifteenth Century and imagining what life was like then. And so, one morning as he sat pondering beside the tombs of the long-dead, Chatterton decided to 'reincarnate' one of their number: Thomas Rowley, priest and poet of the 1400s, who actually had lived in Bristol around that time.

The man Chatterton so respected, Thomas Phillips, was the recipient of the first of many poems supposedly written by Thomas Rowley. Chatterton had of course penned it himself but claimed to have found it among other documents in a parish monument chest in the church he so frequently visited. In fact, such a chest did exist but its contents of manuscripts and parchments from the Fifteenth Century were used only as aids for Chatterton's clever forgery.

Chatterton called his first poem *Elinoure and Juga*. His spidery lines written in brown ink purported to be a dialogue between two girls who lament the death of their lovers in the Wars of the Roses and end up drowning themselves. Deception aside, it was a remarkable piece of work from a boy of Chatterton's age. What was more, it earned him the attention he craved.

When he was fourteen, Chatterton met a local self-made man, a pewter manufacturer named Henry Burgum, who was anxious to trace his family tree. Chatterton 'discovered' old parchments in St Mary Redcliffe Church which included the 'de Bergham' coat of arms and a family tree tracing the Burgums back to the Norman Conquest. He also 'found' a poem by his good friend Thomas Rowley that mentioned a knight called Johan de Berghamme. Adding a bit more colour to his discoveries, he included a branch of his own family that had intermarried with the de Berghams. It had all taken Chatterton time to create but he was well rewarded when a delighted Henry Burgum placed five shillings in his hand. And when Chatterton was introduced to Burgum's partner, George Catcott, he too was the delighted recipient of some of Thomas Rowley's poems.

By now, Chatterton had well and truly slipped into the art of skilful deception. And so, when he met a well-known surgeon called William Barrett who was compiling a work on the history of Bristol, the young forger was more than happy to help. Thus various old parchments and plans of Bristol were 'discovered'. Chatterton found Barrett a stimulating conversationalist as he, a teenager, swapped historical information with the eminent surgeon old enough to be his father. Equally, Barrett made it obvious that he thought highly of the boy. So Chatterton gave him a special token of gratitude: more poems by that Fifteenth Century priest Thomas Rowley. Chatterton also endeared himself to the proud burghers of Bristol by 'discovering' further Rowley works that praised the city and criticised 'cowarde Londonne'.

Chatterton left school when he was sixteen and was apprenticed to a local lawyer, John Lambert, whom he detested. The work was dull for someone with as sharp a mind and appetite for learning as the young lad. He spent his hours copying legal documents, wistfully yearning for a more challenging and rewarding way of life. The only respite from tedium he enjoyed was in the evenings, when he really came into his own. He had gathered a good coterie of friends around him and, already a promising poet, took great pleasure in writing verses to be presented to local girls of his acquaintance.

As a sideline, the bored clerk undertook an interesting escapade when a new footbridge was opened over a river. Chatterton arrived at the offices of the local newspaper with an account of a mayor first crossing the old bridge in 1248. He said he had copied it from a parchment removed by his father from St Mary Redcliffe Church. The newspaper readily published the supposedly historical account.

Only two friends, John Rudhall and Edward Gardner, to whom Chatterton had shown the art of 'ageing' documents, knew the truth. They saw no reason to spoil the local newspaper's pleasure at such a historic discovery. But Gardner later related: 'He would rub a parchment in several places in streaks with yellow ochre, then rub it several times on the ground, which was dirty, and afterwards crumple it in his hand saying that was how to antiquate it.'

The fake Thomas Rowley works that Chatterton produced were written in a pseudo-mediaeval style which seemed genuine enough to local experts who examined them. The language of such poems was not authentic, however, and they were inspired not by mediaeval poets but by Tudor writers like William Shakespeare and Edmund Spenser. Chatterton either invented mediaeval words or found them in dictionaries. Nevertheless, his work, such as the few lines below, convinced Bristol historians they were in possession of important literary discoveries.

When Freedom dreste, yn blodde steyned veste
To everie knyghte her warre songe sunge
Uponne her hedde, wyld wedes were spredde,
A gorie anlace bye her honge.

Chatterton had several of his own works accepted by magazines in 1769, which encouraged him to try to get the Rowley poems published, but without success. He then decided to approach Horace Walpole, author of the 1764 romantic novel *Castle of Otranto*, his translation of a 16th Century Italian romance. The forger presented the great man with *A History of Painting in England* – or *The Ryse of Peyncteyne yn Englande* as it was titled – by one T. Rowleie. Walpole agreed to publish the Rowley manuscripts but became suspicious when he discovered that his correspondent was only sixteen years of age, was from a poor background and was demanding money for his 'discoveries'. Walpole sought the advice of two acquaintances, one being the eminent poet Thomas Gray, and both expressed the opinion that the manuscripts were forgeries.

Walpole wrote to Chatterton suggesting he continue working for John Lambert and that he forget his aspirations to be a great writer. The rejection devastated the teenager. He requested the return of his manuscripts in a bitter reply to Walpole which ran: 'Though I am but sixteen years of age, I have lived long enough to see that poverty attends literature. I am obliged to you, sir, for your advice and will go a little beyond it, by destroying all my useless lumber of literature and by never using my pen but in law.'

Further enraged at neither receiving the courtesy of a reply nor the return of his manuscripts, Chatterton wrote to Walpole again: 'I cannot reconcile your behaviour to me with the notions I once entertained of you. I think myself injured, sir, and did not you know my circumstances, you would not dare to treat me thus. I have twice sent for a copy of the manuscript – no answer from you.

An explanation or excuse for your silence would oblige.' But there was none forthcoming from Horace Walpole.

Reeling from what he saw as the ultimate blow to his pride, the highly sensitive youth sat behind his desk in Lambert's office on April 17, 1770, and wrote: 'The Last Will and Testament of me, Thomas Chatterton of Bristol.' The document was found by his employer and Chatterton was dismissed. He left clutching five pounds and a bundle of unfinished poems.

Chatterton made his way to London in the hope of gaining some recognition, either for work in his own right or for the discovery of that literary priest, Thomas Rowley. At first, he lodged with a cousin in Shoreditch, and his life seemed happy enough as he mixed with writers and politicians, including the radical John Wilkes. He contributed to the Whig opposition party's journals and other publications, and he even had a burlesque opera, *The Revenge*, successfully produced. He also continued producing fake works of the literary priest Thomas Rowley, one poem of which he was particularly proud being *An Excelente Balade of Charitie*.

Chatterton even won himself a female admirer, Esther Saunders. The callow youth was intimidated by her advances and replied to her letters in an abrasive manner but this did not deter Miss Saunders who, in April 1770, wrote to him the following rambling missive.

'Sir, to a Blage you I wright a few lines to you but have not the weakness to Believe all you say of me for you may Say as much to other young Ladys for all I kno But I Cant go out of a Sunday with you for I ham afraid we Shall be seen to go Sir if it aggreable to you I had Take a walk with you in the morning for I be Belive we Shant be Seen about 6 a Clock But we must wait with patient for ther is a Time for all Things.'

Determined to rid himself of Esther Saunders once and for all, Chatterton wrote back: 'There is a time for all things – except marriage my dear.'

Fortune was once more to turn against Chatterton. The Whig journals fell foul of the government and were forced to choose between pursuing a more cautious line or suspending publication. The small payments Chatterton had received became few and far between. Further, having gained a new-found confidence from mixing in London's literary society, Chatterton unwisely turned on his home town Bristol in a satirical poem, *The Exhibition*, in which he pilloried most of his former acquaintances. The result was that he was deserted by his friends, including William Barrett whom Chatterton had held dear.

Friendless and alienated, he rented an attic room in Brooke Street, Holborn. He hardly ate or slept for months as he desperately produced tales, scribblings, songs and poems from Thomas Rowley. He was always hungry and tired and his mental state was becoming troubled. In desperation, he turned to William Barrett for help but his former friend refused him. Yet in his letters home, the now virtually deranged Chatterton pretended all was well in his new life. In one letter he wrote: 'I have an universal acquaintance; my company is courted everywhere....the ladies are not out of my acquaintance. I have a deal of business now, and must therefore bid you adieu...' But Chatterton's real feelings were expressed in his last poem, written two days before he died.

> *Farewell, my mother! — cease my mortal soul.*
> *Nor let Distraction's billow's o'er me roll! —*
> *Have mercy, Heaven! when here I cease to live.*
> *And this last act of wretchedness forgive*

On August 24, 1770, Thomas Chatterton tore all his manuscripts to shreds and swallowed arsenic. He died in excruciating agony at the age of just seventeen. In his will, he wrote: 'I leave my mother and sister to the protection of my friends if I have any...'

Following Chatterton's suicide, greater interest was shown in the work of Thomas Rowley. In Bristol the poems were passed around scholars of mediaeval works and their virtues discussed. Some were even included in Thomas Warton's book *History of English Poetry*.

Horace Walpole learned of Chatterton's death when, at a banquet at London's Royal Academy, he heard Oliver Goldsmith praising some ancient poems that had been found in Bristol. He refused to feel any guilt over the boy – but at that time, he did not know then that he would soon be denounced as the heartless aristocrat who had driven him to suicide.

When the truth about Chatterton's fabrication of work by Thomas Rowley was revealed, he was reviled as a forger but praised as a poet on his own merits. Latter-day critics believe the teenager would have been more accepted by the establishment if it had not been for his humble background. Edward Rushton, a contemporary of Chatterton, boldly defended him. He compared the treatment he received with that of humble poet Thomas Percy and wrote:

'A Common Observer would imagine that both writers were in the same Predicament, but mark the Influence of Wealth and Situation; whilse the One is nothing more than the Innocent Artifice of an Honourable Author, the Other is loudly reprobated as the vile Forger of obscure Charity Boy.'

Others, too, found fine words with which to describe the tragic, talented writer. Dr Samuel Johnson called Chatterton 'the most extraordinary young man'. George Catcott, Chatterton's friend from Bristol, spoke of the young man's 'hawk's eye' through which 'one could see his soul'. Even William Barrett found it in his heart to forgive Chatterton and wrote colourfully: 'I had never seen such eyes, fire rolling at the bottom of them... I sometimes crossed him just to see how wonderfully his eye would strike fire, kindle and blaze up.'

In 1777 the Rowley poems were published by Thomas Tyrwhitt, who left the question of their authorship open. The literary world became divided into those who believed they were forgeries and those who believed they were genuine. Two years later, Horace Walpole published an angry reply to accusations that he had been responsible for Chatterton's suicide. His fiercest accuser was George Catcott. In 1780, Herbert Croft's novel *Love and Madness* caused a sensation. It was based on the murder of Martha Ray, the mistress of the Earl of Sandwich, by a lovesick clergyman called Hackman. It contained a long account of the life of Chatterton and made him a household name.

Arguments over Chatterton's talent and the authenticity of Thomas Rowley's work raged on amongst the literary elite. Thorough examination of the poetry finally revealed it was not written by a Fifteenth Century priest but by a misguided, disillusioned but gifted Bristol boy. Chatterton's work became recognised in its own right. And his life was captured by painters and fellow poets, not least by the words of William Wordsworth:

'...*Chatterton, the marvellous Boy,*
The sleepless soul that perished in his pride.'

Chapter 3

The Unregal Rogue Romanov

At midnight on July 6, 1918, Tsar Nicholas II and his family were awoken by their Bolshevik guards at the house in which they were being held at Ekaterinburg, east of the Ural Mountains. The Tsar was told that anti-revolutionary forces were approaching the town and that orders had come from Moscow that he and his entourage were to be moved. The imperial royal family and their servants were taken to a cellar in the requisitioned merchant's house which served as their prison. There they were told to await transport to a more secure area.

The guards had until two days earlier been peasant soldiers and, while not overly familiar, neither were they unfriendly. However, on July 4 they had been replaced by secret police under the command of fanatical revolutionary Yacov Yurovsky. And his men were not gaolers; they were executioners.

The Tsar and his household gathered in that dingy cellar, with a heavy iron grill protecting its only window, and waited for the transport that never came. Then Yurovsky and his men entered and informed them that they were to be shot. As the Tsar rose to protest, Yurovsky fired a bullet into his head. A fusillade cut down his young wife, the Tsarina Alexandra Feodorovna, and three of her daughters, along with two servants and the family doctor. The soldiers then turned their bayonets on any other adults still standing. The Tsar's son, Alexis, had been wounded and when he stirred he was stamped to death by the soldiers. Yurovsky administered the *coup de grace*, placing his pistol to the boy's ear and firing two shots. Even the family's pet dog had its skull smashed in by a rifle butt.

The bodies were bundled into lorries and driven along the lonely route to a mineshaft, where they were mutilated and buried. They did not remain there long, however, because the anti-revolutionary

White Army was counter-attacking in the area. So a day or two later, the remains of the imperial Romanov dynasty were clumsily removed to a secret resting place deep in the neighbouring forest...

And that is where the legend began of a single royal survivor from the massacre. According to the legend, one of the Tsar's daughters, seventeen-year-old Anastasia, escaped the carnage. And over the years, several women have claimed to be the princess – and hence the heir to the Romanov fortune.

Principal among these was an American, Anna Anderson, and the picture she painted of the horror that overwhelmed 'her family' was even more horrific than the historians' version of events. She said that every member of the group in the dungeon was violently raped before death, with the exception of Prince Alexis, who was saved by the Tsar himself volunteering to submit to the ordeal to protect his son. Anderson claimed that she awoke as she bumped along in the lorry carrying the bodies to the mineshaft. A conscripted peasant soldier heard her soft moans and spirited her away in the darkness. She subsequently bore him a son, later adopted.

Anna first came to public notice when the following brief bulletin was published by Berlin police on February 18, 1920:

> 'Yesterday evening at 9pm a girl of about 20 jumped off the Bendler Bridge into the Landwhehr Canal with the intention of taking her own life. She was saved by a police sergeant and admitted to the Elisabeth Hospital in Lützowstrasse. No papers or valuables of any kind were found in her possession and she refused to make any statements about herself or her motives for attempting suicide.'

Although German speaking, the poor girl refused to give her identity and, at her own request, was committed by police to a mental institution at Daldorf, where she remained for two years. It was not until 1922 that she eventually announced that she was the surviving Romanov, the Tsar's youngest daughter, the Grand Duchess Anastasia.

One or two sceptics suggested that Anna was really Franziska Schanzkowski, a Polish orphan who had disappeared from a Berlin boarding house at the time of the suicide attempt. However, relatives and servants of the Romanovs visited the mysterious claimant in the Daldorf institution and confirmed that she bore a strong resemblance to Anastasia. She certainly had detailed knowledge of the lifestyle of the Romanovs. She had scars that could have been the results of bullet and bayonet wounds. A handwriting expert averred that her writing and that of Anastasia were identical. And the two shared a physical peculiarity: Anastasia's middle finger was the same length as her index and ring fingers.

Naturally, there were many who believed Anna was simply an imposter. These included imperial tutor Pierre Gilliard and his wife Alexandra Tegleva, who had been Anastasia's nanny. Gilliard noted that the woman could not speak or read Russian or English.

After leaving the institution, the claimant, by now something of a celebrity, was taken in by Baron Von Kleist, a Russian émigré who said he believed her tragic story – though some said it was the baron himself who had helped her invent it. Fed up with being put on display, she sought sanctuary with other sympathisers of her cause before finally travelling to the United States and adopting the name Anna Anderson.

She was eventually persuaded to return to Berlin to launch a legal claim on the title, and thirty years of litigation through the German courts followed. If she had been successful, she would have won prestige and riches. The Tsar was always rumoured to have salted away millions in foreign banks in readiness for an escape from the Bolsheviks.

In 1967, however, Anna Anderson sat despondently in a secluded retreat in Germany's Black Forest after her final court action had ended with a judgment that she had been 'unable to provide sufficient proof for recognition'. She said hopelessly: 'All I ever wanted was a name. It's the right of everyone in this world except for me. I suppose the only thing left to do is to die.'

In fact, Anna Anderson did not die for another seventeen years. She had married an American university professor, Dr John Manahan, and they settled down in Charlottesville, Virginia. She died in hospital there in 1984 and her body was cremated twenty-four hours later. Her husband survived her by six years.

Right up to her death, Anna was still believed by many to have been a survivor of the slaughter of Ekaterinburg. It is only since then that scientists have been able to determine if there was any truth in her claims. The reason is two discoveries: one being the introduction of DNA testing or 'genetic fingerprinting', the other the discovery of a secret grave. Even those two breakthroughs could not have totally resolved the mystery without a third chance discovery ... that, despite the obvious destruction of Anna's remains in the cremation, a tiny part of her body had been removed and preserved. Five years before her death, she had had an emergency operation to remove an intestinal blockage. Microscopic slides of her diseased tissue had been kept in paraffin-wax blocks in the pathology department of Charlotte's Martha Jefferson Hospital.

In 1991 a collection of bones were unearthed by accident in a shallow burial pit in the forest twenty miles from Ekaterinburg. Proof that they were those of the Romanov family was achieved by DNA testing, assisted by the British Royal Family. In 1993 genetic scientists studied blood samples from Prince Philip, Duke of Edinburgh, a distant relation of the Russian royal family, and through this they were able to confirm the fate of the Tsar, the Tsarina and three of their five children. However, the DNA tests left a question mark over whether Anastasia and Tsarevich Alexei were among the remains. Tantalisingly, the tests could not at that time distinguish between the sisters.

That is when the lucky discovery in the pathology department of the Charlotte Hospital finally allowed scientists to crack the DNA code. After legal obstructions in America, the slides of the tissue taken from Anna were eventually handed over to genetic investigators in London. At last they were able to match the tissue samples with the Russian bone samples – and match the claims of Anna Anderson against the truth. The seventy-six-year-old mystery was about to be ended.

The jubilant British team passed their findings to their counterparts in Moscow and, on September 6, 1994, Russia's Deputy Prime Minister, Yuri Yarov, revealed the final, foolproof report of the DNA scientists. He announced that the bones found in the burial pit were those of five skeletons. The Tsar, his wife and three of their children had been positively identified – including Anastasia.

So all the 'Anastasias' who had emerged over the decades had been impostors. Despite Anna Anderson's lifelong protestations, she died not a princess but a fake. As one mystery was solved, however, another one opened. If the remains of Anastasia's sister Maria and those of the Tsar's heir Alexis were not in the grave, where were they?

One further clue to that mystery came to light in August 2007 when Russian archaeologist Franziska Schanzkowska announced the discovery of two burned, partial skeletons at a site near Ekaterinburg that appeared to match that once described by a friend of the Romanov family. The bones, found using metal detectors and metal rods as probes, were believed to be from a boy aged between ten and thirteen years and of a young woman roughly aged between eighteen and twenty-three.

Anastastia was seventeen years-old at the time of the assassination, her sister Maria, nineteen years-old and her brother Alexis just coming up to his fourteenth birthday. The two older sisters, Olga and Tatiana, were twenty-two and twenty-one when they died. Along with the remains of the two bodies, archaeologists found 'shards of a container of sulphuric acid, nails, metal strips from a wooden box and bullets of various calibre. And so began another series of tests to try to solve just what happened to all those missing members of the Romanov family.

Chapter 4

Bucking the System for Big Bucks

he tumble of a dice, the turn of a card. For those who seek their fortune through gambling, Lady Luck really is their mistress. But what if you could literally make your own luck? What if you could beat the system and take from casinos just a little of what they take from their gambling clientele every day?

Determination to win without leaving it to chance has led to some elaborate scams in latter years. In 2004, a highly successful trio – a Hungarian woman and two Serbian men – managed to net £1.3million by using a laser scanner linked to a computer. The scanner, hidden in a mobile phone, was allegedly used to gauge numbers likely to come up on the roulette wheel. All this was bad news for London's famous Ritz Casino where the three paid just two visits to secure massive rewards. On the first night, they walked away with £100,000. On a second visit soon afterwards, they left with £1.2million. It was believed that the casino paid £300,000 in cash and paid the balance with a cheque.

A routine review by the casino of its security tapes – common when an abnormally large amount is paid out – led to the three tricksters being arrested. After seizing 'a significant quantity of cash' from a hotel where the team was staying, London's Scotland Yard described the case as 'extremely complex' and specialist detectives from the serious and organised crime group got together to see just how the scam worked. Noone came up with a definite theory, but it is thought the gang's success could have been based on a relatively simple system known as 'sector targeting'. In this, a player determines the point at which the roulette ball is released and the point it passes after one or two spins. These figures can then be used to calculate the ball's 'decaying orbit' and so her man friend eventually split up and, so the story goes, Dawn married and set up her own legitimate business in New Jersey. She looks back at those exhilarating casino days with fondness, saying: 'The men were always talking about different ways of cheating and how they were going to win big one day but I thought it was just boys' talk. We spent a lot and lived the high life. I've no regrets. If you look at the number of lives that are ruined by gambling, I think the casinos were just getting a little of what was coming to them.'

Casinos in South Africa enjoy revenues of more than $333 million a year, but in 1999 there was a bit of blip in profits. Staff at Caesar's Casino in Johannesburg suspected something was wrong when blackjack takings dropped by eleven per cent in three weeks. Security men began studying players and surveying games. They noticed at least five people behaving oddly – either darting their eyes over the decks of cards or making bets of widely differing amounts. It was only when the investigation turned to the cards themselves that it was discovered the patterns on the backs of the 10-cards, Jacks, Queens and Kings were different. Each was found to have a tiny blank space inside a repeated floral pattern on the horizontal edge on the back of the card which was visible to players before the croupier dealt.

The casino said it had received 4,000 of the subtly marked packs, and other casinos were alerted. It was believed that information about the marked cards was sold to gamblers either for a fee or a cut of their winnings. Just who was behind such an audacious scam was never discovered. Involvement was categorically denied by spokespeople for the Protea Playing Cards Company, which had been the sole card supplier to all twenty-two of South Africa's casinos and others in southern Africa for over ten years. Ernie Joubert, Chief Executive of Global resorts, part-owner of Caesar's reckoned that over a year, if the marked card scam had not been discovered, losses across the whole industry would have reached some $10million. He added: 'People always thought that South African blackjack players were the best in the world. Now there may be another, secret reason...'

There seems to be no stopping those who want to buck the system to get big bucks. In 1973, an amateur radio buff employed

anticipate the area of the wheel – or sector – in which the ball is likely to come to rest. The system cannot reliably predict the slot the ball is likely to fall in, but determining the sector greatly sways the odds in the favour of the punter.

Reporting the gambling sting, the *Guardian* newspaper suggested a four-point plan as to how it might work... 1. A laser scanner hidden in a mobile phone which measures velocity is aimed at a roulette wheel as it is spun by the croupier. 2. The laser measures the speed of the ball as it is released and as it passes a second point. The ball's 'decaying orbit' can then be calculated. 3. The two figures are relayed to a computer which works out where the ball is likely to rest. It would almost certainly not be able to predict the slot but may be able to work out the sector, improving the odds for the gambler. 4. The computer's prediction is relayed back to the mobile phone. The bet or bets are placed before the cut-off point of three turns of the roulette wheel. The whole operation takes two or three seconds.

The team's scam was picked up when staff at the Ritz Casino played back video tapes. The pay-out cheque was then frozen. But incredibly, going against all belief that crime does not pay, the three cheats, all in their thirties, were eventually allowed to keep their winnings. In December 2004, police officially announced that the team had not broken the law, the case was closed, no charges had been brought and the money was rightly theirs.

The laws which cover gambling date back to the Nineteenth Century when the possibility of sophisticated scams could never have been dreamed of. In Britain, the Gaming Act of 1845 forbids 'unlawful devices'. The 1960s Theft Act makes it an offence to go 'equipped to cheat'. However, just as was the case with the Ritz gang, perpetrators have successfully argued that they had not interfered with a game but had simply used a system to win.

It was only natural that the Ritz Casino reviewed its security after such an embarrassing high-profile case, when it was seen for once to be the big loser. But it did not want to comment on the affair, and it was left to journalists and other curious parties to visit the casino's website which stated that the Ritz placed 'great emphasis on ensuring the highest standards of operation procedures are constantly upheld'. It added, tellingly, that the game of roulette is 'ideally suited to "system" players who note down number sequences to detect patterns. No other game of chance allows players to win so much, so fast.' No one could argue with that.

The public imagination has always been fired by gamblers smart and brave enough to cheat. The two most common ways are by being in collusion with a croupier or by 'card counting' – famously used by the autistic character Raymond, played by Dustin Hoffman, in the movie *Rain Man*. Card counting, in which skilful blackjack players keep track of which cards have been played to calculate which are left, is not illegal. It is, in any case hard to prove. But if a casino suspects this is happening, it can ask a player to leave.

In the mid 1990s, a team of American science students from the Massachusetts Institute of Technology scooped millions of dollars at Las Vegas casinos by using the technique. One of the gamblers, Anthony Curtis, subsequently confessed: 'The buzz for me was the potential. It was unlimited and I could make more money without punching a clock. I could have a ton of fun. Certainly women were going to love me and it was great.' This was not the opinion of the casinos, of course. In a BBC television *Horizon* programme on the subject in 2004, Roy Ramm, compliance and security director for casino group London Clubs International, said card counters often made themselves obvious. He said: 'They usually occupy a certain part of the table and may stare intently at the cards. They tend to irritate the other players.' Mr Ramm added that card counters sometimes carried a device 'in their boots' and that the use of technology in casinos was a bit of a 'grey area'.

Really big heists rarely happen in real life, despite the complex and colourful plans put into operation in such movies as the *Ocean's 11* series, in which mega million-dollar stings take place. But there have been some notable cases. In 2003, a croupier in Melbourne, Australia, was jailed for her part in a sophisticated scam that defrauded a casino of $1.8million Australian dollars. The baccarat dealer had met a man who apparently showed her how to shuffle cards in such a way that the face could be seen. A high-roller at her table won $1.4million, with the rest of the casino's loss made up of people who copied his bids.

One of the most ingenious casino scams of all time involved a team who not only were never caught, but who were clever enough to remain anonymous. In 1992, New York girl 'Dawn' was dating an ophthalmologist who was hooked on gambling. This meant the young woman spent most of her time with him as a 'blackjack widow' while he spent hours at the table. She played with dollar bills and he gambled away thousands with his high-rolling friends in Las Vegas. Eventually he and his buddies realised the only way to win back some of the money they had lost in casinos was to cheat.

One night, the eye specialist showed Dawn a pair of lightly tinted green contact lenses, a small bottle of liquid and a pack of playing cards. She recalled: 'He tapped some of the liquid onto the cards and, when I was wearing the contact lenses, I could see a fingerprint glowing in a kind of greenish colour where he had touched the card.' The man told Dawn he had created the inky liquid himself and, because it was colourless and odourless and faded after an hour, it was completely undetectable.

He asked her to go to a blackjack table and mark high-scoring cards with the ink but she couldn't do it quickly enough on her own, so she recruited a girlfriend. Describing their antics much later, Dawn said: 'We'd dress up very provocatively and play a table for maybe an hour at a time, flirting with the dealers. I'd have taken the contents out of a powder compact and glued in a little sponge. I would put the invisible ink solution on the sponge and keep the middle finger of my right hand wetted with it so that when the dealer dealt me a face card, a ten or an ace, I would tap the card and leave a print.' As soon as the right cards were marked, the women would leave the table to make room for the ophthalmologist and his friend to take their places. Wearing the lenses, the men could know exactly when high cards were coming up and could adjust their betting accordingly. So they started winning, giving twenty-five per cent of their money to the two women.

The scam ran for two years until the couple started to worry about their luck running out and getting caught. But by that time, Dawn had made $2million just through her share alone and had bought a house which turned out to be a good investment. She and

as a roulette dealer at the casino in France's upmarket resort town of Deauville, built a radio transmitter into a pack of Marlboro cigarettes. He then embedded a tiny receiver into a roulette ball he sneaked into play. His brother-in-law placed the bets while his sister softly pressed an invisible button on the cigarette pack as the ball was spinning, sending it into a controlled dive that resulted in the ball's landing in groups of six numbers with ninety per cent accuracy. In a week, the Casino Deauville lost five million francs ($1 million at the time).

The owners of the casino knew something was up but could not work out exactly what. First, they thought the wheel itself was defective and called in experts to completely dismantle it while examining every working piece integral to the ball's spinning around the disk and the wheel's revolutions in the opposite direction. When the wheel was found to be in perfect balance, and without even the slightest imperfection which could produce biased outcomes, the finger of suspicion fell on the dealer. He was watched secretly from above, but his motion was the same every time. He was doing nothing out of the ordinary to control the movement of the ball. It always made the same number of revolutions before going into its descent.

What proved the team's downfall had nothing to do with the discovery of gadgetry aids. It was the interest of the casino owner in the sister – a particularly striking woman. After she rebuffed his advances, he began to look at her in a different light, wondering why she was always at the casino seemingly alone, always at the same table and why she only placed an occasional bet during the lengthy times she spent playing roulette. He further pondered whether the mystery woman had anything to do with the casino's losses. Eventually suspecting some kind of radio interference with the roulette wheel, he called in an expert debugging team to sweep the casino when the wheel was in play. The game was finally up.

Not all gambling cheats are loveable rogues. American Dennis Sean McAndrew – born Dennis Nikrasch in 1941 – has been called the greatest slot machine cheat in gambling history. He masterminded several slot machine cheating rings over twenty years, accumulating around $16 million from jackpots, mostly in

Nevada and Atlantic City. Despite the security precautions and surveillance cameras used by casinos to ensure all was fair, McAndrew found a way to beat the system. He worked out how it was possible electronically to manipulate the computer chips that govern slot machines – the chips that guarantee the random nature of play of the machines. Working with his carefully-selected slot-cheating teams, McAndrew used high-tech tools to set up his own jackpot wins. While team members acted as lookouts and carefully positioned themselves to shield what they were up to from casino cameras, McAndrew opened up the machines and rigged them. Then one of his team would play them and become an instant big winner.

It didn't always go McAndrew's way. In the 1970s, he was arrested and found guilty of rigging mechanical reel slots. In 1986, he was sent to prison for being part of a gang that cheated Las Vegas casinos out of $10million. Out on parole in January 1991, McAndrew soon found a way to beat what were considered advanced cheat-proof slot machines. But it was McAndrew's unpleasant character that brought him down. He treated those who worked for him so badly, forever haggling over their cut of the wins, that they helped set up a sting of their own – with the FBI. McAndrew was arrested in November 1998 while going for a $17million 'Megabucks' jackpot. A deal was struck between the FBI, Nevada gaming officials and McAndrew, whereby he would receive a reduced prison sentence in exchange for his slot machine secrets. McAndrew is now listed in Nevada's Black Book of people banned from the state's casinos – but it didn't stop his merry band of thieves carrying on where he left off, of course.

One of the most successful casino cheats ever was Richard Marcus, who worked the casinos in Las Vegas and around the world for thirty years. His reward was millions of dollars without ever getting arrested. He didn't just stick to one game. Roulette, craps, baccarat and blackjack were all favourites. One of Marcus's top tricks was what casino cheaters call 'posting', a simple method but one which demands dexterity and nerves of steel. It works, by putting, for example five $10 chips at a roulette table. If your number does not come up then obviously you lose. But if it does, you discreetly add a high-denomination chip to the bottom of the lower ones you placed earlier. Marcus explained: 'When the croupier pays your bet, you say something like, "Hey, you paid me too little. I bet $1,050 not $60". And when the croupier examines your wager, he will see that it consists of five $10 chips plus one $1,000 chip and not the six $10 chips he first thought.'

This particular trick faded out in the 1980s when casinos started installing cameras above every table so they could see what every player did all the time. This should have put an end to 'posting' but Richard Marcus invented a way to beat the cameras. It was called 'The Savannah' and was hailed as one of the most brilliant casino tricks ever devised. Named after a favourite lap dancer, 'The Savannah' was created in 1995 when Marcus was in his kitchen trying to come up with fresh cheating ideas.

He recalled: 'I took a few red $5 chips and put them down on top of a $5,000 chip so that they were like a shark's jaw hanging out. I put my right-hand man, Pat, in the dealer's position and experimented until we'd conceived the right angle. Then me and Pat looked at each other in shock, because we knew we had stumbled upon the greatest discovery in casino cheating.

'How it would work is this. On the layout, I put a $5,000 chocolate chip and two $5 reds on top. Pat stands at the wheel. If the bet doesn't come in, Pat shouts "Damn" and I pick the bet right up and it's gone. We thought the dealer would see that every time but he only saw it one in five times. If he caught me, I would just do my "drunk" routine, pretending I didn't know what was happening. In my right hand are three $5 chips and I put that stack down. The dealer thinks that's what it was anyway.

'If the bet comes in, Pat stays quiet and I go, "Yeah. I just won five grand!" The dealer lifts the two reds and – Boom! The $5,000 chip is there. But the dealer can't just pay it. That's a huge bet. So she calls over the pit boss who comes over and demands that they play back the surveillance tape. They run back the tape... and it's a legitimate bet!'

Marcus's love of cheating began very early on when he was tricked into losing his entire baseball card collection to another boy. From then on, he was determined to be the one who duped others. Long before he hit the casinos, Marcus was cheating. One of his early favourites was the gas-station scam when he would drive into a garage and as he paid for fuel, suddenly drop to his hands and knees. Recalled Marcus: 'I'd be going, "Oh shit". I'd say to the attendant: "My grandparents gave me a diamond ring; damn thing must have cost $2,000, and now I've lost it. I'm going to be at this bar watching a football game so if you find it just call me and I'll give you $500".'

Marcus would then have a partner-in-crime drive up half-an-hour or so later and just happen to find the 'diamond' ring. Happily surprised, the gas station attendant would start offering money for the ring – something in the region of $150 or $200, believing he would make a profit when it was returned to its rightful owner. Of course, the ring was fake and Marcus wasn't sitting in a bar but probably at another gas station pulling the same stunt. He later confessed: 'That scam kept me in gambling through my teens. We must have done it 150 times. It preyed upon human greed. The attendant was trying to scam us but we scammed him.'

It was, however, gambling that provided the greatest lure for Marcus. He admitted: 'I woke up gambling and went to sleep gambling.' But he did not start off a winner. On his first trip to Las Vegas, he played baccarat at the Riviera Hotel and won $100,000 in a week – then lost it all. He later trained as a dealer during a ten-month 'apprenticeship' at a casino, and then put his skills to use as part of a team which hit casinos from Atlantic City to Monte Carlo, from Las Vegas to London.

Marcus was last heard of living a blissful, non-working life on the French Riviera. In an interview he gave to *Inside Poker* magazine, he said he would only come out of retirement if 'Miami beach opens casinos. It would be bigger than Las Vegas, with all those beautiful high-rise hotels and the drug money. Not really boasting, but I could probably make $1million in a weekend. It would be a rampage.'

Chapter 5

Harry Houdini: Trick or Cheat?

I t was the basis on which he became a performing legend: 'No one wants to see a man fall 100ft to his death – but they do want to be there when it happens...' There have been many imitators since, but none has grabbed the world's attention so completely as Houdini, escapologist extraordinaire, whose heart-stopping acts earned him top billing as the 'Genius of Escape Who Will Startle and Amaze'.

But was he really the death-defying daredevil who pushed human endurance to the limit – or an illusionist who shattered everyone's illusions? For the 'Genius of Escape' relied on clever con-tricks, slight of hand and a close team of colluding confidantes just as much as his own ability to break free of tight bonds.

The legendary escapologist was born Ehrich Weisz on March 24, 1874, in Budapest, the son of Mayer Samuel, a Hungarian rabbi, and his wife Cecilia. The family emigrated to America four years later. But Houdini's origins are as mystifying as his stage act. Some reports have his birth some years later. Houdini himself claimed he was born in Appleton, Wisconsin, on April 6, 1874.

Houdini might have been the one who made his mark in the world, but he was by no means the only Weisz child. There were brothers Nathan, Gottfried, Theodore (who also found fame on stage) and Leopold, a sister Gladys and a half-brother Herman. Shortly after he was born, Ehrich Weisz was nicknamed 'Ehrie' or 'Harry.'

At first, the family enjoyed a reasonable lifestyle when Mayer served as a rabbi of the Zion Reform Jewish Congregation. But the family's fortunes began to fail when he lost his tenure and moved to New York to set up a Hebrew school. Once he was settled, the family followed but money was tight and, one by one, the children were forced to earn their keep. The young Ehrich took several jobs including an assistant cutter at a neck-tie manufacturer. But even in those early days, he aspired to physical fitness, becoming a champion cross-country runner and an excellent swimmer.

It is believed that Ehrich became interested in trickery through a family member who was the first magician invited to perform at the White House. As a child, he made his public debut in a trapeze act, calling himself 'Ehrich, the Prince of the Air'. At seventeen, when he became a full-time illusionist, Ehrich changed his name to Harry Houdini because of his fascination with a French magician of the time, Jean Eugene Robert-Houdin.

Like most newcomers to the entertainment world, Houdini struggled to gain recognition. He performed in 'dime museums' and sideshows, and even doubled as 'the Wild Man' at a circus. Houdini initially focused on traditional card tricks, at one point billing himself as the 'King of Cards'. But he soon began experimenting with escape acts.

Always fascinated by locks, Houdini taught himself to unpick the various makes of handcuffs that were around at the time, using nothing more than tiny pieces of wire. His big break came in 1899 when he met theatre booker Martin Beck, who advised him to concentrate on his escape acts and booked him on the Orpheum vaudeville circuit. Gradually, Houdini built up a dramatic routine, his gimmick being an element of suspense. It certainly worked, for within months Houdini was performing at the top vaudeville houses in the country.

In 1900, Beck arranged for Houdini to tour Europe with his act, which by now included escaping from an old straitjacket donated by the director of a lunatic asylum. Perfection of this show-stopping act was made possible by Houdini's loyal wife Bess. The couple had met in 1894 when Houdini performed a show at her school, and they had married within a week. Before that meeting, Houdini's brother Theodore, also known as 'Dash', had helped on stage. Now it was Bess, his new stage assistant, who buckled the escapologist into his straightjacket every night and watched him struggle, sometimes hour after hour, in a bid to free himself and complete the ultimate suspense act.

The rehearsals for this feat would involve Houdini lying

exhausted on the floor until eventually he succeeded. Though every limb ached, his fingers were bleeding and his strength sapped, Houdini managed to bring his arms to the front of his body, undo the sleeve buckles with his teeth and reach behind to unfasten the rest of the buckles through the canvas of the jacket.

Though much of Houdini's act was fake, there is no doubt that his shortness (he was just 5ft 5ins), his bow legs, his physical fitness, and a unique muscular ability to create a little 'slack' when tied up all helped him manoeuvre himself from the most restrictive bonds.

In the 1996 biography, *Houdini!!!: The Career of Ehrich Weiss*, author Kenneth Silverman summarised how reporters described Houdini's appearance during his early career. They stressed his smallness – 'somewhat undersized' – and angular, vivid features: 'He is smooth-shaven with a keen, sharp-chinned, sharp-cheekboned face, bright blue eyes and thick, curly, black hair'. Some sensed how much his complexly expressive smile was the outlet of his charismatic stage presence. It communicated to audiences at once warm amiability, pleasure in performing and, more subtly, imperious self-assurance. Several reporters tried to capture the charming effect, describing him as 'happy-looking', 'pleasant-faced', 'good natured at all times', 'the young Hungarian magician with the pleasant smile and easy confidence'.

There was no doubting the excruciating physical pain Houdini would put himself through. When tied down with ropes or encased in straitjackets, he gained 'wiggle room' by enlarging his shoulders and chest, moving his arms slightly away from his body, and then dislocating his shoulders.

Houdini's straitjacket escape was originally performed behind curtains, with him popping out free at the end. But he changed this after his brother, also an escape artist, billing himself as Theodore Hardeen, was accused of having someone sneak in and let him out. Theodore was challenged to escape without the curtain. The brothers thus discovered that audiences were more impressed and entertained when the curtains were eliminated so they could watch trapped escapologists struggle to get out.

All this was impressive, of course. But Harry Houdini had other tricks, although not exactly up his sleeve, to enable him to break free. In one of his books, *Handcuff Secrets*, Houdini later revealed that many locks and handcuffs could be opened with properly applied force, others with a shoestring. At other times, he carried concealed lock picks or keys, being able to regurgitate small keys at will. He also taught himself to be ambidextrous and once admitted: 'When at table, I practised using the left hand persistently until I could use it almost as easily as the right.'

All this dedication to the art of escapology resulted in Houdini becoming a sensation. Now billed as 'The Handcuff King', he toured England, Scotland, the Netherlands, Germany and France. In each city where he was appearing, he would challenge local police to restrain him with shackles and lock him in their jails. In many of these challenges, Houdini would first be stripped nude and searched. Sometimes he would ask a doctor to search him for concealed keys or lock-picks before having his arms chained behind his back, being manacled at the ankles and all limbs tied together with ten pairs of handcuffs. Houdini would then be carried to a cupboard – which had been 'searched' for any signs of escape beforehand – and locked in. Less than ten minutes later, he would reappear.

The Great Houdini was not without his critics, however. His arrival in Britain in 1900 was greeted with cynicism. Many were suspicious of him and even believed the American police so corrupt they colluded with Houdini's act. A disbelieving audience at London's famous Alhambra Variety Theatre sat down to watch Scotland's Yard Superintendent William Melville handcuff Houdini round a metal pillar and announce he would be back in an hour to release him. But Houdini was free before Melville had even reached the door.

At the same theatre on opening night, Houdini was challenged on stage by a member of the audience who accused him of being a fraud. The stranger claimed to be 'Cirnoc' the 'original Handcuff King'. Houdini bravely challenged his rival to a release feat involving the Bean Giant, handcuffs with a lock positioned so that even with the key, it was impossible to undo them. Houdini went first and stunned his audience into silence with his incredible escape. Cirnoc failed. What no-one knew was that Houdini had secreted a specially-designed key on himself, enabling the Bean Giant lock to be undone. Cirnoc had to make do with the key that Houdini had pretended he had used.

In 1909, the London *Daily Mirror* newspaper challenged Houdini to escape from a special handcuff that it claimed had taken Nathaniel Hart, a locksmith from Hertfordshire, five years to make. Houdini accepted the challenge for a matinee performance on March 20 at London's Hippodrome theatre. It was reported that 4,000 people and more than 100 journalists turned out for the much-hyped event. The escape attempt dragged on for over an hour, during which Houdini emerged from his 'ghost house' (a small screen used to conceal the method of his escape) several times. On one occasion, he asked if the cuff could be removed so he could take off his coat. The request was refused on the grounds that Houdini could gain an advantage if he saw how the cuff was unlocked. Houdini promptly took out a pen-knife and used it to cut his coat from his body.

Then, fifty-six minutes later, Bess appeared on stage and gave her husband an encouraging kiss. It is believed that in her mouth was the key to unlock the special handcuff. Houdini then went back behind the curtain. After an hour and ten minutes, Houdini emerged free. As he was paraded on the shoulders of the cheering crowd, he broke down and wept. Houdini later said it was the most difficult escape of his career.

After Houdini's death, his friend Will Goldstone wrote in his book *Sensational Tales of Mystery Men* that the escapologist knew he was beaten that day and appealed to Bess for help. Goldstone went on to claim that she begged the key from the *Mirror* representative, then slipped it to Houdini in a glass of water. Some Houdini biographers have claimed the whole challenge was pre-arranged by Houdini and the newspaper and that his tortuous struggle to escape was just another example of the dramatic showmanship for which he had become famous.

After two months in Britain, Houdini left for Germany and performed in such prestigious theatres as the Berlin Wintergarten where he proudly showed off a sensational new act in which he escaped from leg-irons and manacles that had 40lb weights attached to them.

Houdini got used to challenges by disbelievers who brought along various manacles and locks for him to open. He always beat them, thanks to his detailed knowledge and the selection of fine picks he always carried. While in Berlin, he worked alongside a locksmith and happily perfected the trade. He later wrote: 'I would pass six to ten hours daily picking locks and soon I could open any lock that contained the five or six Chubb levers.'

In Cologne, Houdini sued a police officer, Werner Graff, who claimed he made his escapes via bribery. Houdini won the case when he opened the judge's safe (he would later say the judge had forgotten to lock it). But his most controversial act in Germany was to be thrown handcuffed from a boat and free himself under water. The German police tried to ban this stunt but Houdini insisted on performing it. It was to become one of his legendary acts.

In Moscow, Houdini escaped from a Siberian prison transport van. Realising the high value of sensational self-publicity, he stated that, had he been unable to free himself, he would have had to travel to Siberia, where the only key was kept.

Houdini returned to the US in 1904 and continued to enjoy incredible success. He regularly altered his act but always including the same amazing escapes – from jails, handcuffs, chains, ropes and a straitjacket – often while hanging from a rope in public. One of Houdini's most popular publicity stunts was to have himself strapped into a regulation straitjacket and suspended by his ankles from a tall building or crane. He would then make his escape in full view of the assembled crowd, often numbering thousands, who would bring city traffic to a standstill. In New York City, Houdini performed the suspended straitjacket escape from a crane being used in the construction of the New York subway. Film footage of him performing the escape in Dayton, Ohio, exists in the Library of Congress. After being battered against a building in high winds during one escape, Houdini preformed the escape with a visible safety wire on his ankle so that he could be pulled away from the building if necessary.

After a while, however, something even more breathtaking was required to keep Houdini on top. He was in competition with other similar acts, and audiences were demanding greater feats. Houdini knew something with an element of death was what was needed, so in 1908 reworked his daring underwater escape act, this time using a tightly locked water-filled milk can. In this, Houdini would be handcuffed and sealed inside the over-sized can with water. He would then make his escape behind a curtain. For added effect, he would invite members of the audience to hold their breath along with him while he was inside the can. Advertised with dramatic posters that proclaimed 'Failure Means a Drowning Death', it proved a sensation.

Houdini modified the act yet again, this time to include the can being locked inside a wooden chest. The escape was included in his show for four years but his brother Theodore continued to perform it well into the 1940s. Just like all the others, this escape was made possible through intervention that was more human than divine. The rivets holding the top were filed down inside. After escapologist and can were covered, the rivets were pushed out from inside, the lid removed, the trickster climbed out and the lid and rivets were replaced.

But the possibility of death and failure was just what the Edwardian audiences wanted to see. Houdini moved this act on even more, inviting the public to devise contraptions to hold him, such as nailed packing cases (sometimes dropped into water), riveted boilers, wet sheets, mailbags and even the stomach of a whale which had washed up on shore.

In 1912, Houdini introduced perhaps his most famous act, the Chinese Water Torture Cell, in which his feet were locked in stocks and he was lowered upside down into a tank filled with water. The mahogany and metal cell featured a glass front, through which audiences could clearly see Houdini. The stocks would be locked to the top of the cell, and a curtain would conceal his escape. In the earliest version of the Torture Cell, a metal cage was lowered into the cell, and Houdini was further enclosed inside that. While making the escape more difficult (the cage prevented Houdini from turning), the cage bars also offered protection should the glass front break.

The first public performance was at the Circus Busch in Berlin on September 21, 1912. The act required that Houdini hold his breath for more than three minutes. Houdini performed the escape for the rest of his career, and, although two Hollywood movies would later depict Houdini's demise in the Torture Cell, this was not how his career was to end.

Houdini's colourful, controversial and challenging escapades made him an obvious choice as a heroic and daring film star. Following two early, obscure silent films, he was signed up for three Hollywood blockbusters, a fifteen-part serial titled *The Master Mystery* (1919), and the movies *The Grim Game* (1919) and *Terror Island* (1920). While filming an aerial stunt for *The Grim Game*, two biplanes collided in mid-air with a stuntman doubling Houdini suspended by a rope from one of the planes. Publicity was geared heavily toward promoting this dramatic 'caught on film' moment, claiming it was Houdini himself dangling from the plane.

Along with his act as a headliner in vaudeville, Houdini was for many years the highest-paid performer in American variety. In his final years, he presented what he billed as 'Three Shows in One: Magic, Escapes, and Fraud Mediums Exposed'. This earned him many enemies because, following the death of his beloved mother, Cecilia, he turned his energies toward debunking self-proclaimed psychics and mediums. His magical training allowed him to expose fraudsters who had successfully duped even scientists and academics. As his fame as a 'ghost buster' grew, Houdini took to attending séances in disguise, accompanied by a reporter and police officer. Possibly the most famous charlatan whom he debunked was the Boston medium Mina Crandon, also known as 'Margery', whom he exposed in his book *A Magician Among the Spirits*.

Houdini was a member of a 'Scientific American Committee', which offered a cash prize to any medium who could successfully demonstrate supernatural abilities. Thanks to Houdini's own knowledge (and practice) of fakery, he was able to ensure that the prize was never collected.

A book published at the time, *The Secret Life of Houdini*, forecast that it would be revenging spirits and not a dangerous stage act that would finally put paid to the amazing life of Harry Houdini. In fact, it was Houdini's foolish bravado that eventually killed him...

In 1926, Houdini was reclining on a couch after one of his performances as an art student sketched him. Three other students were present, one of whom, Gordon Whitehead, asked Houdini if it was true he could take a blow to the stomach and not flinch or be harmed. When Houdini said it was, Whitehead hit him three times and then carried on punching despite Houdini's protests.

Houdini did not know it, but when he arrived at the Garrick Theatre in Detroit on October 24, 1926, it would be for his last ever daring escape act. He had a fever of 104 degrees F and was dying from peritonitis caused by a ruptured appendix. Seven days later, the great Houdini died in the arms of his loving and loyal wife Bess at 1.26pm on October 31 at Detroit's Grace Hospital. He was fifty-two. Bess held yearly séances on that date every year – Halloween – for ten years after Houdini's death, but her beloved husband never appeared. In 1936, after a last unsuccessful séance on the roof of the Knickerbocker Hotel, she put out the candle that she had kept burning beside a photograph of Houdini since his death, later saying: 'Ten years is long enough to wait for any man.' The tradition of holding a séance for Houdini is continued by magicians throughout the world to this day

Houdini's funeral was held on November 4, 1926, in New York, with more than 2,000 mourners in attendance. He was interred in the Machpelah Cemetery in Queens, New York, with the crest of the Society of American Magicians inscribed on his gravesite. To this day, the society holds its 'Broken Wand' ceremony at the gravesite on the anniversary of his death.

Houdini was as controversial in death as in life. Fearing that spiritualists would pretend to contact him after his death, he left his wife a secret ten-word code that he would use to contact her from the afterlife. This proved worthwhile when Spiritualist ministers attempted to bring alleged messages from Houdini and his mother back from the afterlife. The resulting row drove Bess to depression and attempted suicide.

In Houdini's will, his vast library was offered to the American Society for Psychical Research on the condition that research officer and editor of the ASPR Journal, J. Malcolm Bird, resign. Bird refused and the collection went instead to the Library of Congress.

Some of Houdini's followers believed he had been poisoned by

Spiritualists, who held a grudge against him for his constant exposure of their supposed trickery. The row rumbled on for decades. In 2007, some of Houdini's descendants and several notable forensic pathologists tried to gain permission to exhume his remains and search for evidence of poisoning. Dr. Michael Baden, who chaired panels re-investigating the deaths of President John F. Kennedy and civil rights leader Martin Luther King Jr, pointed out an oddity in Houdini's death certificate: it noted that his appendix was on the left side, rather than the right.

Houdini's loyal wife Bess died in February 1943 and was not permitted to be interred with him at Machpelah Cemetery because she was a gentile. Instead, Bess Houdini is interred at Gate of Heaven Cemetery in Hawthorne, New York. At the time, it was criticised as a cruel gesture towards a woman who had devoted her life to her husband's success. Others wondered whether, with a little trickery, Houdini might escape his own burial chamber to pay her a visit.

Chapter 6

The Man Who Created 2,500 'Sexton Blakes'

Tom Keating had cheating down to a fine art – literally. For two decades, he recreated on canvas the paintings of more than a hundred famous artists. His output of about 2,500 fakes was an incredible feat, worthy of admiration in the eyes of anyone but the art world and, of course, the law. But what was even more amazing was the fact none of the fashionable dealers who handled his prodigious output recognised these blatant forgeries. And unlike many other hoaxers, Keating did not wish to reap huge financial reward for his handiwork. He simply wanted to make a point among the self-styled elite who run galleries and art shops.

Born into poverty in Forest Hill, London, in 1917, Keating left home when he was only fourteen to pursue a painting career – although at this stage he confined his brush work to the outside of houses. He was following the trade of his father but later decided to better himself by attending evening classes in signwriting and commercial art. His artistic ambitions were halted, however, with the outbreak of the Second World War. The young art student now had to turn his hand to being a stoker in the Royal Navy, serving in the Far East where he narrowly escaped capture by the Japanese following the fall of Singapore. Keating was invalided out of the Navy in 1944 because of nervous strain, and his wartime experiences were forever to blight his life with poor health.

Awarded a grant, Keating gained admission to London's prestigious Goldsmiths College but, to his bitter disappointment, he failed to gain a diploma in art. His work, he was told somewhat ironically, 'lacked original composition'. An acquaintance was later to state: 'Keating feels, like many art forgers before him, a resentment against the system, and undoubtedly the extreme poverty of his childhood stimulated his sense of grievance. For a man with sufficient talent to knock off a Renoir in a couple of hours, the disappointment of being refused a final diploma from Goldsmiths College must have been the last straw.'

If it was this early setback that made Keating bitter and cynical about the art world, he was never to admit it. But his struggles as a young painter made him angry at the lack of respect he felt artists had to suffer. One particularly frustrating incident was when a gallery offered to exhibit Keating's paintings but he was unable to afford frames for his work.

He also became enraged over the vast profits dealers made from artists, selling on paintings for as much as one hundred per cent more than they had bought them for. He maintained that he was a regular victim of the dealers' greed, which was robbing him of the living he needed to support the wife and two children he now had. He once proclaimed: 'Those dealers are just East End blokes in West End suits. They don't give a damn about the paintings. All they're after is the profit.'

And so he set out to ridicule them all – and in doing so, cracked the veneer of the art dealers' world. His limited success as an artist in his own right steered him towards a vocation which was to nurture his revenge. He became an art restorer and, after his marriage ended, went to live in Scotland where he diligently learned the finer points of his craft and gleaned more knowledge through visits to Scottish castles and stately homes. Keating did not really approve of the need for art restorers, especially if several generations of them had already had a go at a painting. He once declared: 'How authentic can you then say it is? If the old boys walked the earth again, they would not recognise their own work!'

By 1950, Keating was primed to produce his first faultless fakes. He had already practised copying the work of famous painters and even sent the odd canvas to auction, but he claimed that his first fake was as much a shock to him as it was later to prove to be to the so-called experts. He said he awoke one morning to find what looked like a Degas self-portrait resting on his easel – and assumed that he must have done it in his sleep. Nevertheless, he was wide awake when he commenced what was to be his twenty-year 'fake period'. Indeed, Keating quite happily referred to his works of art as 'Sexton Blakes' – London Cockney rhyming slang for fakes. He became a master at imitating the styles of Rembrandt, Goya, Constable, Turner, Gainsborough and Renoir.

Keating returned to London in 1960 for his most important commission: restoring the pictures in Marlborough House, which had been empty since the death of Queen Mary in 1953. One day, as he was carrying out the restoration of a giant painting of the Duke of Marlborough, by Laguerre, he was visited by the Queen. In his book, *The Fake's Progress*, Keating recalled: 'The Queen came up the stairs and gazed in astonishment. She turned to me and mentioned that she had run up and down the stairs hundreds of times as a little girl but had not been aware these beautiful pictures were on the wall. "Well they are madam," I said. "And there's a lot more under the black varnish on the other walls."' Then, according to Keating, the Queen watched him use a solvent to clean a section of the painting. Had anyone tried cleaning one of Keating's fakes in such a way, he would have immediately been exposed – for the paint would have simply lifted off!

The restoration work at Marlborough House was just a necessary job for hard-up Keating. Most of the time he spent turning out his 'Sexton Blakes' by the score. What he didn't sell through auction rooms he gave away. He said one went to a tramp and another to a harassed mother of six he bumped into in a Woolworths store.

This cavalier attitude may explain why it took so long for Keating to be exposed. For the recipients of his gifts would probably have sold them to junk shops and it would often take years before the painting surfaced to more conventional art outlets. In any case, nobody took the trouble to check the paintings were real. With a constant need for new pictures by dead artists, the art world of the 1950s and 1960s often considered it wisest not to delve too deeply into a painting's origin.

All it would have taken to discover Keating's fakes was closer inspection and an X-ray test. He would write in white lead paint the word 'fake', or sign his own name, or even write a rude word on the canvas before he painted over it. The words would clearly be visible under X-ray. In his fake Impressionist pictures, he often included tiny portraits of the artist whose work he was forging. His paintings were also coated with gelatine – hence the lifting of paint if cleaning was attempted.

In 1963, Keating met Jane Kelly, a pretty convent-educated schoolgirl who was studying for her exams. In Bohemian coffee bars, she and her friends would gather around the painter, treating him almost as a guru. After the death of her boyfriend in a road accident, Jane and Keating fell in love. She was seventeen and he was forty-six. The couple moved to historic Wattisfield Hall, in Suffolk, where Jane restored pictures and Keating carried on with his own creative brushwork.

It was in 1963, too, that Keating read a book on the Nineteenth Century artist Samuel Palmer and became captivated by him. He scoured the art galleries for examples of Palmer's work to copy. At the Tate Gallery, said Keating, he touched one 'and a strange sensation went through me like an electric shock'. Keating claimed the spirit of Palmer would guide his hand. 'I'd sit in my little sketching room waiting for it to happen,' he explained. 'I have never drawn a sheep from life but then Palmer's sheep would begin to appear on the paper. Then came *Valley of Vision Watched Over by the Good Shepherd in the Shadow of Shoreham Church*. With Sam's permission, I sometimes signed them with his own name, but they were his not mine. It was his hand that guided the pen.'

The fickle art world was so delighted that a market for Samuel Palmer had been created – thus allowing for inflation of the prices asked for his work – that if dealers had any doubts about the authenticity of the work, they kept them to themselves.

Keating had indeed become an art expert in his own way. He enjoyed his work with a passion. One reporter, Geraldine Norman, was later to write: 'I learned more in two weeks interviewing Tom than in seven years as *The Times* saleroom correspondent.' Supporting his claim of painting with a guiding hand, she added: 'The spirit of the artist whose style Tom was imitating at the time seemed to possess him as he worked.' In fact, it was Geraldine Norman who pieced together the clues that led to Keating's exposure as an old faker. She investigated the release of thirteen previously unknown Samuel Palmers onto the market in 1976.

Examination of the paper used revealed it was modern.

The game was up. But Keating just shrugged off his sudden notoriety. He even happily co-operated with Geraldine Norman on *The Fake's Progress*, a tongue-in-cheek account of his career. And he willingly admitted: 'My aim was to get back at unscrupulous galleries and dealers. Five or six times, dealers approached me to do copies and I did them. I was conned. Once a gentleman offered £65 to do two pictures after the style of Krieghoff. He gave me £7.50 for them and hours later they were in a Bond Street gallery being offered at £1,500.'

Keating went on to claim that certain dealers had false signatures put on the paintings he had faked. Proving the ease with which a forged painting could be 'knocked out', Keating was later to appear in a television documentary producing a 'Samuel Palmer' in front of the camera.

Tom Keating appeared at London's Old Bailey in 1977 charged with criminal deception. The case was abandoned after five weeks because of his ill health. The stress of the trial, plus years of heavy smoking and the effects of breathing in the fumes of chemicals used in art restoration, had taken their toll. But there had been some entertaining moments in court when Keating, white-bearded and with a wicked sense of humour, took the witness box.

At one point, he was shown his most famous fake: a sepia ink-wash of *Sepham Barn* sold as a genuine Samuel Palmer for £9,400. Keating turned to the jury and said: 'I am ashamed of this work.' He had no recollection of painting it, he said. Contrary to his usual attention to detail, the picture had been done using modern materials. The main figure of a shepherd was 'un-Palmerish' and the flock of sheep 'unsheep like'. It was the sort of painting, he confessed, that he would normally have burned or thrown away. In fact, *Sepham Barn* did have some significance for Keating. After its sale, he and Jane had gone to live in Tenerife. There, Jane had met a Canadian whom she had married. Her appearance at the Old Bailey to give evidence was the first time Keating had seen her in seven years.

Presented in court with another work subsequently sold for £2,550, Keating appeared bemused and said: 'That must have taken me about half an hour. It's just a doodle. It has the ingredients of Palmer, but not his technical ability or aesthetic appeal.' The 'doodle', of a barn at Shoreham, had been sold at a country auction for £35. It was later sold by a London gallery for £2,550 after restoration work by the National Gallery. As well as Keating's own revelations, the court heard colourful evidence exposing crooked dealers and ignorant experts. The discomfiture of the art establishment, so ridiculed and acutely embarrassed in court, was immense.

Having escaped sentence, Keating became a celebrity, though those who wrote about him were careful not to call him a 'forger'. An article in *The Times* described him as 'an artist and imitator of other painters'. Meanwhile, he continued turning out his paintings – but only for the right price. In fact, his notoriety had won him what he always craved as an artist: recognition. His works became highly prized. As one gallery owner said: 'Suddenly everyone wants to own a Keating. Prices have doubled in a month. His paintings are going around the world.'

Keating was offered a £250,000 contract from one London gallery and a £30,000 commission for a single portrait. He turned down both offers. 'I have enough work to make me rich beyond my wildest dreams,' he said. 'But I have met many millionaires and they have all been miserable. All I have ever wanted is to paint. I would give all the damn things away if I could afford to. Painting is God's gift, not mine, and it should be used to bring pleasure.'

In December 1983, Keating had the satisfaction of seeing Christie's auction house sell 150 of his paintings for almost £100,000. Sadly, he died two months later. The stress induced by the court case had taken its toll, but contributing factors were his years of chain smoking and the effects of breathing in the fumes of chemicals used in art restoring, including ammonia, turpentine and methyl alcohol.

His demise denied him the pleasure of seeing himself on television giving a colourful account of his life and times. TV director Rex Bloomstein, who got to know Keating well, said: 'He was a very emotional man. When painting, he would cry and shiver He was the most fascinating, complex person I have ever met.'

In 1984 there was a major sale of Keating's work. It had been expected that many of the paintings would fetch between £100 and £200 but interest in the artist, described as 'staggering' by Christie's, made them revise their estimates and they finally sold 204 works for a total of over a quarter of a million pounds – four times the amount his paintings had fetched a year earlier. Top prices were paid for a 'Monet' and a 'Van Gogh', which sold for £16,000 each. A self-portrait – ironically, the only 'genuine' painting in the sale – went for £7,500. Keating had made it as an artist in his own right at last!

In February 1992 a London pawnbroker bought what he believed to be a genuine 'fake' by Keating, only to find that it was a fake 'fake'. The artist who succeeded in exposing the sham of the art world could not have wished for a better accolade. After all, throughout his life, he had proved that imitation was the sincerest form of flattery.

Chapter 7

Past Masters of the Art Trickster's Trade

T here is nothing new about the forgery of works of art. Disgruntled painters and craftsmen throughout history have passed off their fakes as genuine, effortlessly capitalising on the gullibility, ignorance and often greed of the luminaries of the art world.

History's best known artist, Michelangelo di Lodovico Buonarroti Simoni, not only created masterpieces such as the marble sculpture of *David* and the painting of the Sistine Chapel, he also dabbled in fakery. He first came to fame when he sold a marble Cupid to Cardinal San Giorgio, who then summoned him to Rome in 1496. It produced much needed funds for the struggling young artist. What he never told the cardinal was that he had first stained and buried the statue to 'age' it as an antique.

One of the most prolific sculptors of all time was Giovanni Bastianini – and every one of his works was a fake. The Nineteenth Century Florentine forger turned out terracotta busts by the dozen for a crooked art dealer. Before his death in 1868, Bastianini was heartened to see them displayed in museums and galleries around the globe. According to London's Victoria and Albert Museum, which took two of the forgeries, the faker's works were 'perfect examples of Renaissance sculpture'.

A pair of forgers fell out over one particular work of art. The Tiara of Saitaphernes was an intricate golden headdress which reposed in the Louvre, Paris, admired by all and sundry as one of the minor wonders of the ancient world. In 1902, however, a Parisian painter claimed to have been the creator of this beautiful work of art. Administrators of the Louvre fiercely denied the claim, insisting that the artefact was genuine.

The row created great publicity, reaching even Russia, where the newspaper reports of the scandal were read by a goldsmith, Israel Rouchomowsky. He knew that the headdress was a fake – and was equally certain that it was not the work of the Parisian claimant. For the creator of the forgery was Rouchomowsky himself! The goldsmith travelled to Paris to lay claim to the dubious honour and, when Louvre officials adamantly refused to give him credit for his work, he produced his original designs for the tiara, which he had drawn up eight years earlier. Rouchomowsky finally proved the origins of the golden tiara beyond all doubt – by creating yet another one, as a perfect match for the Louvre's most embarrassing fake.

Another artist who laid claim to his own work was an amateur sculptor who found his creation proudly displayed in Harrods, the top people's store in London's Knightsbridge. Their antiques department is staffed by some of the leading experts in their various fields. But even they were bamboozled by the work of Frank Sedgwick, a forty-seven-year-old ex-fitter whose hobby was woodwork and who had knocked up an 'antique' in less than a fortnight in his garden shed in Kent. The honest Mr Sedgwick had sold his wooden sculpture of a kneeling stag for £165 in 1972. It changed hands several times over the following five years until it turned up on display at Harrods with a price tag of £9,800. It was labelled as a 'carving from a French chateau, dated circa 1580'. In 1977 Sedgwick walked into the store and told the astonished assistant: 'That's all my own work.' Harrods removed it instantly.

Modern technology, rather than masterful knowledge, uncovered a fake that had been displayed as one of the most prized possessions of America's Cleveland Museum of Art. The museum believed that their wooden *Madonna And Child* had been carved in Italy in the thirteenth century. In fact, the work was indeed that of an Italian – having been carved by art restorer Alceo Dossena in 1920. In 1927 the *Madonna And Child* was X-rayed to discover whether such an ancient work was due for restoration. The discovery of modern nails embedded in the wood prompted the statue's sudden removal to the museum basement.

Within three weeks, the Cleveland museum authorities had found a suitable replacement for the fake *Madonna And Child*. They purchased a marble statue of *Athena* for $120,000. Unfortunately, it too was the work of Alceo Dossena, master forger! Sadly for Dossena, his expertise never made him a fortune. The Italian stonecutter-turned-sculptor produced a mass of sculptures during the early years of the Twentieth Century but sold them all through a pair of clever confidence tricksters. Jeweller Alberto Fasoliu and antique dealer Romano Palesi set up a studio in Rome for the young sculptor and paid him a small salary. There he spent ten years slaving away at his forgeries for a pittance, while his crooked agents made themselves a small fortune.

Another gallery which paid handsomely for a string of fakes was the renowned New York Metropolitan Museum of Art. One particular statue, a two-metre tall figure of an Etruscan warrior, held pride of place. One arm was missing, as was the thumb of his other hand. This was not surprising, as the statue had supposedly been buried since pre-Roman days. The museum had paid $40,000 for the Etruscan warrior in 1918. It was not until 1960 that Alfredo Fioravanti announced that he and five accomplices had created it half a century before. To prove that he was indeed the sculptor, Fioravanti produced the warrior's missing thumb ... which fitted perfectly!

The Metropolitan Museum was again in trouble in 1975 when one of its most popular attractions, a beautiful bronze horse supposedly of the Greek period, was shown to be a fake and had to be withdrawn. In 1984 the museum was forced to re-examine many of its masterwork, including elegant gold pieces embellished with jewels in the style of Benvenuto Cellini, the Sixteenth Century Florentine goldsmith, sculptor and engraver. The alarm was raised when a museum curator came upon working sketches by a Nineteenth Century German craftsman, Reinhold Vasters, for a gold cup depicting a jewel-studded dragon. It prompted the museum to make further examination of their own treasured gold cups – and realise that they had been soldered together in a modern manner. Vasters, and not Cellini, was the artist, and the embarrassed Met was forced to admit that no fewer than forty-five of their golden treasures were mere fakes.

Perhaps the most publicly embarrassing scandal over fake artworks occurred in Germany in the 1950s. It involved an art restorer turned forger named Dietrich Fey. Despite warnings that Fey was not to be trusted, he was nevertheless given the prestigious job of working on the frescoes of the Marienkirche in Lübeck. Scraps of the original Thirteenth Century frescoes had come to light during the Second World War as bombs gutted the church. When his work was complete, Fey proudly declared that he had 'added nothing but merely preserved what had survived'. The work was unveiled before West German Chancellor Konrad Adenauer in September 1951. It was a momentous occasion, not only for art experts and historians but for Christians too. For the frescoes showed Biblical scenes and saints as well as mythical beasts. A special five pfennig stamp was even issued to commemorate the event.

Fey appeared to have done too good a job, and it was only when he was awarded the federal Cross of Merit for his work that a fellow art restorer on the project, Lothar Malskat, pulled his own masterstroke. Malskat was believed to have faked Chagalls and other modern masters before the war, and to have given them to Fey to sell. Now, embittered over lack of recognition for projects he had worked on, Malskat stepped forward in May 1952 to announce that the frescoes were all his own work. The claim threatened to throw the art world into turmoil but, after much debate, Malskat was simply dismissed as a troublemaker. Most critics agreed that neither Malskat nor Fey could possibly have created work of such beauty. Above all, the West German Association for the Preservation of Ancient Monuments did not want the embarrassment of knowing it had possibly spent £25,000 on dubious restoration work.

Even more frustrated that no one believed his confession, Malskat took drastic and incredible action. He instructed his lawyer to file charges against himself and Fey! At the court hearing, Malskat produced a film proving that the walls of the church had been almost entirely bare when he and Fey had begun work on them. He said the original paintings were so fragile they had crumbled to dust at the mere touch of a restoration brush. The only thing to do after that, he said, was to create the artwork from scratch.

Even after this confession, there were those who refused to believe what they were hearing – but Malskat had one final trick up his sleeve to convince them. He led members of the court to the church walls and pointed out how the heavenly faces of a choir on the frescoes bore remarkable similarities to the not-so-saintly likes of Marlene Dietrich, Rasputin, Genghis Khan and even Malskat's own sister. If that wasn't enough proof, Malskat told the astonished gathering, they could always visit Schleswig Cathedral and see his 'ancient' painting of a turkey – a bird unknown in Europe until after the discovery of America!

Dietrich Fey was sentenced to twenty months in jail and Lothar Malskat was sentenced to eighteen months. After his release, and satisfied with his revenge on Fey, Malskat returned to art restoration – but in an honest way.

Another quick-on-the draw artist was David Stein, who for a brief but mind-boggling four-year reign was undisputed king of the art forgers. Indeed, his total income from his fakes was around one million pounds. Born near Paris in 1935, Stein was a gifted artist, but he felt payments for his works simply were not enough, especially when he heard about the high prices other painters were receiving. It was too much of a temptation to resist. Working in watercolours or oils, he recreated the styles of some of the world's best-known artists, both living and dead.

The dead gave David Stein no trouble, but reproducing the living led to his downfall. On one occasion, while living in New York, he rushed off three watercolours 'by French artist Marc Chagall', which he had promised to a dealer. Working furiously in his apartment, the whole fateful operation took just seven hours. During that time, he treated the paper with cold tea to give it the impression of ageing, perfectly captured Chagall's style, and added to each painting the finishing touch of the artist's signature. He finished at 6am in the morning, and by lunchtime that same day he was handing his 'genuine' works of art, each with its own certificate of authentication, to a delighted art dealer. The dealer was so proud of his new acquisitions that he decided to show them to someone who just arrived in New York – Marc Chagall himself. Chagall's reaction was first bewilderment and then horror. 'They are not mine,' he said. 'And they are diabolical.'

Had Stein stuck to recreating Cezannes, Renoirs or Manets, he would have got away with it. Impersonating Chagall, who was alive and well and more than likely to come face-to-face with his faked work, was bad judgment. It meant he had to abandon his New York gallery, financed of course by his ill-gotten gains. As the police arrived at Stein's front door, he fled out the back, taking his wife Anne-Marie and their small child with him. They ended up in California – but there Stein's luck ran out. He was arrested and confessed to his handiwork. 'If only I had stuck to dead men,' he moaned as he was charged with ninety-seven counts of grand larceny and counterfeiting. In January 1969 he was sentenced to three years in Sing Sing Prison.

While in jail, Stein shared his knowledge of forgery with the New York Police Department, helping them to create a special art forgery squad. With remission, he served just sixteen months. His time in prison had also given him the time to think about a legitimate, money-making venture. Stein had hit upon the idea of painting famous people in the style of well-known artists. Only this time, he would declare his work as a genuine gimmick. For instance, from a single, three-hour sitting he painted actress Brigitte Bardot in twenty-five different styles, ranging from Picasso to Van Gogh. Unfortunately for Stein, he then made the big mistake of setting up business in France. The French police still wanted to interview him about his previous lifestyle. And following that interview, Stein was back in jail – this time for two-and-a-half years.

Upon his release, Stein concentrated only on paintings by Stein. But he was still bitter about what he considered the fickleness of so-called art experts. And he still reckoned he had had the last laugh. 'A lot of the art world is fake,' he said. 'And they may not know it, but there are about two or three hundred of my forgeries still on the market listed as originals.'

A touring exhibition of Expressionist works was one of the art world's most remarkable success stories of the early Nineties. American students flocked to see the fifty-eight paintings, intrigued by the notion that these were works of degenerate art that Hitler had sought to burn but which had miraculously escaped the Nazi torch. It was only when the paintings were on their twelfth stop, near Chicago, that a visiting art dealer called the police and alleged that all fifty-eight were fakes. The tour was halted, the pictures impounded and one of the most astonishing art frauds of all time began to fall apart at the seams.

The tour of American colleges had been the brainwave of Bryn

Lloyd Williams, a former art dealer from Chalfont St Giles, in the English Home Counties. He had already induced eighty-seven Irish art investors to put up £3.2million to buy 'Old Masters' by the likes of Rubens, Rembrandt and Sir Joshua Reynolds, which they were to sell on to guaranteed buyers for double the price. The pictures were modern fakes or nineteenth-century copies, yet enough money rolled in to enable Williams to acquire his next collection of worthless fakes: the supposed 'art treasures' condemned by the Nazis but rescued by a Jewish nobleman who had fled Germany in 1938.

To raise the value of the fifty-eight Expressionist works, Williams sent some on a tour of Germany, while the others went the rounds of American universities, where the cream of America's art academia lavished praise on them. When finally exposed as fakes, the German police also impounded the European exhibition. The law finally caught up with Williams six years later when, in London's High Court in 1998, his long-suffering investors succesfully sued the faker.

Most art fakers' talents are hidden, for obvious reasons. Eric Hebborn was different. The genial Englishman was among the most successful and prolific artists of his generation. His drawings can still be found in great private collections and in galleries and museums around the world. Yet Hebborn could never be honoured for his services to art. Instead, he was destined to become known as one of the greatest fakers of all time.

Hebborn copied almost every important European painter from the Fourteenth to the Twentieth Century and created more than 1,000 'Old Master' drawings which have been attributed to the likes of Van Dyck, Gainsborough, Poussin and Degas. In *The Art Forgers Handbook*, which he wrote a year before his death in Italy in 1996, he described his craft as 'a glorious game', a way of entertaining himself as well as of making money. Hebborn, an ex-Borstal boy who started his fakery as a penniless London art student, always insisted that he was no conman because none of his drawings was a copy; each was a fresh work that recreated the style of a past great artist. But he admitted his glee at deceiving the pundits. 'I have never tried to fool the man in the street,' he once said. 'Only the "experts" are worth fooling – and the greater the expert the greater the satisfaction.'

But it is art cheat Elmyr de Hory who is the recipient of the greatest accolade of anyone in his line of business. He was the subject of a book called *Fake*. Not only that, it was written by fellow forger Clifford Irving, who was the creator of the 'Howard Hughes autobiography' in the 1970s.

De Hory was a stateless Hungarian who was a fine artist in his own right. He was born in 1911, the only child of land-owning parents who divorced when he was sixteen. De Hory went first to an art school in Budapest, then the Akademie Heimann in Munich and finally to the Académie de la Grande Chaumière in Paris. He was a homosexual whose charm soon won him friends from the world of famous artists including Matisse and Picasso – two friends he would later have no qualms about imitating for financial gain.

Although he was making a good living and gaining in reputation as an artist, de Hory was to suffer a cruel fate. After returning to Budapest in 1938 after Hitler's annexation of Austria, he was arrested as a political undesirable. He was interned first in Transylvania and then moved to a concentration camp in Germany where he suffered badly at the hands of the Gestapo. The end of the war saw de Hory a broken and penniless refugee subsisting in Paris. However, a chance remark by a visitor to his studio was to set him on the road to profitable forgeries. Spotting a line-drawing by de Hory of a young girl's head, the visitor asked: 'Is that a Picasso?' De Hory did not demur. Instead he accepted the equivalent of £50 for the picture – then went on to paint another half a dozen 'Picassos'.

In fact, de Hory became so adept at recreating Picasso's work that the great man himself was once fooled. De Hory had the cheek to ask Picasso to authenticate one of his nude fakes. Looking at the painting, and readily putting his name to it, Picasso remarked: 'I remember painting her. It did take rather a long time to complete as I could not resist making love to her.'

After falling out with a partner in his crooked business, de Hory fled, first to Brazil, then New York and finally to Los Angeles. The same attributes that had won him friends in Paris soon earned him a place in Hollywood's smart set. He quickly realised that here was real money to be had. So he changed his name to Baron de Hory and turned out paintings by Matisse and Renoir which were quickly snapped up by the rich residents of Hollywood.

In 1952, when a sharp-eyed dealer spotted a fake Modigliani, de Hory was forced to flee back to New York, where he sold three fake Matisse drawings for £500 each. Deciding to start a new life for himself, de Hory went to Miami and attempted to exist only on his own work. But when times got hard, he fell back on producing fake paintings of famous artists. He claimed he could paint a portrait in forty-five minutes, draw a 'Modigliani' in ten and then immediately knock off a 'Matisse.' Over the next two years, de Hory made nearly £200,000 from his fakes. And his colourful life continued. He was arrested and then freed after being suspected of a homosexual murder in Mexico City; he threw fabulous parties attended by glittering stars such as Marilyn Monroe, and he attempted suicide after his criminal activities were exposed.

He said: 'The art dealers, the experts and the critics resent my talent because they don't want it shown how easily they can be fooled. I have tarnished the infallible image they rely upon for their fortunes.'

De Hory finally settled on the island of Ibiza. But he was not to find peace. He was in the clutches of a conman called Ferdinand Legros who controlled him and made a fortune out of his illicit work. The artist's tragic end came in December 1976 when all his misdeeds caught up with him. Everyone knew he was a crook, art dealers were demanding their money back and he had spent three months in jail on charges ranging from homosexuality to consorting with known criminals. All this painted a future too grim for Elmyr de Hory, the expert art faker. In a fit of depression, he killed himself.

We'll let another art forger have the final word. 'You can sell anything to Americans and Englishmen,' said the grandson of French painter Jean François Millet when convicted of forgery in 1935. 'They know nothing about art. Even their experts know nothing. All you have to do is to ask a fabulous price.' Many forgers before and since would agree with Millet's verdict on the gullibility of the leading lights of the art world. The forgers' only argument with Millet might be that the trade in fakes is not confined 'to Americans and Englishmen', nor, as we have seen, is it peculiar to the twentieth century. Fakes have been with us for as long as a talented rogue has picked up a paintbrush!

Chapter 8

Fastest Fake Cowboy in the West

Tales from the Wild West never fail to fire the imagination; pictures of cowboys riding across cactus-strewn deserts, gunfights, Indians and galloping horses all come to mind and have inspired some of the greatest Wild West legends.

The story of Frank T. Hopkins is just one of those legends. And quite rightly. For he fought against all the adversities of the time and quite literally rode into the annals of cowboy history... or so it was believed until Hopkins's life was re-examined in the rather more cynical Twenty-first Century.

Hopkins always boasted of his heritage and exploits (including being the only white survivor of Custer's Last Stand) but his greatest claim to fame was a long way from home – competing in a legendary sixty-eight-day race across 2,860 miles of Arabian Desert and winning. Now, however, nothing Hopkins built his reputation on appears to be true. It seems he was a cowboy conman and a mustang-riding master of lies.

The story starts with Hopkins being born in a log cabin in Fort Laramie, Wyoming, shortly after the American Civil War. He claimed to have been the son of an Army scout and Sioux mother, whose father was a Sioux chief. Hopkins also claimed to have been a long-distance US Cavalry rider by the age of twelve.

His love of horses helped forge a link with the Indians with whom Hopkins is reported to have ridden, capturing and breaking mustangs. The story continues that Hopkins rode dispatch for well-known Generals Nelson Appleton Miles and George Cook, American Civil War legends and both foes of the Indian tribes. Hopkins was then a buffalo hunter and worked with Great Plains trailblazer and Wild West showman Charles Jesse 'Buffalo' Jones and 'Buffalo' Bill Cody.

The Hopkins legend continues with his success as a breeder of mustangs after he acquired a small, white mustang mare in the most extraordinary circumstances. It was 1877 and a time when the army was coming down hard on the northern Indian tribes. When some of the Sioux Indians had been herded onto the Pine Ridge reservation, General Cook ordered all the captured ponies to be shot, except two for each tepee. Hopkins told the story that a Sioux chief named Red Calf, who had been a childhood friend of his, told him to buy a certain white-eyed mustang before she was shot. Later, Hopkins bought a pinto mustang stallion which he bred with the white mare – thus beginning a successful blood line known as the White-y Family.

Hopkins got into endurance racing through his success at breaking and riding a stallion which he took on buffalo runs. In the summer of 1886, an endurance race was proposed from Galveston, Texas, to Rutland, Vermont. Hopkins' friend, Buffalo Jones, agreed to finance the 1,799-mile ride if Hopkins entered with his mustang stallion Joe. Only one horse was allowed for each rider and a day's journey was not to exceed ten hours, and route judges were positioned along the way to keep a tally of the riders' times on cards that they each carried.

One record of Hopkins' ride goes thus:

'I passed twelve more tired horses. Joe was feeling fine. When I took his saddle off at the end of the day, he would swing his head and let his heels drive at me. On the seventeenth day, Joe passed the last horse and rider. We were in the Mississippi country where there had been a heavy rain and the yellow mud stuck to Joe's feet but he was still happy to shake his head, jump and play at the close of the day. Our route was marked with red paint daubed on trees and stones and was easy to follow. On this ride, I weighed 152 pounds. My saddle, blanket and slicker weighed thirty-four pounds and Joe weighed 800.'

Hopkins and Joe won the race and the $3,000 prize. It was said that Hopkins and Joe were in Rutland thirteen days before the second horse and rider came in. He had made the journey in thirty-one days with an average distance of 57.7 miles a day.

This amazing exploit set Hopkins on the road to horse-riding fame. Bill Cody, now touring in the famous Buffalo Bill Wild West Show, invited Hopkins to join his troupe, where he stayed for thirty years, becoming an established figure in the elite Congress of Riders. It was while he was with the show in Paris for the World's Fair in 1889 that Hopkins supposedly heard about an epic race, known as the 'Ocean of Fire', across almost 3,000 miles of Arabian Desert.

In the past, only desert-bred horses had competed in the legendary race but a rich Arab businessman called Rau Rasmussen, who had become fascinated by Western horses and their riders, was anxious to pit an American mustang against the Arabian horses. According to Hopkins's story, the prestigious race had taken place annually for a thousand years and a non-Arab rider had never competed before. Hopkins was at first reluctant to take up the challenge – not for fear of losing face but because of the lost earnings while he was taking part. He changed his mind when the Congress of Riders of the World stepped in to finance him.

Hopkins shipped three of his mustang stallions to Aden. All were half-brothers bred from the White-y line but his favourite, and the horse destined to tackle the gruelling race, was a white pinto called Hidalgo. This horse was eight years old and, wrote Hopkins in his diary, 'as fine a looker as could be found. I had ridden him on some hard rides and knew what he could do if called upon'.

The Ocean of Fire race started in Aden and headed north for more than two months across the inhospitable Arabian Desert. Much of the ride was over treacherous limestone where food and water were scarce. Camels accompanied the horsemen and carried barley for the horses, which sometimes went without water for up to two days. Sandstorms regularly blinded both men and animals and forced them to stop.

As Hopkins told it, over a hundred horses started the race but just a handful were left after the first week. By Day 14, Hidalgo and its rider were easily passing other horses and eventually took the lead. They reached the finishing line an amazing sixty-eight days later, more than a full day ahead of the next rider. Against all the odds, Hopkins and Hidalgo had won. Only three other horses officially finished the race. One observer was quoted by Hopkins as saying: 'It seemed as though the tougher the environment, the better Hidalgo performed. As a distant relative to the Arabian horses he had competed against, Hidalgo had finally come home at last.'

That's Hopkins's story – but how much of it is backed by contemporary evidence? How much of it was elaborated upon by the egotistical champion? Did Hopkins want glory so badly that he was prepared to fabricate his epic victory? Was there even an Ocean of Fire race at all?

It is not a popular occupation debunking heroes, especially cowboy kings of the Wild West. And when, more than a century later, plans were announced for a movie version of the Hopkins saga, there were few who at first voiced doubts about the desert victory of an all-American horseman against a bunch of Arabs. One critic wrote:

'A true legend, Frank T. Hopkins and his mighty Hidalgo live on in American horse history as the greatest pair of endurance racers ever. Over a hundred years ago have passed since that infamous race but their memory lives on even today. When we need to reach out to our heroes for inspiration, Hopkins and Hidalgo are still there – proving once again that nothing is impossible if you want it bad enough.'

In 2004, Walt Disney released its movie about Hopkins and the race. The £50 million blockbuster, titled *Hidalgo*, featured stunning scenes of sandstorms swirling around the lone horseman Hopkins character as he rode, drenched in sweat across the windswept desert. It was, Disney promised, an adventure film appealing to both young and old who appreciated true daring exploits.

But by this time, there were claims that *Hidalgo* could be telling a fictional tale of achievement rather than a factual one. The Long Riders' Guild, an American organisation that honours epic equestrian achievement, promised to investigate the story. After a year's research, the guild came to the conclusion that Hopkins was a counterfeit cowboy with an imagination that galloped faster than any horse he claimed to have ridden.

Two of the guild's founder members, Basha and CuChullaine O'Reilly, devoted considerable time to proving Hopkins was a sham and his story a lie. The two edited and published an annotated version of *Hidalgo and other Stories* by Frank T. Hopkins. In the book, they refuted Hopkins' claims point by point, enlisting the support of more than fifty curators, criminologists, equestrians and other experts. They said they could find no record of anyone by the name of Rau Rasmussen in Aden and pointed out it was unlikely Hopkins travelled to Paris with the Wild West show, since he never worked with them – not for a week, never mind the claimed thirty years! And they could find no mention of him in the carefully-kept records of the US Cavalry. Further, several of the victories Hopkins said he had enjoyed in long-distance races were a little dubious, either because the alleged route was unlikely or because the race just did not exist.

Basha O'Reilly concluded that Hopkins was 'one of history's great hoaxers'. CuChullaine added: 'Hopkins's fantasies are in no way an autobiographic account. They are the deluded ramblings of a very sick man.' He claimed that the only known image of Hopkins in cowboy gear showed him sitting on a stool, and remarked: 'The idea that there is no documented photo of Hopkins in the saddle is staggering.' The two authors were determined to debunk the Hopkins legend, even sending several letters of complaint to filmmakers Touchstone and Disney, saying it was wrong to advertise the movie *Hidalgo* as a 'true story'. They got no replies.

Researchers at the History Channel who were planning a television documentary of Hopkins also felt they had been saddled with an equestrian myth rather than a true tale. Said producer Bill Brummel: 'Everything seems to go back to Hopkins's own writings. As documentarians, we look for multiple sources to back up factual material. We couldn't find a thing.'

The non-discovery of any record (other than Hopkins' own) about the Ocean of Fire and other races snowballed. Casey Greene, curator of the Rosenburg Library in Galveston, said: 'I've referenced every newspaper between 1880 and 1890 but there is no mention of Frank Hopkins or a race from Galveston to Vermont.' Dr Juri Winchester, considered to be the world's leading expert on Buffalo Bill, could not find any references either. 'I looked for a record of Hopkins but never found any mention of him among the vast list of friends, acquaintances or work colleagues of Buffalo Bill. In my opinion, the man was a fraud. If Hopkins was the "ringmaster" for the Wild West, why do we not find his name listed as such, when even the pile drivers and dishwashers get their names in the programmes?'

So did Frank T. Hopkins achieve any of what he claimed? Did the Ocean of Fire race even exist? The screenwriter behind *Hidalgo*, John Fusco, insisted both were real. However, it was revealed that he had based some of his film account on two chapters about the race found in a book called *Blood of the Arab* by a writer named Albert W. Harris. And Harris had based his account on letters Hopkins wrote him in 1940.

Fusco responded: 'Having taken place in 1890 and the Bedu culture being of oral tradition, I was not bothered by lack of contemporary documentation.' A horseman himself, he said he had researched the Hopkins story in America for over twelve years, mainly by recording oral histories from members of the Lakota and Blackfoot tribes and by seeking out articles, mostly from mid-Twentieth Century equestrian magazines that recounted different aspects of Hopkins' tale. Fusco said he speaks the Lakota language and that tribal elders had told him 'the story of the small pinto mustang that had won many long-distance races under a half-breed cowboy'. Those elders had also heard about the great victory in a long-distance race in Arabia. Added Fusco protectively of his *Hidalgo* account:

> 'This story is a major thorn in the side of elitist groups who don't like the idea of a humble cowboy achieving what he did. I believe the thrust of the story is true, although I had to take creative licence with a sketchy story. Myth and legend infuse the film.'

Peter Harrigan, a journalist stationed in Saudi Arabia, saw an early *Hidalgo* script and began to wonder about the Ocean of Fire race. While writing a series of articles about it in the *Arab News*, Harrigan contacted Yemen's Ghalib Al-Quaiti, the last ruling sultan of the area including Aden, and an Oxford and Cambridge educated historian. His answer was very direct. 'There is absolutely no record of any horse race in the past staged from Aden or from anywhere in that part of Arabia. Southern Arabia has never been known for its horses.' Harrigan himself said the likes of Disney and John Fusco would prefer to believe that Arabs relied exclusively on an 'oral tradition'.

So what is the truth? A Frank T. Hopkins did live from 1865 to 1951. Employment records show he was a foreman digging subway tunnels on the East Coast, a shipyard boilermaker and a horse-handler for the Ringling Brothers' Circus in the Thirties. A rather murky picture of Buffalo Bill's Wild West Show from 1898 shows a young man who could be him. But if that's the case, he showed scant reverence for the great showman... In his 'memoirs', Hopkins called Buffalo Bill 'a stinking drunk'.

The legend that was to become Frank T. Hopkins actually seems to have started not in the 1800s but the late 1930s when Hopkins met a pulp-fiction writer from Denver called Charles B. Roth. Roth listened in a bar as Hopkins recounted his tales of long-distance races and turned them into an article in *Horse* magazine in 1936. The article began: 'Mr Hopkins does not list himself among the great riders, but in my opinion, he not only belongs in the list, he belongs at the head of it.'

The article then went on to list Hopkins's 'achievements', including 400 long-distance races and the Ocean of Fire race. Roth and Hopkins went on to sell thousands of copies of their books and raked in 'a tidy fortune', according to newspaper accounts of the time.

But what appears to be a pretty wild account of a so-called Wild West hero will always continue to court controversy. As author David Dary, a University of Oklahoma professor and expert in the Wild West, said: 'The American West was full of people such as Hopkins who spun yarns. His tale is an elaborate hoax.'

Where Hopkins ended his days in unclear but it is thought he was buried in a pauper's grave on Long Island, New York. His death was perhaps the only journey that was never in doubt.

Chapter 9

Swansong of the Phantom Pianist

Many performers suffer for their art. But pianist Joyce Hatto, producing flawless recordings while dying from cancer, touched the hearts of music-lovers everywhere. And while her fans listened in awe to the masterful performances, experts were amazed at her faultless playing of works by Brahms, Liszt, Mozart and Beethoven. More poignantly, all 107 recordings were produced by her husband in Hatto's dying years.

But instead of winning praise for his efforts, William Barrington-Coupe was exposed as a fraudster when it was discovered that many of the works were actually performed by other artists. Hatto had won international acclaim for a musical talent that wasn't hers. 'There has never been a music scandal quite like it,' was how one aficionado summed up the fiasco.

So just why did Barrington-Coupe do such a thing? He claimed it was an act of love, giving his wife an end to a career he felt was 'unfairly overlooked'. He denied his wife knew anything about the dishonesty and said little money had been made from the recordings.

Even before the scandal broke, in the months following her death at the age of seventy-seven in 2006, Joyce Hatto's life had been checkered. Born in Kilburn, North-West London, in 1928, she was the daughter of a music-loving confectioner. She always maintained she carried on with her piano practice even when German bombs rained down on the city. The only reason she did not get into the Royal Academy of Music, she would later tell people, was because a tutor had scoffed at her musical interest, saying: 'It is more important for a girl like you to cook roast dinner than play piano.'

This could have all been an invention, of course; Hatto always liked to suggest she came from a middle-class background and that her father was an antiques dealer, but there was noone left alive to verify or deny this story. 'My father played the piano himself really quite well,' she told one music critic. 'Even before I could read, he would play to me every evening before I went to sleep. He was a devotee of Rachmaninov and never missed an opportunity to hear him play. It was almost as if Rachmaninov was a relative.'

Whether Hatto did in fact cook roast dinners on a regular basis, as her tutor had suggested, is not known. But she did give concerts in London from the 1950s, encouraged, she said, by influential composer Sir Granville Bannock, who described her as 'a born performer'. Legendary composer Sir Michael Tippett had also, allegedly, urged her to devote her life to Bach.

Hatto later claimed to have been in contact with some of the greatest musicians of the time including Victor de Sabata, Thomas Beecham, Wilhelm Furtwangler, Sviatoslav Richter, Alfred Cortot, Benno Moiseiwitsch, Frederic Lamond, Paul Hindemith and Michael Tippett. Was any of this true? As writer Ates Orga said: 'She mentions all the big names but they are long since dead.'

Hatto's early musical career was not greatly recognised. One critic was particularly harsh reviewing her performance at Chelsea Town Hall in October 1953, writing: 'Joyce Hatto grappled doggedly with too hasty tempi in Mozart's D Minor Piano Concerto and was impeded from conveying significant feelings towards the work, especially in quick figuration.'

Hatto and Barrington-Coupe met when he set himself up as a concert agent after leaving the army. He advertised for clients in the *Daily Telegraph* and Hatto answered. Recalled Barrington-Coupe: 'She was seen by a friend who said she was exceptional. I rang and got her mother, who asked me if I was Joyce's boyfriend. Eventually Joyce rang back and we talked for an hour about Shakespeare and music. By the time I put the phone down, I couldn't wait to hear her voice again.'

By the time she married Barrington-Coupe in 1956, Hatto had not received the accolades she felt she deserved. She played at prestigious venues such as the Royal Festival Hall but the concerts were organised by her husband and again the reviews were lukewarm. In 1961, in *Gramophone* magazine, critic Trevor Harvey wrote of her recording of Rachmaninov's Piano Concerto No2:

> 'One wonders... whether her technique is really on top of the difficulties of this music... She shows a musical sense of give and take with the orchestra but it remains a small, rather pallid performance.'

Hatto supplemented her income by teaching piano at Crofton Grange, a girls' boarding school in Hertfordshire. There were also concerts by 'pupils of Joyce Hatto'. As Hatto attempted to make her name, Barrington-Coupe began to dabble in the music industry himself, setting off on the road to rogue recordings.

In 1960, after the collapse of a company he was involved in called Saga Films, he created the Lyrique record label. An acquaintance, Marcel Rodd, had a record-pressing factory and it was at this time that Barrington-Coupe first began to release records by artists under different pseudonyms – a practice not unheard of at the time.

One of Barrington-Coupe's former colleagues, Ted Perry, said: 'The repertoire was from the variety of master tapes in Rodd's tape library. It was also, possibly, from some of Coupe's own tapes, since he always seemed to have a lot of recorded material of unknown, not to say dubious, provenance.'

Barrington-Coupe went on to set up another record label, Triumph Records. His partner this time was Joe Meek, a producer best known for the 1962 hit *Telstar* by The Tornados. Meek also hit the news when first charged with importuning for immoral purposes, and when facing police interviews about a suitcase containing the mutilated body of a rent boy. In 1967, Meek fatally shot his landlady before killing himself.

When Barrington-Coupe's company went into liquidation, he looked for another money-making venture. This ended with what was then the longest-running and most expensive trial at the Old Bailey. For he formed a company, W.H. Barrington-Coupe Ltd, which imported radios from Hong Kong to sell at London markets and through mail order – but which overlooked the paying of purchase tax.

On May 17, 1966, Barrington-Coupe and four others were found guilty of failing to pay £84,000 in purchase tax on imported records – the equivalent of £1million today. Barrington-Coupe was fined £3,600 and jailed for a year. His company was fined £4,000 and was wound up. Said Judge Alan King-Hamilton: 'These were blatant and impertinent frauds, carried out in my opinion rather clumsily. But such was your conceit that you thought yourself smart enough to get away with it.'

While Barrington-Coupe was in jail, Hatto continued her rather unremarkable piano-playing career, carrying out tours of Poland, Russia and Scandinavia. She only ever once played in America, rather good-naturedly confessing: 'Noone came.'

When Barrington-Coupe was released, the two stayed together, she now gaining some reputation for her recitals of Chopin and Liszt, while he 'retired' from business dealings.

In 1970, Hatto was offered the chance to work with conductor Dr Vernon Handley on the *Bax Symphonic Variations* with the Guildford Philharmonic Orchestra. Although not the easiest musician to work with, Hatto nevertheless turned in an acceptable performance. Dr Handley's personal view of Hatto's talents varied. When the performance was recorded at EMI's Abbey Road studio for Barrington-Coupe's latest record label, Revolution, he said: 'She was very, very good as a solo player and a very nice person but she had a very doubtful sense of rhythm. The recording of the *Bax* was a tremendous labour.'

Some years later, Dr Handley was altogether kinder. 'As a solo pianist, she was absolutely marvellous,' he said. 'She had ten wonderful fingers and she could get round anything. Also she was an extraordinarily charming person to work with, even if she could be very difficult.'

It was at this time that Hatto was said to be suffering from ovarian cancer, though no mention of this was made to Dr Handley. Her husband said she went straight from the recording studio to hospital for surgery, which was then refused because of her low blood count. Barrington-Coupe said Hatto's determination to complete the recordings and perform with the orchestra was admirable, because one of her doctors had commented that the pianist was 'not in a fit state to do either'.

Strangely, a consultant radiologist who saw Hatto every six weeks for the last eight years of her life said she was first treated for ovarian cancer only fourteen years before her death in June 2006, and had no previous history of the disease.

The *Bax* recording won Hatto a rare favourable review. 'Joyce Hatto gives a highly commendable account of the demanding piano part,' wrote Robert Layton in *Gramophone* in 1971. In 1972, Hatto embarked on an ambitious project to play the eight complete works of Liszt in London. She achieved this in the famous Wigmore Hall, which she described as 'rather like a morgue or a chapel of rest, don't you think?'

Hatto gave up public performances in 1976. Barrington-Coupe claimed this was because she was so badly hurt when a critic said it was 'impolite to look ill'. This review cannot be traced.

Although it would be thirty years before the couple would make the news again, they were not idle. Living as virtual recluses, they made no less than 103 recordings of Hatto's piano-playing, making her one of the most prolific artists of all time.

The first of these, on Barrington-Coupe's label, Concert Artist, was released in 2002. More followed. They came from a 20ft-square shed at the rear of a house owned by sound engineer Roger Chatterton, who some time before had worked with well-known bands. Chatterton said he first met Barrington-Coupe in 2003 and was unaware he was to be involved in deception. The first recording to be worked on was a *Bax*. Recalling this work with Barrington-Coupe, Chatterton told the *Daily Mail* newspaper:

'William was looking for a recording studio that had Dolby A, a noise-reducing system. I didn't actually have that system but he started bringing other bits around and we just started general editing and file copying together. He would give me basic audio files of various recordings, maybe fifteen tracks for a particular album, and my job was to make sure they came together. The music might have been recorded in different venues, for instance, so I would have to adjust the tone, sound level and so on to make it sound like they were all recorded at the same time and in the same place. It was the icing on the cake, if you will.

'William was an engineer or producer who had been involved

in those recordings. That is what he told me. To be honest, I don't know where the rights lay with this music. It was not my concern. Then William would bring in these unmarked CDs and digital audio tapes with Joyce's music on. I would ask him where they were recorded, to get an audio image to work with. William would choose the best versions to bring in to save studio time. He would bring them in here and one track might not match the preceding or succeeding track. Usually, it was not orchestral, but we did do some Rachmaninov and the Brahms tape with Rene Kohler that they are making all the fuss over.'

The reason a fuss was being made was because Rene Kohler could not be traced. The sleeve notes on the CD said he had studied at the Jagiellonian University of Krakow but the university knew noone of that name. In fact, the university did not even have a music department.

Later, when challenged about the mysterious conductor, Barrington-Coupe said Kohler was not the family name and that he had been given a room by a member of tutorial staff at the university for a short stay. Yet there were no photographs of him. Despite a written, detailed biography, Rene Kohler did not exist. Neither did orchestras such as the National Philharmonic and the Warsaw Philharmonia which also got mentions on the recordings.

The outpouring of recordings included the complete sonatas of Beethoven, Mozart and Mendelssohn and most of Chopin's compositions, along with rarer works such as the complete Godowsky Chopin Studies.

From 2003, the year Barrington-Coupe teamed up with Roger Chatterton, the recordings attributed to Hatto began to receive enthusiastic praise from a small number of participants on various mailing lists and web forums, sparked by a 'blind listening' test posted on a website featuring her recording of Liszt's Mephisto Waltz. Specialist record review magazines and websites such as *Gramophone*, *Music Web* and *Classics Today*, as well as some newspapers, eventually discovered Hatto, reviewed the recordings in a mostly favourable light and published interviews and appreciations of her career. One described her as 'the greatest living pianist that almost noone has ever heard off'.

Then, in May 2005, a sharp-eared 'musicologist', Marc-Andre Roberge, reported on a website that in Hatto's version of the Chopin-Godowsky Studies on the Concert Artist label, a misreading of a chord was identical to one on the Carlo Grante recording released in 1993. Unfortunately, this did not prompt Roberge to investigate further.

More skeptical analysis came later, in early 2006, when more listeners cast doubts on the Hatto recordings. Some found it hard to believe that a pianist who had not performed in public for so long and who was said to be fighting cancer should produce, in her seventies, a large number of such high-quality recordings. Details of the recordings could not be confirmed. Yet even then, music critic Jeremy Nicholas, writing in *Gramophone*, challenged the cynics, saying he had evidence the Hatto recordings were legitimate.

Joyce Hatto died at the couple's home in Royston, Hertfordshire, on June 30, 2006. She was seventy-seven. Strangely, for a performer then being hailed as 'one of the greatest pianists Britain has ever produced', only a handful of people attended her funeral at Cambridge Crematorium. Among the twenty-five present at the humanist service was Roger Chatterton. There was no reception afterwards.

'William said he didn't want any music people there at all,' said Chatterton. 'He always made it clear that they were outside the music establishment. Joyce did not go along with the thinking of the Royal Academy. She was not taught in this country but went abroad and she was doing quite well. I think that the Royal Academy was not very happy with them. Well, at least that was what William told me.'

In fact, rumours about the bogus Hatto recordings had already started. The full extent of the fraud was revealed eight months after Joyce Hatto's death.

In December 2006, Radio New Zealand re-broadcast an hour-long programme of glowing appreciation of the Concert Artist Hatto CDs. The programme included excerpts from a phone interview with Hatto conducted on April 6 in which she made no indication that the recordings were not what they seemed. But she did fondly describe her husband as a very good critic, saying: 'He has a better idea of sound than myself. He always says what is right for me or the music, so therefore I can trust his opinion.' All this generated a boost in sales for the Concert Artists CDs. In 2006, one online retailer did £50,000 worth of business with Barrington-Coupe.

It was to be new technology, once a boon to Barrington-Coupe's musical cheating, that proved his downfall. Financial analyst Brian Ventura decided to listen to a Hatto recording of Liszt's Transcendental Etudes at his New York home. He put the CD into his computer – which automatically identified it as a recording by the pianist Laszlo Simon. The same thing happened with five other recordings. Electronic comparisons showed that the pitch, volume and tempo of Hatto's supposed music was identical to that of other artists.

Mr Ventura then contacted Jed Distler, a critic for *Classics Today* and *Gramophone* who had praised many of the recordings purportedly made by Hatto. The critic will not forget the day he was asked to check out such a monumental musical mishap. He said:

'When I received Brian Ventura's e-mail, I decided to investigate further. After careful comparison of the actual Simon performances to the Hatto, it appeared to me that ten out of twelve tracks showed remarkable similarity in terms of tempi, accents, dynamics, balances, etc. By contrast, track five, Feux Follets, sounded different between the two sources. I reported my findings to Mr Ventura and he told Classicstoday.com editor David Hurwitz. I told *Gramophone* editor James Inverne, plus three of my *Gramophone* colleagues who had written about Hatto.

'Then I wrote to Mr Barrington-Coupe. He quickly replied, claiming not to know what had happened and to be as puzzled as I was. At James Inverne's suggestion, Andrew Rose, of the audio-restoration business Pristine Audio, contacted me and I uploaded three MP3s from the Hatto Liszt disc. Andrew's research confirmed what my ears suspected – at least two Liszt tracks were identical between the record label BIS and Concert Artist, while at least one was not.'

Andrew Rose was later to write about his startling discovery: 'I was flabbergasted. I was on the phone to Jed and had lined up the

Hatto and the Simon so they'd start at the same time and play together. Holding the phone to the loudspeaker, I hit play and we both heard for the first time, the two playing together – apparently identical. It was an amazing moment and one which appeared to prove that all was not what it seemed.'

Further investigation by Andrew Rose followed. In the end, there was only one conclusion: 'These were deliberate hoaxes.'

An identification of the source of another recording, which had been in preparation for some months, was released the following day by the AHRC Research Centre for the History and Analysis of Record Music (CHARM) at London's Royal Holloway College, as part of research on performances of Chopin's Mazurkas. As a result, an initial story was posted on the *Gramophone* website on February 15, announcing that CDs ascribed to Hatto had been found to contain copies, in some cases digitally manipulated, of published commercial recordings made by other artists. Within a week, the sources for some twenty of Hatto's Concert Artist CDs had been identified.

The conductors whose work was represented on the concerto recordings credited to the mysterious Rene Kohler were, in fact, rather better known ones – such as Esa-Pekka Salonen, Andre Previn and Bernard Haitink. The National Philharmonic-Symphony and the Warsaw Philharmonia were actually the prestigious Vienna Philharmonic, The Philharmonia and the Royal Philharmonic.

One 'victim' of the fraud, classical pianist David Owen Norris, learned that his 1988 rare solo piano recording of Elgar's *Symphony No 1 in A flat major, opus 55*, had been passed off as Hatto's work. 'I'm just very sad,' he said. 'I think it's pathetic that somebody should be reduced to this.'

Somewhere, there is a silent band of musicians who took part in the bogus recordings but whose identities will probably now never be revealed.

But the big question still remained: how much was Hatto herself involved in the music fraud? Did she know that each time she sat down at her Steinway piano, she really was not that accomplished a player? Did she revel in her unwarranted recognition, believing that at last, being described as a 'national treasure' was no less than she deserved? Some even believed that Hatto deliberately took part in the fraud to take revenge on the classical music industry she felt had treated her unfairly.

Arts critic Denis Dutton was emphatic that Hatto knew exactly what she was doing. 'It is a palpable absurdity to imagine she did not,' he said.

Barrington-Coupe claimed the deception was an act of love to give his dying wife a great end to an 'unfairly overlooked career'. He said it had been his decision to record his wife's performances, but that she was in so much pain as the cancer took hold that her gasps could be heard. Because of this, he inserted parts of other artists' recordings, at first small sections, then longer and longer ones.

While she was still alive, he had claimed: 'She doesn't want to play in public because she never knows when the pain will start or when it will stop and she refuses to take drugs. Nothing has stopped her and I believe the illness has added a third dimension to her playing. She gets at what is inside the music, what lies behind it.'

Barrington-Coupe at first denied any wrong-doing but later admitted the fraud in a letter to Robert von Bahr, the head of the Swedish BIS recording label that had originally issued some of the recordings plagiarised by Concert Artist. He admitted acting 'stupidly, dishonestly and unlawfully'.

This confession was posted on the website of *Gramophone* and later in the magazine, with a comment from critic James Inverne who said about Barrington-Coupe: 'What music lovers will want, and what he must surely now provide (together, where possible, with witnesses who can verify), is a full and accurate list of which Joyce Hatto recordings actually feature Joyce Hatto, and which other artists were involved, where appropriate. Only then will we know how good she actually was, and only then can at least some of her reputation be salvaged.

'When asked to do this, Barrington-Coupe replied that he didn't want to go down that road, adding, "I'm tired, I'm not very well. I've closed the operation down, I've had the stock completely destroyed, and I'm not producing any more. Now I just want a little bit of peace".'

Barrington-Coupe denied making a lot of money from the music fraud, claiming he only sold 5,595 records since April 1996, compared to 3,051 in 1995 alone.

Mr Van Bahr said it was unlikely he would take action, as proving a financial loss would be difficult. He said: 'I'm not moved to seek revenge. But I'm very glad the truth is at last known.'

For a while, Joyce Hatto's ashes sat on her piano stool in the sitting room of the home the couple shared. It was all a sad end to a career that once promised accolades but instead ended in shame. Some say Barrington-Coupe's only real crime was loving his wife so much.

Some dubbed the whole sorry affair 'Hattogate'. But Barrington-Coupe was no longer gloating over his ability to fool the world of music. He said: 'It wasn't something I liked doing. But Joyce's music was everything to her – and to me too.'

Chapter 10

Ageless Charm of Saint-Germain

He breezed in from nowhere and captivated the courts of Europe. Graceful, charming, dressed like a dandy, his pockets full of glittering diamonds, he became one of history's most enigmatic men – not least because he claimed to be over 150 years old!

The Count of Saint-Germain first appeared on the European social scene in the mid-Eighteenth Century. He was guaranteed to make an impression with the flowing black and white silk clothes he habitually wore, an austere display for times when brightly coloured dress was the fashion. He set off his sombre clothes, however, with a magnificent array of diamonds which he wore on his shoe buckles and on his fingers and which decorated his snuff box. He boasted of always carrying them in his pockets in lieu of money.

He was quick-witted and charming, but it was his allusions to his own immortality which drew to him the attention of Europe's intellectual and social elite. To many he was a charlatan, a clever talker, an eccentric. To others, among them the great French poet and dramatist Voltaire, he was 'a man who knows everything and never dies'.

Even now, the story of the man who called himself Count Saint-Germain remains a mystery, because it is difficult to separate fact from fiction in the many accounts written about his life. He has been variously described as a magician, alchemist, inventor, pianist, violinist, composer, courtier, adventurer and charlatan. Even the title he bestowed upon himself provides no clues to his true identity; he may well have invented it as a French version of the Latin *Sanctus Germanus*, meaning 'Holy Brother'. For, as will become clear, the phoney nobleman did not suffer from false modesty!

So where did the mysterious Count Saint-Germain come from? One report says that he was born in Italy in 1710, the son of a tax collector. Another has him born in Bohemia, the son of an occultist. Little is known of his early life, apart from his own reports of his travels and experiments in alchemy. Certainly he was master of more than six foreign languages and there is no reason to disbelieve his claim that he studied jewellery and art design at the court of the Shah of Persia.

If his younger years were indeed spent absorbing the mysteries of the occult in faraway places, it would explain why there is so little independent record of him before his rise to fame in Eighteenth Century Austria. In 1740, historical records describe him as a mature man, somewhere between forty-five and fifty years old, whose charming manner won him recognition among the higher echelons of Austrian society. The first of many to fall under his spell were Count Zabor and Count Lobkowitz, two leading Viennese socialites and dictators of fashion, who took him under their wing. For whatever reason, they generously installed him in a stylish apartment.

By now well known for his astonishing claims to have powers over death, Saint-Germain was sought out by a sick general, the Maréchal de Belle-Isle. The nature of his ailment was not recorded, but it seems that after a visit from Saint-Germain he was completely cured. In gratitude, Belle-Isle funded Saint-Germain on a trip to Paris and set him up in a laboratory. There he embarked on his weird alchemy studies.

It was in Paris in the 1740's that the legend of Count Saint-Germain really became celebrated. Parisian society was fascinated by him, despite knowing little about his antecedents. His age, it is recorded, appeared to be about fifty – although he claimed to be over 100! We know this from the anecdote of an aged French countess who, upon meeting the mysterious newcomer, recalled that as a young woman in 1670 she had heard the name Saint-Germain announced by a footman. 'Was that your father?' asked the countess. 'No, Madame, that was me,' he replied. Astonished, the countess told him that it was impossible. The Saint-Germain she had known was then about fifty and would now be over 120 years of age. Saint-Germain said that he well recalled her beauty from that ancient meeting and concluded: 'Madame, I am very old.'

The story helped Saint-Germain in one of the two goals he was pursuing in Paris – the search for the elixir of life, or 'the secrets of eternal wealth and eternal beauty,' as he once described it. His other obsession was as far fetched, if equally predictable: the pursuit, as old as time itself, of the secret of turning base metals into gold. These and many other astonishing claims he was to make guaranteed that he became the talk of Paris, some in society pronouncing him a genius, others a devil.

It was inevitable that his renown should come to the attention of the omnipotent Louis XV. In 1743 the Bourbon king summoned Count Saint-Germain to his opulent Palace of Versailles where the monarch and his mistress, Madame de Pompadour, questioned him at length about his outrageous claims. They both ended up totally entranced by the alchemist as he related to them his tales of mysterious meetings with Italian occultists and Indian mystics. He also related to them how he had unravelled the secrets of the Pyramids.

Perhaps Saint-Germain wished he had kept his boastful mouth shut. For Louis XV immediately employed this supposed globe-roving genius – as a spy. The count travelled to England at a time when revolution was being fomented to reintroduce the Roman Catholic Stuart family to the throne. With help from Louis XV, Charles Stuart – 'Bonnie Prince Charlie' – had rallied an army in the Scottish Highlands and launched the Jacobite Rebellion, eventually savagely crushed at the Battle of Culloden in 1746.

At this unsettled time, spy fever swept the nervous English aristocracy. Every French-speaking stranger was seen as a Jacobite sympathiser and many were arrested, including the count. On him were found pro-Stuart letters. In the case of any normal man, retribution would have been swift and final. But amazingly Count Saint-Germain sweet-talked his prosecutors and convinced them that the letters had been planted on him. Not only did he escape with his head, but he began to attract the curiosity of English society and politicians, one of whom, Horace Walpole, wrote of him: 'The other day they seized an odd man who goes by the name of Count Saint-Germain. He has been here these two years and will not tell who he is or whence, but professes that he does not go by his right name. He sings and plays on the violin wonderfully, is mad and not very sensible.'

The count could have been as big a star in England as he had been at the French court. But wanderlust overtook him and he moved back 'home' to Austria, where he made his base a new laboratory in Vienna, funded by wealthy patrons. From there he travelled twice to India, in 1747 and 1756, where he boasted about learning new arts from Indian mystics. In one letter to Louis XV, he claimed that he had perfected the arts of alchemy and could now 'melt jewels'. The hint that he was on the verge of a breakthrough in his attempt to turn base metals into gold was sufficient to bring a fresh summons from a rapt French court.

Saint-Germain again settled in Paris, where Louis funded a new laboratory for his experiments that never quite came to fruition. There was another commission for the count, however. Louis sent him on a mission to Holland in 1760 to raise support money for France's Seven Years War against Britain. Again, the scheming count failed to realise when he was onto a good thing. Instead of helping his French patrons make war, he made secret representations to English diplomats, supposedly seeking peace between the two countries. The count's conspiracy was uncovered by the French foreign minister at the Hague, the Duc de Choiseul, who reported back to Louis. The king was furious and ordered Saint-Germain arrested and sent back to Paris. The count, as ever, was one step ahead of his foes. He took ship to England until the fuss died down.

In 1764 he felt safe enough to return to Holland, where he remained for two years, opening laboratories which produced a myriad coloured paints and dyes but no gold. When again his patrons demanded some tangible results from their investments, he fled to Belgium under the name of the 'Marquis de Monferrat'. After a year there, he was off again, on an amazing odyssey across Europe, his first stop being the court of Catherine the Great. In 1768 the Russian Empress had declared war on Turkey, and the glib-tongued traveller soon found himself advising a spellbound Catherine on the conduct of the war. In recognition of his services, he was given a title, and the name he chose for himself was 'General Welldone'.

His tour of Europe continued from 1774. In Germany he raised fresh funds and established laboratories in Nuremberg, which became his base. From there he travelled to Berlin, Frankfurt and Dresden, dabbling widely in Freemasonry and the occult, as well as his alchemy. On one of these trips he encountered one of the few people to have dismissed Saint-Germain as a phoney. He went to Prince Frederick Augustus of Brunswick, claiming to be a Mason. The prince knew his claim was false, however – because he himself was Grand Master of the Prussian Masonic lodges.

The brazen count also tried to reintroduce himself to the French court, now under the old king's successor, Louis XVI. He sent a warning to the king and his wife Marie Antoinette of a 'gigantic conspiracy' which would overtake them and sweep away the old order of things. Saint-Germain was showing remarkable foresight, for in 1789 the French Revolution broke out and four years later dispatched them to the guillotine.

Count Saint-Germain's final port of call was Eckenförde, in Schleswig, Germany, the home of Prince Charles of Hesse-Cassel. The count, by now well into his sixties, is said to have died there in 1784. Certainly a tombstone in the local churchyard records: 'He who called himself the Comte de Saint-Germain and Welldone, of whom there is no other information, has been buried in this church.'

And that was the end of the story of Count Saint-Germain. Or was it? A year after his death a group of occultists holding a conference at Wilhemsbad reported that he had appeared before them. In 1788 he was supposedly warning the French nobility of the looming peasants' revolt. In 1789 he was said to be at the court of King Gustavus III of Sweden. And an old friend, Madame d'Adhémar, said she continued to be visited by the count, the last occasion being in 1820. That would have made him more than 100 years of age!

French Emperor Louis Napoleon III was so obsessed by the legend of Count Saint-Germain that he instituted a special commission to study his life and works. The findings of this inquiry were destroyed in a fire in 1871. The latter-day followers of the count believe that this was no accident but an act for which the count himself was responsible!

Adventurer, explorer, inventor, alchemist, mystic, healer, clairvoyant, diplomat and socialite … or spy, dandy, leech, fraud and confidence trickster? History has not provided us with the answer to the question of whether the charismatic Count Saint-Germain was merely a charlatan or an eccentric genius – or, more probably, both.

Chapter 11

2,000-Year-Old Count Cagliostro

I f the story of the Count of Saint-Germain seemed implausible (see previous chapter), then the case of cunning Count Alessandro di Cagliostro will stretch credulity still further. For this phoney nobleman arrived on the scene only a short while after Saint-Germain and equally successfully bamboozled the courts of Europe.

Count Cagliostro was described by one of his contemporaries thus:

'While not actually handsome, his face was the most remarkable I have ever seen. His eyes were indescribable – all fire and yet all ice.' No wonder he beguiled and bewitched European society in the latter part of the 18th century. Perhaps the awe in which the nobility held him would have been tempered had they known that the grandiose title he had bestowed on himself was not his real name, and that the title 'Count' should really have been 'King ... of Liars'.

Cagliostro's real name was Giuseppe Balsamo, born in poverty to a Sicilian peasant family in 1743. He embarked on his career of criminality by stealing from his own family and from the church poor box in his Sicilian village. With sufficient money to flee the island, he briefly became a monk before being defrocked as a novitiate for unexplained 'blasphemies'. He then attached himself to the coat-tails of the Greek alchemist Altotas, and practised the ingenuous art in Egypt until the supply of gullible investors ran out. Back in Italy, he settled down to a life of lucrative crime.

Balsamo married an incredibly beautiful girl he discovered living in rags in a slum area of Rome. His bride, Lorenza, was fourteen;

he was twenty-six. She saw him as her way out of the gutter and he saw her as the beautiful bait that would hook wealthy victims. Despite her background, and because of her obvious attractions, Lorenza became Balsamo's key to the higher echelons of 18th-century Rome society. After a stint of passing counterfeit coinage – and a sideline dabbling in the production of phoney aphrodisiacs – the couple embarked on a tour of Europe.

First stop was France, where they met the world's most famous lover, Casanova. Balsamo and Lorenza's confidence tricks had earned them money enough to mould themselves into the roles of aristocrats, and Casanova immediately fell for their charade. To him, they could belong nowhere else but within the circles of high society. It is not known whether Casanova worked his infamous seducer's charm on Lorenza but it is certainly likely. What is known is that Lorenza was seduced by a Monsieur Duplessis when her husband was in jail over unpaid debts. So outraged was Balsamo that he complained to the highest authorities and Lorenza suddenly found herself in prison.

Amazingly, the couple forgot and forgave. Realising that as a twosome they were a force to be reckoned with in the world of deception, they agreed to stay together. And so, now calling himself Marchese Pellegrini, Balsamo set off back to Italy accompanied by Lorenza. The next ten years were spent masterminding a series of spectacular confidence tricks which were to take them as far afield as North Africa.

The couple found themselves in London in 1776 and, with a string of victims on their tail, it was now time for a change of name. They became 'Count Alessandro Di Cagliostro and Countess Serafina'. To add a little colour to their background, Balsamo said he had stolen the countess from an oriental harem and made her his wife. No one challenged the unlikely origins of such an aristocratic lady. Neither did they question the couple's source of wealth when rumour spread that the count could turn common metals into gold.

So the couple were welcomed into society and enjoyed themselves immensely. They wore rich clothes and extravagant jewellery. They had liveried servants at their beck and call. And they rode in elegant coaches pulled by beautifully groomed horses. In fact, the count and countess's sole wealth was the £3,000 they had made in their foreign escapades.

Balsamo wangled himself an introduction to the Freemasons and found the secret society to be the perfect setting for his faker's magic. He virtually took over the London lodge of which he was a member, claiming powers of second sight and soothsaying. It was not long before he was made Grand Master of his lodge, a bizarre but envied position that was to open many doors for him throughout Europe. In Paris, he had much fun creating the 'Egyptian Rite of Freemasonry' and appointed himself Grand Cophta. It also meant he was in charge of collecting membership fees and monies paid by initiates to the lodge's strange initiation ceremonies.

With no one daring to usurp Balsamo's power, he soon created a leading Freemasonry role for Lorenza too. She was appointed the new 'Queen of Sheba' in charge of a female lodge. This was a controversial move, not just because of Lorenza's new-found authority, but because up until now the Freemasons had been a strictly male order. Despite this, the wealthy elite of Parisian society flocked to their 'queen'. Lorenza would earnestly take duchesses and fellow countesses aside and confide in them that, although she looked only thirty, she was in fact sixty years old. A magic elixir concocted by her husband had held back the years.

Her rich and noble confidantes swore to keep the 'queen's' secret – in exchange, of course, for bottles of the age-defying potion. It also encouraged both men and women followers alike to part with their money for other powerful remedies. They could not help but be impressed by the count's personal attention, even carefully wrapping the pills he prescribed in fine gold leaf. The cunning count made sure he gave out nothing that was dangerous. Indeed, any of the magical cures bought by his wealthy patients could have been obtained from a doctor at a fraction of the price, for they were simply herbal remedies.

The Grand Master was fast winning a reputation as a genius in the field of medicine, and it was inevitable that his fame would spread. His presence was demanded across Europe. In Leipzig,

Germany, Balsamo got quite carried away, declaring that if the local Freemason lodge failed to observe the Egyptian Rite, its master would incur the wrath of God. Coincidentally, the master killed himself shortly afterwards and there was mass hysteria at Balsamo's divine powers. In the Baltic state of Courland, nobles wanted to make Balsamo their king. He sensibly declined the invitation. In Moscow, Balsamo recruited young boys and girls as 'soothsayers'.

Hearing of the presence of the 'count and countess', one of the Tsar's ministers begged Balsamo to cure his insane brother. At first Balsamo was reluctant, then agreed to examine him. The brother was brought before Balsamo, tightly bound to prevent doing himself and others harm. Balsamo ordered that the man be untied and was greeted with protests. Did he not realise the patient was a lunatic, liable to attack people? The Russian wardens were eventually persuaded to release their patient, who immediately leaped towards Balsamo. The count coolly pushed him aside and instructed that he be thrown into an ice-cold river. Perhaps it was the shock of finding himself immersed in freezing waters but the madman emerged sensible and profusely sorry for his behaviour.

The count and his beautiful countess arrived in the French spa of Strasbourg in September 1780. As usual, they made their appearance in fine style, with liveried servants on black horses. Realising that there was now no end to what people would believe, Balsamo extended and elaborated his mystical powers to an incredible degree. He claimed to have been born before the great flood of Noah, to have been a pupil of Socrates; to have been on close terms with Moses, Solomon and Roman emperors and to have drunk wine at a wedding feast in biblical Galilee. If anyone dared to look askance at these ridiculous stories, Balsamo would whip out a bundle of letters dated 550 BC.

Balsamo continued to administer his pills, potions and promises of eternal life. To answer claims of being an impostor milking money from the vulnerable, Balsamo took daily walks distributing alms to the poor. And despite investigations ordered by the French government into his alleged powers, no respected member of the medical profession could declare him a phoney. Confident of his hallowed standing, he boldly told revered philosopher Lavater: 'If your science is greater than mine, you have no need of my acquaintance; if mine is the greater, I have no need of yours.' Lavater immediately became one of the great count's disciples.

Another recruit of Balsamo was Cardinal de Rohan, confidante to Queen Marie Antoinette. Balsamo's initial attitude towards de Rohan was as insulting as it had been to Lavater. When de Rohan sent a servant to him to demand an audience, Balsamo sent the message: 'If the prince is ill, let him come to me and I will cure him. If he is not ill, he has no need of me and I have no need of him.' The cardinal was enraged by the impudence but was nevertheless curious enough to pay Balsamo a visit. The two men forged a close friendship. Balsamo cured de Rohan's brother, Prince de Soubise, of scarlet fever when all other doctors had failed. This won him God-like adulation, with his face appearing on snuffboxes, buckles, rings and other jewellery.

However, Balsamo's closeness to de Rohan was also to be his downfall. Balsamo and Lorenza had decided to go to Paris to escape increasing hostility from more orthodox physicians. There, they learned that de Rohan had fallen out with Marie Antoinette and was desperate to win favour once more with the French queen. The couple became embroiled in de Rohan's plot to steal a diamond necklace he knew she coveted. The plan involved forging the queen's signature, and when King Louis XVI was informed, he ordered that de Rohan, Lorenza and Balsamo be thrown into the dungeons of the Bastille.

At a subsequent trial, the count and countess were cleared of all conspiracy charges and were given their freedom. They left the Bastille in a parade of thousands of cheering followers. But the scandal had left its mark on the hitherto unblemished reputation of this amazing, aristocratic couple. For harsh interrogation had forced Lorenza to reveal one too many secrets about her husband's success – and the news quickly spread that gullible innocents throughout Europe and across the world had been victims of a cruel impostor.

Despite their phoney titles, Lorenza and Balsamo were no longer fêted by the rich and noble classes. King Louis eventually ordered that they leave France, never to return. The couple spent aimless months wandering around Europe, their relationship slowly falling apart. For with the trappings of their former grand life long gone, Lorenza saw little attraction in her middle-aged (or was it 2,000-year-old!) husband.

Lorenza persuaded Balsamo to return to Rome in the hope that some of their old tricks might win them back their glorious lifestyle. It was 1789 and Balsamo believed that creating a new Egyptian Rite Masonic Lodge could be the answer to their prayers. It was a monumental mistake. Any Roman Catholic joining the Freemasons was subject to excommunication as a heretic. Three years later, Balsamo was seized by the papal police. On April 7, 1791, he was found guilty of heresy and sentenced to death. This time Lorenza did not stand by her husband. She denounced him in the hope that her life would be spared. Her sentence was to spend the rest of her days locked away in a convent, where she died in 1794.

Balsamo survived, however. The Pope commuted his death sentence to life imprisonment and he was taken to the dungeons of the Castel San Leo. He died there on August 26, 1795, it being rumoured that he had been murdered. The fake mystic, Grand Master and medicine man who claimed to be immortal, had reached the end of his cheating life at the age of fifty-two.

Chapter 12

A Truly Giant-Sized Hoax

With his massive limbs and rugged features, the 'fossilised' giant unearthed on a farm in New York State on October 16, 1869, was literally a gargantuan discovery. Weighing 3,000 pounds, the stone figure was indeed larger than life. His incredible proportions included feet that were nearly two feet long, thighs thirteen feet in diameter and shoulders measuring more than three feet across.

The discovery of this recumbent Goliath had epic significance for historians and archaeologists at the time – for the man mountain gave credence to tales of an ancient race of giants. The find was hailed by some as a prehistoric petrified man; indeed, four local doctors declared it to be a petrified body. Other supposed experts believed it to be an ancient Phoenician idol – supporting their theory that Phoenicians had reached America. The central debate, however, was between those who thought it was a petrified man and those who thought it to be an ancient statue. The 'petrifactionists' believed that it was one of the giants mentioned in the Bible, in Genesis 6:4, which states: "There were giants in the earth in those days." Those who promoted the statue theory followed the lead of Dr John F. Boynton, who speculated that a Jesuit missionary had carved it sometime during the Seventeenth Century to impress the local tribes.

But the interest shown by archaeologists was nothing compared to the excitement of the good people of the sleepy town of Cardiff, where the discovery was made, and visitors arrived in their hundreds. Even when scientists at Yale University raised doubts over the giant's authenticity, sightseers kept on coming. It meant boom time for Cardiff, with its population of 200 now boosted by tourists who arrived by rail and wagon to stay in their town, patronise its two hotels and, most important of all, spend money.

As the people flooded in, new restaurants were opened and stalls selling cider were set up by Cardiff folk in front of their homes. It seemed the influx of curious visitors would never end. Week after week they crowded in, more than happy to pay their fifty cents to peer into the pit and take a peek at the Cardiff Giant. On one Sunday alone, 2,500 people came to stare.

Some time passed before the true origin of this amazing archaeological discovery was revealed. It was all the creation of George Hull, who had thought big and pulled off one of the most over-sized hoaxes in history. The cigar maker and conman, who came from Binghamton, New York, had hit upon the idea of creating a giant three years earlier. He had visited Iowa in 1866 and fallen into conversation with a travelling preacher. From him he learned about the giants mentioned in the Book of Genesis. Hull went away and read up on the giants, and it did not take him long to realise that if anyone unearthed one of these ancient breed, he would surely make a fortune.

No real giants being available, Hull decided to make his own. On a return trip to Iowa, he visited the gypsum quarries near Fort Dodge, taking with him his partner, a Mr H. B. Martin. The two bought a stone block twelve feet high by four feet wide and had it shipped to Chicago where it took two sculptors three months to shape it into a man standing ten feet tall. Then, with a clever bit of 'ageing' using wet sand, ink and sulphuric acid, the 'fossilised' man, as George Hull was keen to describe it, was ready. He looked to all the world like a giant who had been buried for millions of years. The whole operation had cost him about $2,500.

Hull shipped the figure to his cousin, William 'Stub' Newell, who with great difficulty managed to bury it five feet deep on his farm. The conspirators decided to bide their time before 'discovering' the giant. Then the main thrust of the huge forgery began to take shape. Newell would pretend to drill for water on his farm, sinking wells all over his land. It would be during this drilling that the 'Cardiff Giant' would become their surprise find.

No one suspected a thing when the discovery was eventually made. Newell erected a tent over the pit where the giant was found and soon began charging members of the public to take a look. Hull kept well away from the farm, fearing too many questions but he made sure Newell regularly paid him his cut of the admission fees. So successful was the venture that Hull got Newell to raise the admission price to one dollar. People still crowded to the farm site to see the Cardiff Giant with their very own eyes.

Hull then sat down and wrote pages of 'scientific' notes on the discovery. He somehow managed to persuade the reluctant and far from eloquent farmer to give a worthy lecture on the ancient figure, using Hull's 'authoritative' notes, of course. Hull had no qualms about hailing the Cardiff Giant as the Eighth World of the World.

Stories vary on just how Hull was finally exposed as a fraudster. One version has it that when an archaeological expert, Oliver Wendell Holmes, bored a hole in the skull, he found it to be solid. Another report says a private investigator traced the connection between Hull and Newell and found out about a giant block of gypsum being shipped from Iowa to Chicago. Yet another declares that the end for Hull came when the giant was moved to Syracuse, where it could be better displayed. There it was studied by Yale palaeontologist Othniel C. Marsh, who observed plainly visible chisel marks which should have worn away if the giant had been in the ground for any length of time. Other experts pointed out that gypsum was neither an ancient stone, nor local to where the figure was found. Therefore the Cardiff Giant was one big fake.

None of this mattered to Hull, for he had already extricated himself from the scam. Sensing he was soon to be exposed, he had sold his interest in the figure to a local businessman for $37,500. He had, of course, already made a great deal of money from the gullible folk who had paid to see the ancient figure.

Incredibly, even when the truth came out about the Cardiff Giant, people still flocked to see it, despite it now being nicknamed 'Old Hoaxey'. Another great fraudster, Phineas T. Barnum, made a replica of it for his New York City exhibition. Hull had refused to sell him the original for $60,000 but that didn't stop Barnum saying his giant was the 'real' fake when he put it on show. Soon the replica was drawing larger crowds than the original.

This competition prompted the owners of the giant to file a lawsuit against Barnum, but the judge refused to hear their case

n. Since this
l.
t is currently
eum, outside
s Museum at
ill enjoys the
who queue to

m Bard

rk by history's greatest
cries of derision; that
m Shakespeare should
the actors performing
he curtain came down
ockery is o'er.'
was indeed 'o'er' for
ry Ireland, creator of
and Rowena. All he
erary fraud.
ere planted at a very
ild sired by his father
ever married, despite
el was a prosperous
bookshop owner. He
ollecting anything he
l. But with so many
uch time for his son.
head for learning. So
father asked him to
on to Shakespeare's
father bought a chair
blet carved from a
nd a purse presented
tratford dealers were
h his request for such
was doubtful that the
nuine. He did note,

Chapter 13

Odes That Went Fro
to Worse

I t was almost beyond belief that a wc
playwright should be greeted with
words spilled from the quill of Willia
be drowned out by raucous laughter. Finally
the dubious dialogue were booed off stage as
at the utterance of the line: 'And when this x

At that humiliating moment, the mocker
an 18th-century forger named William He
this 'lost' Shakespeare masterpiece *Vortiger*
could do now was confess to his stunning li

The seeds of Ireland's career as a faker
early age. He was born in 1777, the third c
Samuel and his housekeeper, whom he r
always referring to her as his wife. Sam
architect, painter, author of travel guides an
was also a devotee of Shakespeare, avidly
could lay his hands on relating to the Ba
interests in his busy life, Samuel never had

William was dismissed as a dullard with n
he was surprised but delighted when his
accompany him from their home in Lor
birthplace of Stratford-upon-Avon. There hi
that once belonged to Shakespeare, a g
mulberry tree planted by the Bard himself
to him by his wife, Anne Hathaway. The
more than happy to oblige Samuel Ireland w
treasures, but William, then aged eighteen,
relics he saw his father being sold were g

however, the joy Samuel Ireland showed over his purchases. And an idea started to germinate...

William began to take even less interest in his job as a solicitor's clerk in London's New Inn. Instead his thoughts turned to Thomas Chatterton, the astonishing young faker who had pulled off a literary fraud some thirty years before. William researched all he could about Chatterton. Then he decided to have similar fun with Shakespeare.

William bought some books which had been printed during the reign of Queen Elizabeth I, the text sandwiched between several sheets of blank paper. William carefully cut them out; they were important to his scheme, having been around in Shakespeare's time. Taking a bookseller into his confidence, William asked what kind of ink Shakespeare would have used and what it contained. When he discovered the correct ingredients, he bought them from a pharmacist's shop and set about the first stages of his literary fraud, mixing the ingredients of this 'ancient' ink.

This was just a practise run, and William knew he should tread cautiously. Forgetting Shakespeare for a while, he took one of the Elizabethan volumes and carefully wrote a 'dedication' from its author to the good queen. He presented the book to his father, who was overjoyed with the gift. Basking in that rare display of affection, William decided to find another suitable gift for his father. That turned out to be a terracotta relief head of Oliver Cromwell, accompanied by an old parchment letter saying that it had been presented by Cromwell to John Bradshaw, president of the court that condemned Charles I to death. Again his father was deeply moved by the present – while at the same time proving that he was not as learned as he made out to be, for according to historians, there was great animosity between Cromwell and Bradshaw.

It was time for William to move on to greater things. He had often heard his father quote a scholar named J. A. Boaden who had written a book about Shakespeare, in which he described the nation's passion for the Bard and expressed disappointment that so little was known about him and that so few documents or writings relating to him seemed to exist. Boaden included a list of these documents which he felt must be hidden away somewhere. This was the key to William's scheme. He could react to Boaden's longing for Shakespearian relics by finding some. At the same time, he would find a place in his father's heart forever.

Dipping his quill into his home-made 'ancient' ink, William practised Shakespeare's signature and handwriting until he achieved near-perfect results. Then, with his confidence growing, he wrote what purported to be a love letter from Shakespeare to his wife Anne Hathaway. Then he wrote a business letter about a property deal between Shakespeare and an actor called John Heminge and provided a receipt for some money Shakespeare might have received. William realised he could not produce these historically significant items without providing a story to go with them, so he told his father he had met up with an aristocratic gentleman in a coffee house. He and his new friend had got into conversation and their talk had turned to Shakespeare. Hearing of the Ireland family's interest in the Bard, the old gent had then invited William to his chambers to look through a chest of documents.

'I have one or two things I think might interest you,' the gentleman had supposedly remarked to him. Then, William related excitedly to his father, came the biggest surprise of his life. For there, stored away in one of the rooms, was a mass of documents written by Shakespeare – the literary 'treasure trove' J. A. Boaden believed must exist somewhere. And incredibly, added William, this generous, wealthy man said he would allow him to take away one of the documents to show his father if Samuel expressed sufficient interest.

Naturally, this news enthused Samuel Ireland no end. He begged to be given the name of the remarkable gentleman with the incredible literary hoard but William explained that the old man wished to be known only as 'Mr W. H.'. Samuel Ireland did not question this, accepting that his son's new friend had good reason to wish to remain anonymous or was perhaps an aristocratic eccentric. All he was really concerned about was seeing one of these Shakespearian documents for himself.

Two weeks later, William brought home the property document: a deed of mortgage made between Michael Fraser and his wife,

John Heminge and William Shakespeare. So overcome was Samuel at what he held in his hands that he could barely find words to thank his son. Instead, he grabbed the bunch of his library keys, thrust them into William's hand and begged him to take whatever books he wished. It was a double moment of triumph for William. He had created a fine forgery and he had won over his father at last.

Word of the precious document now in Samuel Ireland's possession soon spread. All his literary and artistic friends suddenly found reasons to call upon him and they were all duly impressed. The forgery was convincing. It was written on parchment of the right period, Shakespeare's signature was unmistakable, and the seal was authentic enough. The document was declared genuine and an extraordinary, exciting discovery. This spurred William on to produce the five guinea receipt he had said was amongst the mystery gentleman's Shakespearian collection. To keep his story convincing, the receipt was from John Heminge and related to other business involving him and Shakespeare.

Samuel Ireland could barely contain himself. But now he was becoming greedy and curious. He implored William to tell him the full contents of this man's 'treasure chest'. William held back. Instead, he produced a letter from Shakespeare to his patron, the Earl of Southampton, and a reply from Southampton. Southampton's letter was written with William using his left hand in case the two sets of handwriting bore too much similarity. When Samuel Ireland's friends examined the Shakespeare letter and made loud exclamations about his genius, William was tempted to shout out: 'It's me. It is I who am the genius!' But he bit his lip and carried on writing fake texts on Shakespeare's behalf.

His next historical document was a letter from the Bard professing his devotion to the Church of England. This was particularly significant and guaranteed to send his father reeling, because William had often heard Samuel pondering over whether Shakespeare had been a Roman Catholic. Indeed, it had been the cause of great debate amongst scholars. Now here was the proof against that theory. In Shakespeare's hand, William wrote what he considered to be just the right degree of piety:

O Manne whatte arte though whye considereste thou thyselfe

thus greatlye where are thye great thye boasted attrybutes loste forr everre inne colde Deathe…

Even eminent Shakespeare scholars Joseph Warton and Samuel Parr failed to pick up on William's amateur attempts at the Bard's 300-word religious statement. Elizabethans did not put 'e' at the end of every word. And they paid more care to their punctuation!

With all these incredible manuscripts in his collection, Samuel Ireland became famous. The London bookshop he ran near The Strand became a mecca for Shakespearian enthusiasts. Even the Prince of Wales (later George IV) paid a visit. From time to time, William added to the growing collection of relics. One of these additions was a lock of hair, said to have come from the head of the Bard. Then he told his father he had seen a full-length portrait of Shakespeare and that his friend 'Mr W. H.' had generously said he could have that for his collection too at some later date. William also acquired a collection of Elizabethan books and presented them to his father, saying they were from Shakespeare's library. Among them was a three-volume history of England, Scotland and Ireland titled *Holinshed's Chronicles*, a work which was later to prove very useful to the forger as well as to his parent.

William was now an expert, not only at forging Shakespeare's writing, but also at producing the kind of documents he might have received. One of these was to Shakespeare from Queen Elizabeth, thanking him for some of his '*prettye Verses*'. It nearly proved William's downfall, for 'the Queen' referred to the Earl of Leicester and his presence at The Globe Theatre – yet the earl had died six years before the Globe was opened!

Incredibly, none of the so-called experts who regularly called at Samuel Ireland's bookshop to gaze in awe at his collection picked up on these discrepancies. Only one man voiced his suspicions. Author and critic Edmond Malone, who was preparing a work titled *Inquiry into the Validity of the Papers Attributed to Shakespeare*, was critical of Ireland's Shakespearian spelling. Referring to the alleged deed between Shakespeare and Heminge, Malone said: 'It is to be observed that we are not told where the deed was first discovered. It is said in a mansion house, but where situated is not stated.'

None of this stopped the flow of 'Shakespearian gifts' from William to his father. They included a drawing of Shakespeare's head from the hand of the Bard himself, a watercolour of Shakespeare in the role of Bassanio and a couple more love letters to Anne Hathaway. There was also a love poem that began:

> *Is there inne heavenne aught more rare*
> *Thanne thou sweete nymphe of Avon Fayre*
> *Is there onne arthe a Manne more trewe*
> *Thanne Willy Shakespeare is to you.*

One wonders how anyone could believe those words came from England's most celebrated playwright. Yet Samuel Ireland's appetite was insatiable and therefore William's output unstoppable – even when he was caught at work by a fellow clerk, Montague Talbot. Talbot had always believed William was up to no good. But instead of exposing him, he found the world William had created such fun that he became a willing supporter.

It is hard to comprehend how Samuel Ireland was so happy to accept such a succession of Shakespearian mementos without fully investigating their source or authenticity. Why should a complete stranger hand over such treasures? Why wasn't the whole splendid hoard delivered in one go? And why, at a time when England was consumed with a 'Shakespeare revival', was this mystery man not demanding exorbitant prices for the Bard's bounty? None of this seemed to matter to Samuel Ireland. And when one day he mused out loud over the possibility of there being an actual, hitherto undiscovered Shakespeare play in existence, his son was more than happy to oblige.

First, however, William teased his father with fragments of genuine Shakespeare plays: first drafts written in the Bard's hand, complete with 'alterations' and 'deletions'. Thus Samuel Ireland found himself reading 'original' drafts of *King Lear* and *Hamlet*, all free of any bawdy language which his son feared might offend him! Some critics who saw the manuscripts scoffed at them. Derisory reports were written about them in newspapers, together with parodies of this early Shakespearian style. Nevertheless, they convinced many. Diarist and biographer James Boswell saw them and fell on his knees and kissed them. He declared: 'I now kiss the invaluable relics of our Bard to thank God that I have lived to see them.' Boswell was particularly taken with Shakespeare's *Profession of Faith*.

One element of public speculation alarmed William somewhat: should these papers not belong to Shakespeare's own descendants? The problem was quickly solved. William supplied a Deed of Gift from Shakespeare to a contemporary who had once saved him from drowning. Amazingly, it did the trick.

It was now time to fulfil his father's greatest desire: the discovery of an original, 'hidden' Shakespeare play. William's inspiration was found by way of a painting in his father's study. It depicted the Anglo-Saxon king Vortigern being offered a goblet of wine by his mistress Rowena. William read up on the story of Vortigern in *Holinshed's Chronicles*. It seemed only reasonable, he reckoned, to use such a source of reference, for Shakespeare had found inspiration for the plots of some of his historical plays from the very same pages. And, of course, the *Chronicles* had been so helpful at the start of William's master-plan.

William soon had his play mapped out in his mind. It was titled *Vortigern and Rowena*. And he was confident enough of his giant hoax to cut corners. Not willing to spend the time writing the play in Shakespeare's forged hand, he wrote it in his own. William told his father that he was copying it piecemeal from the original. 'Mr W. H.' did not want to relinquish this piece of Shakespearian history but was prepared to let William copy it. William, for his part, was enthused by his work. He was later to say of his play: 'I became fired with the idea of possessing genius to which I had never aspired.'

Great interest was shown in *Vortigern and Rowena*. Drama experts said it was definitely penned by Shakespeare, but perhaps in his earliest period before he had developed his style. Theatrical managers clamoured to produce the play. The 'lucky' man to score this coup was Richard Brinsley Sheridan, manager of the Drury Lane Theatre. After reading the manuscript, Sheridan admitted that, although the work contained 'some bold ideas', it probably wasn't the Bard's best piece of writing. He said: 'It is very odd. One would be led to think that Shakespeare must have been very, very young when he wrote the play. As to the doubting whether it be really his or not, who can possibly look at the papers and not believe them to be ancient?'

Sheridan decreed that, for a successful public performance, the play would have to be shortened. The task was given to William, and so for the first time he actually got paid for his efforts, his father acting on his behalf in drawing up the contract. Sheridan agreed to pay the Irelands £300 plus fifty per cent of the net profits. Highlighting Samuel Ireland's greed, William was actually to receive only £60 out of the £300 payment. Nevertheless, William was so overwhelmed at his literary success that he dashed off another Shakespeare play, *Henry II.*

Richard Brinsley Sheridan originally agreed to present *Vortigern and Rowena* at Drury Lane on December 15, 1795, but having spent some time reading the play closely, he began to feel uneasy and kept postponing the date of the production. This discomfort was not helped by Samuel Ireland's publication *Miscellaneous Papers of William Shakespeare*, including the new version of *King Lear.* The publication was ridiculed.

A further drawback threatened William Ireland's Shakespeare play making it to the stage. An historian unearthed an authentic deed signed by the actor John Heminge. Comparing the signature with that on the deed in Samuel Ireland's possession, he immediately saw they were vastly different. William had to think quickly. He said he would go away and get an explanation from 'Mr W. H.' William was all smiles when he returned. He had solved the mystery, he said. There were two John Heminges, one of whom had been attached to the Globe Theatre and the other to the Curtain Theatre. Both, by an amazing coincidence, had had dealings with Shakespeare.

Preparations for the staging of *Vortigern and Rowena* continued, although actor-manager John Kemble did not have his heart in the project. Having grave doubts about its authenticity, he wanted opening night to be April 1, 1796, so that everyone would see the joke! However, *Vortigern and Rowena* finally made it to the stage a day later, on April 2.

The First Act passed off reasonably well. Audiences were used to actors such as David Garrick rewriting Shakespeare and the often ridiculous result. And as William had used *Macbeth* as his model for *Vortigern and Rowena,* some of the scenes had a comfortable feel about them. So the play passed happily into Act Two, the audience a little bemused but prepared to give it a chance. It was in Act Three that things began to go disastrously wrong...

An actor with a high tenor voice had to declaim: 'Nay, stop not there, but let them bellow on til with their clamourous noise they sham the thunder.' It brought the house down. Not with wild applause but with hoots of laughter. And once the audience had discovered the play's unintentional comedy, they seemed to find everything about it amusing – especially when a comedian with an enormous nose who had been chosen to play a death scene flapped around the stage when the curtain accidentally fell on his neck. As far as the audience was concerned, the finale came with the next few lines:

> *O! then doest ope wide thy boney jaws*
> *And with rude laughter and fantastic tricks*
> *Thou clapp'st thy rattling fingers to thy sides*
> *And when this solemn mockery is o'er*

Somehow the actors managed to make it to the end. The audience was having a wonderful time – until the announcement came that the play would be repeated the next night. Then there was uproar and people starting fighting with each other. *Vortigern and Rowena* would never be staged again, but the evening did reap some financial reward. Sheridan and Samuel each made £103 from it. William again fared worst with his £30 share.

The demise of *Vortigern and Rowena* also halted William's intention to complete a series of Shakespeare histories, covering all those periods the Bard had missed. Recalling this idea much later, William said: 'Had the play *Vortigern* succeeded with the public, and the manuscripts been acknowledged as genuine, it was my intention to have completed a series of plays from the reign of William the Conqueror to that of Queen Elizabeth; that is to say I should have planned a drama on every reign the subject of which had not been treated by Shakespeare.'

Following the spectacular failure of *Vortigern and Rowena,* the critics revelled in their caustic reviews. There was a strong suggestion that the play was a joke, the work of a prankster who had fooled everyone. What hurt Samuel Ireland most was speculation that he was the one behind this dramatic fraud.

The moment William had long dreaded finally came. He was confronted by his father and forced to confess to his catalogue of forgeries. His father stood there, transfixed as the whole story came tumbling out. But to William's amazement, Samuel Ireland did not threaten to cut him out of his life for good. Instead, he simply accused William of 'arrogance and vanity' and of trying to be the centre of attention.

Taken aback by his father's reaction, William decided to escape from the whole embarrassing affair. He told him that a rich, beautiful girl had fallen desperately in love with him and they were going to get married. For good measure, he added that, despite what the critics said, his good friend 'Mr W.H.' had sent all the actors in *Vortigern and Rowena* splendid presents and had decided to give William £300-a-year allowance. In these circumstances, William told his father, he would be off to make a life on his own. It was just a pity, he told him, that he would not be around to see *Henry II* performed at Covent Garden. Even Samuel Ireland began to realise his son was probably entering the realms of fantasy. When he paid a visit to Covent Garden, he was told no one knew anything about the staging of *Henry II*.

Finally incurring his father's full wrath, William placed advertisements in newspapers stating that the terrible Shakespeare fraud that had been perpetrated was all down to him and that his father was completely blameless in all respects. Despite this, his trusting parent still refused completely to believe that his son was capable of such a monumental confidence trick.

William Ireland left the family house in Norfolk Street, London, never to return. In a letter, he made one final effort to convince his father it really was he who had created the bogus Shakespeare documents. It did no good. Samuel Ireland wrote back accusing his son of 'gross and deliberate impositions'. Father and son were never to communicate again.

William was still only twenty, making his forgery achievements quite remarkable. They had, however, earned him very little money.

He lived off loans from family friends, secretly made without his father's knowledge, and, far from the beautiful female he had claimed was his true love, William married a short, ugly girl called Alice Crudge.

In a bid to earn some money with which to keep himself and his wife, William Ireland wrote a pamphlet called *Authentic Account of the Shakespearian Manuscripts*. It was so badly written that it only seemed to confirm Samuel Ireland's belief that his son was an arrogant liar living in a world of his own. Even worse, the inferior pamphlet convinced the public and many historians that William could not have had anything to with the forgeries – and therefore Samuel Ireland had to be responsible. Samuel hit back by publishing a pamphlet defending himself. One would have thought he had had enough of the whole sorry saga but, for reasons known only to himself, he actually published the finished work of *Henry II*. Just like *Vortigern and Rowena* before, it was greeted with derision. Samuel Ireland died in 1800, a bitter and frustrated man.

William, meanwhile, had made his home in France where he embarked on a string of legitimate literary efforts. The year before his father's death, he published a three-volume novel, *The Abbess*, which heralded a successful writing career for him at last. Sixty other books followed, including a three-volume work on the life of Napoleon. There was also a long poem, *The Neglected Genius*, containing an account of his hero, Thomas Chatterton. However, a book detailing his Shakespeare forgeries caused only a ripple of interest. Everyone seemed to have become bored with the episode.

William died in 1835. His life had been a strange one, most of it lived vicariously through a brilliant playwright from a previous century. Indeed, such a plot of scheming, misunderstandings and trickery would have been worthy of the Bard himself.

Chapter 14

Just a Big 'Kid' Who Never Grew Up?

Many children are told that school is the happiest time of our lives. And perhaps when we are adult, we hanker after days spent in classrooms and games fields, all responsibility taken by others. But sadly, none of that can come back. Or can it? Could it be possible to turn back the clock, lose years and become a kid again? American James Hogue did just that. Aged twenty-seven, he enrolled at a school as a sixteen-year-old. Hogue then went on to create his own school of learning – with his top subjects being: impostor, conman and thief.

James Arthur Hogue was born on October 22, 1959, in Kansas City, the son of Eugene and Maria. Little is known about his early years at home, though one childhood friend, Keith Mark, said young Hogue had an 'incredible drive' and developed a love of running when just a boy.

Clues to just how Hogue would conduct his life were given by Mark's recollection that 'you never knew what to expect from him because he was always changing. One day he'd have long hair, the next day it was short'. Hogue attended Washington High School in his home town from 1975 to 1977, where he took part in the school cross-country team and set a national four-mile record. In 1977 he led the team to its second consecutive league title and won the Kansas City individual title. A high school track coach remembered Hogue as 'highly intelligent, ambitious and determined to attend college.'

Hogue graduated that same year and, because of his natural running ability, was recruited to run at the University of Wyoming in Laramie, then one of the nation's top collegiate running programmes. He was at the university for two years, competing in the cross-country team and training with a number of world-class

Kenyan runners – a situation that left him angry and frustrated. For the Kenyans were a mix of some who had competed in the Olympics and others waiting to do so. Hogue was good, but they were in a class of their own.

He took to gruelling methods of training, such as tying himself to a car and running alongside it in a bid to match the men he saw not as team mates but rivals. He still only managed to be fifth best long-distance runner on his team. Hogue dropped out of Wyoming and returned to Kansas City. Could this have been the turning point? Was the seeming loss of such a sporting skill what led him to run off the straight and narrow?

Between 1979 and 1984, Hogue was briefly enrolled in a community college and later the University of Texas at Austin, where he studied chemical engineering but failed to graduate. Hogue's erratic college attendance and attitude were already changing his character. In 1983, he was arrested for theft and placed on probation for three years.

Perhaps it was during a short stay in Colorado that Hogue formulated a plan to recapture his earlier moments of sporting glory – by going back to school and doing it all again. On September 10, 1985, Hogue enrolled in the senior class of the Palo Alto High School, California, under the name of Jay Mitchell Huntsman. He pretended to be a sixteen-year-old, self-taught orphan from a Nevada commune. His parents, he said, had died in a mysterious car crash in Bolivia.

Less than a month after joining the school as Jay Huntsman, Hogue won the prestigious Stanford Invitational Cross-Country Meet as a member of the school's cross-country team. He apparently told classmates that his goal was to win a track scholarship to Stanford University.

What they made of Hogue and his sporting ambition, we don't know. For he had already earned the nickname 'Mystery Boy' for his rather strange physical appearance and unwillingness to talk about himself. Fellow pupils found him aloof and generally unapproachable.

Hogue was not to achieve his goal. On October 25, 1984, Palo Alto police revealed his true identity and the fact that the name Jay Huntsman had come from a baby boy who had died from pneumonia shortly after birth in 1969. Their revelation followed a tip-off from a suspicious local reporter, Jason Cole. Hogue was asked to leave the school and was briefly held in juvenile custody. Seven months later, he was arrested for forging cheques and received a ninety-day jail sentence. A warrant was issued for his arrest after he violated his probation.

For the next year, Hogue taught running at a Cross Training Clinic in Vail, Colorado, after falsely claiming to have a PhD in bio-engineering from Stanford University. Always keeping on the move, he then went to work with a custom bicycle frame builder called Dave Tesch in San Marcos, California – and stole £10,000 of tools and bike frames from the man who had taken him in and befriended him.

After taking flight to St George, in Utah, Hogue in 1988 applied to Princeton University, using the alias Alexi Indris Santana. This time, he claimed to be a self-taught eighteen-year-old orphan ranch hand from Utah. He also said in his application that he had slept outside in the Grand Canyon, raising sheep and reading philosophers. A documentary film made some years later about Hogue showed just how easy it was for him to be accepted at the prestigious university.

After seeing various press reports attesting to 'Santana's extraordinary running times', Larry Ellis, the coach of Princeton's track team, was ready to give him an athletic scholarship on the spot. Sadly for him, Hogue had to defer admission for one year following his arrest at a lock-up garage in St George where police found Dave Tesche's stolen bike frames. Hague pleaded guilty to receiving stolen property and served six months' in the Utah State Prison. Leading the investigation, detective Matt Jacobson also discovered applications to various Ivy League universities bearing the name Alexi Indris Santana.

Meanwhile, Princeton, desperate to ensure this sporting marvel came to them, was more than happy to pay for the trickster's cross-Atlantic flight to visit his mother 'who was dying of leukemia in Switzerland' – the story Hogue told to explain why, although he was delighted at being accepted, he couldn't join the university for another year. He was also delighted with the £7,500 scholarship it had awarded him.

After his release, Hogue had to serve a six-month term at a halfway house in Salt Lake City, from where he absconded and made his way to Princeton. In that summer of 1989, Hogue worked with a university grounds crew and participated in the Freshman Summer Orientation Programme. The local paper, *The Trenton Times*, caused a small hiccup for Hogue when it published an article about the incoming Princeton student and star runner Alexi Santana under the headline 'A Different Path to Glory: Princeton's Self-Educated Santana Blazing a new Trail'. Hogue's face was recognised and the State of Utah issued a fugitive warrant for his arrest.

Incredibly, Hogue finally managed to enter Princeton University in September 1989 and for two years lived as the student called Alexi Santana – who not only scored A and B grades, but was also a highly-regarded member of the track team and the Ivy Club, Princeton's most selective private eating club.

However, while he was competing at the Harvard-Yale-Princeton Track Meet in New Haven, Connecticut, in February 1991, Hogue was exposed again. Yale senior Renee Pacheco recognised him from Palo Alto High School and told her former track coach who in turn notified Jason Cole, a reporter on the *Peninsula Times Tribute*. He tipped off Princeton University officials that the young sporting hero was not who he said he was.

Hogue was arrested in the university's geology lab and charged with defrauding the university of $30,000 in financial aid, forgery, wrongful impersonation and falsifying records. Initially denying the charges, Hogue eventually pleaded guilty to theft-by-deception in a plea bargain a year later, on February 10, 1992. He was later to describe his time at Princeton as 'nothing but smoke and mirrors', adding that living with any guilt was easy enough because ultimately his main aim was to attain a degree.

While awaiting sentencing, Hogue managed to enroll in a Harvard University Extension programme and to be hired by the Harvard Mineralogical Museum. On October 23, 1992, Hogue was given a 270-day sentence and five years' probation. He was also ordered he pay restitution to Princeton University.

On May 16, 1993, Hogue made headlines again through his

association with Harvard University. Having once more lied about his identity, he was able to take a job as a security guard in one of Harvard's on-campus museums. A few months into his tenure, museum officials noticed that several gemstones on exhibit had been replaced with cheap fakes. Somerville police seized Hogue in his home and charged him with grand larceny to the tune of $50,000 after recovering gemstones, microscopes and other scientific equipment.

At a hearing at Somerville District Court in December that year, Hogue was convicted of larceny and receiving stolen property. He was jailed in Massachusetts until his transfer to New Jersey in January when he found himself at the Mercer County Correctional Facility. He was further charged with violating his parole.

Did any of this teach Hogue a lesson? Did he re-think his life of imposter? Sadly, not.

Out of jail in 1996, Hogue simply carried on where he left off. He took on another identity, that of graduate student Jim MacArthur, and headed back to Princeton University, again violating the conditions of his parole. This time, he was not officially enrolled but hung around the campus attending social events and eating in the cafeteria. When finally recognised as Hogue the conman by one of the students, he was arrested by Princeton Borough Police who let him out on bail after charging him with trespass. Another term at the Mercer County Correctional Facility followed. When released, Hogue went to Aspen, Colorado, where he was arrested for bicycle theft and sentenced to one year in jail.

Here, the trail of Hogue goes cold. He vanished from the public eye for two years and was reluctant to fill anyone in on what he was doing during that time. But he was very much high-profile again when film director Jesse Moss tracked him down in 1999 to make a documentary about his criminal and colourful life. The result was *Con Man: The True Life of an Ivy League Imposter*, released in 2001. Making of the film was not without its problems. Six months after agreeing to co-operate with Moss, Hogue was arrested by the Telluride Police Department and convicted of theft.

Hogue may have tired of pretending to be someone else, but he never lost the desire to steal. In January 2005, police armed with a search warrant raided Hogue's home in San Miguel County, Colorado, and found 7,000 stolen items worth almost $100,000. They had all come from nearby homes in which Hogue had worked as a repairman, and included rugs, bikes and antique furniture. Some of Hogue's clients had suspected him of pilfering from their houses, and one witness saw Hogue trying to hide stolen wares beneath a water tower at a local lake. Hogue's hoarded items, remarked one of the police team, 'packed his house and a small compartment he'd built'.

Hogue was not present to hear this, as he had fled the area. Over a year later, he was finally apprehended in Tucson, Arizona, when a US marshal and several deputies surrounded him as he surfed the internet in the café of a Barnes & Noble bookshop. He had been recognised as a wanted man by a member of staff, his daily pattern of using the café proving to be his downfall. During his interrogation, Hogue waived all his rights, preferring to answer all the questions put to him. It was, an observer remarked later, perhaps the only instance Hogue was ever honest.

On March 12, 2007, forty-seven-year-old Hogue pleaded guilty to a single felony count, of theft of more than $10,000, in exchange for a prison sentence not to exceed ten years and prosecutors' agreement to drop other theft and habitual criminal charges. Hogue, with a life of crime behind him, had a lucky break that day in court, with the threat of a longer jail term now removed.

Two victims of Hogue's theft took the stand to reinforce the prosecution's hope that Hogue should receive the full ten years. Deputy District Attorney Keri Yoder told the court that Hogue had struck fear into the heart of the local community of Mountain Village. He said: 'It's not just about stealing items – anything the defendant could get his hands on. People were really scared.'

Incredibly, the court received three letters asking for leniency for Hogue. And his public defender, Harvey Palefsky, challenged this, saying: 'Mr Hogue has become a myth, a creation – in large part created by the media for their own ends. He's the famous con man of Cinemax fame. I don't think there's anyone that can argue that prison will be very good for anybody. This was theft. He's not a dangerous man.' He described any lengthy sentence as being 'a waste of Hogue's talent and brain power'.

On May 17, 2007, Hogue officially received his ten-year prison sentence. He appeared in court looking nothing like the smart student he had once purported to be. His hair was lank and his wrists were contained in handcuffs. Hogue's demise was described by reporter Reilly Capps: 'The sentencing hearing for James Arthur Hogue was a small window into the life of one of America's most infamous conmen, a man who seemed at once greedy and generous, compassionate and cold-hearted; a man whom the prosecutor painted as remorseless and his defence lawyer described as a media-created myth.'

When given his chance to speak, Hogue did so in a whisper. There was no reference to his multi-identities, merely remorse for the string of thefts. Hogue said: 'I do apologise for all the trouble I've caused. I've stolen things and I've also purchased some things that turned out to be stolen. I think I believed them to be stolen when I bought them. It's hard to explain why I do this. It's nothing that I can really understand myself. It's some sort of collection compulsion, I guess. I never disposed of any of the things. I never made any profit.'

District Judge James W. Schum said the ten-year sentence was an attempt to 'get Hogue's attention'. He added: 'This is apparently some sort of mental illness you suffer from, some sort of obsessive personality trait that you have. But it is offensive and threatening and it has to be stopped.'

An insight to Hogue's mental state and compulsion to distort the truth was provided in a series of telephone calls he made and which were recorded by police. In them, Hogue seemed resigned to a long jail sentence and bizarrely was mostly concerned about a mystery woman in Russia who he claimed was his fiancée. 'I'm just trying to think about the girl,' Hogue told a friend. He then went on to worry about the woman getting a visa to come and visit him in America and how she would take the news that he was in jail.

In another call, Hogue's nephew advises him to 'come clean' with the woman.

'How am I gonna do that? I don't know how to explain it. She's a really, really nice person and I have to figure out a way to get her out of this,' replies Hogue before coming up with a solution to his dilemma. 'The only thing I think I can do is tell her I was killed in a car crash or a coma. I just can't keep her tied up like that. I might as well be dead to her.' Both Hogue's friend and nephew refuse to lie for him.

Detective Robert Wallraven, in charge of Hogue's arrest, said that rather than feel sympathy for Hogue, one should realise the calls simply revealed his continuing criminality. Said Wallraven: 'He's not worried about all that criminal behaviour. All he's worried about is what lie and con he can say to someone he claims to love. His behaviour has not changed for over twenty years. The only gaps in his criminal records are when he wasn't caught.'

Having served 465 days in jail before sentencing, Hogue was told that he would be eligible for parole before half of his ten-year sentence is completed.

The reasons for Hogue's life of crime and hoaxes are a mystery. His unique sporting skills would have found him success without the extraordinary web of lies and deceit he spun. He could so easily have become someone special in his own right. Instead, he ended up both failing to capitalise on his abilities and failing to make crime pay.

During interrogation by police immediately after his Princeton arrest, Hogue had been asked the simple question: 'Why?' He answered: 'I just wanted to start all over again without the burdens of my past.' But when finally walking free from jail, would Hogue the long-distance champion have anywhere left to run?

Chapter 15

The Greatest Fairy Story
of All

I t is the grandest fairy tale ever, standing out from all those much-loved by children over the years. For the Cottingley Fairies story actually seemed true at one time – proof that the tiny, sparkling little creatures from folklore actually were real. Indeed, there were even photographs.

A splendid mix born from a desire for it all to be fact and the final revelation that it was all fiction, the Cottingley Fairies hoax has gone down in history, partly because it was perpetrated by two young girls. Frances Griffiths and her cousin Elsie Wright were the two culprits who wanted the world to know there really were fairies at the bottom of their garden. And it helped that the great detective writer Sir Arthur Conan Doyle became involved. He, like most others, was taken in by the sweet little Yorkshire lasses and even went on lecture tours to proclaim that here, at last, was evidence fairies really did exist.

Looking back at the infamous photographs today, it is hard to believe that anyone could have been convinced by the flimsy evidence. But perhaps it was the promise of magic in the bleak early 1900s that made the girls' hoax so plausible.

Elsie, aged sixteen at the peak of the trick and six years older than Frances, was certainly the main instigator. Born in 1901 to Arthur and Polly Wright, she developed into a gifted and accomplished artist, painting portraits and local landscapes, mainly in colour. She attended Bradford Art College from the age of thirteen and later found work in a photographic laboratory and a greeting cards factory. It was during her photography experience that the young Elsie perfected the art of creating composite pictures of fallen World War One soldiers alongside pictures of their loved ones. She also worked with plate cameras. Elsie and Frances became firm friends when Frances, born in 1907 to Sergeant Arthur Griffith and Annie Griffith in South Africa, moved to live with her cousin in Cottingley.

The story of the fairies began in 1917. Elsie borrowed her father's camera – a Butcher Midge No 1 Magazine Type Falling Plate quarter-plate – to take pictures of Frances with fairies dancing right under her nose in their garden in Cottingley. The veins in the wings were clearly visible. The photographs were developed by Elsie's father and Frances even cheekily sent a couple to a friend, Johanna Parvin, in South Africa. On the back of one she scribbled the message: 'Elsie and I are ever friendly with the beck stream fairies. It is funny, I never used to see them in Africa. It must be too hot for them there.'

Her accompanying letter said: "I hope you are quite well. I wrote a letter before only I lost it or it got mislaid. Do you play with Elsie and Nora Biddles? I am learning French, Geometry, Cookery and Algebra at school now. Dad came home from France the other week after being there ten months and we all think the war will be over in a few days. We are going to get our flags to hang upstairs in our bedroom I am sending two photos, both of me, one of me in a bathing costume in our back yard. Uncle Arthur took that while the other is me with some fairies up the beck. Elsie took that one. Rosebud is as fat as ever and I have made her some new clothes. How are Teddy and dolly? Elsie and I are very friendly with the beck Fairies."

Mr Wright was not impressed, however. He immediately declared as fakes the first pictures, which included Frances looking into the camera as a troop of fairies danced on a branch at Cottingley Beck. When he developed a second, similar, batch, he banned Elsie from using the camera again.

But Elsie's mother, who took great interest in the occult, believed the photographs deserved showing to an expert. In 1919 she took them to Edward Gardner, president of the London branch of the Theosophical Society at an evening when the society's theme for the talk was 'Fairy Life'. He accepted the pictures as genuine. So too did Harold Snelling, a photographic expert, who commented in a letter to Gardner dated July 31, 1920: 'These two negatives are entirely genuine unfaked photographs of single exposure, open-air work, show movement in all the fairy figures, and there is no trace whatever of studio work involving card or paper models, dark backgrounds, painted figures, etc. In my opinion, they are both straight untouched pictures.' He added: 'What gets me most is that all these figures have moved during exposure.'

Because the original pictures were somewhat faded and ill-defined, Gardner asked Harold Snelling to produce sharper reprints which would satisfy a growing public curiosity in them. It was the dark, grim days after the First World War, and the story of the Cottingley Fairies were just what a depressed Britain needed. Sir Arthur Conan Doyle, who had lost his son in the war and was eager to believe in the supernatural, heard about the fairy pictures while preparing an article on fairies for the *Strand* magazine.

Conan Doyle asked Gardner for further proof of the authenticity of the images, and the latter approached the Kodak photographic company's British manager. Kodak put the pictures before a panel of their experts and all agreed that the negatives were single exposure and that the plates showed no sign of being faked work. However, they were sufficiently wary of their professional reputations to decline to issue a certificate of authentication.

Still convinced, Conan Doyle next sent Gardner to Yorkshire to meet the two perpetrators of this monumental hoax: In his book, *Fairies: A Book of Real Fairies*, published in 1945, Gardner recalled this meeting: 'I went off to Cottingley again, taking the two cameras and plates from London, and met the family and explained to the two girls the simple working of the cameras, giving one each to keep. The cameras were loaded and my final advice was that they need go up to the glen only on fine days as they had been accustomed to do before and 'tice the fairies, as they called their way of attracting them, and see what they could get. I suggested the most obvious and easy precautions about lighting and distance, for I knew it was essential they should feel free and unhampered and have no burden of responsibility. If nothing came of it all, I told them, they were not to mind a bit.'

Elsie and Frances were convincing about their 'friends' the fairies. They played with them often, they said. The tiny visitors were 'very shy but could be great fun'.

Elsie's mother was still convinced that the pictures were genuine but her father was still cautious. Mr Wright told Gardner that, at first, he had been so suspicious that he had searched for clues in the glen where the photographs were taken, as well as in his daughter's bedroom. He had found nothing. He agreed to an article appearing in the London-based *Strand* magazine, as long as full names were not used. And, astonishingly, he declined the offer of payment by Conan Doyle, on the grounds that if the photographs were genuine they shouldn't require remuneration.

Elsie and Frances's families handed over the photographic plates and, although the girls themselves refused to swear their story on the Bible, they did offer to take more photographs. Three more were produced, one showing a fairy offering Elsie flowers. The pictures, together with the girls' original ones, appeared alongside articles by Sir Arthur in *Strand* magazine in November 1920 and March 1921. The headline on the first article was: 'An Epoch-making Event Described by A. Conan Doyle'. In the second, Sir Arthur wrote: 'It is at the lowest, an interesting speculation which gives an added charm to the silence of the woods and the wilderness of the moorland.'

Reaction was mixed. The tiny creatures were exactly what romantics imagined fairies to be and people wanted to believe there really were such gentle creatures. Others thought the detective writer should have known better. One photographic expert, Kenneth Styles, declared the pictures to be 'a most patent fraud'. Cynics said the fairies appeared to have been cut from a children's book and others pointed out the similarity between the Cottingley fairies and those that appeared in an advertisement for 'Price's Night Lights'. Another critic, radium expert Major Hall-Edwards, declared: 'On the evidence I have no hesitation in saying that these photographs could have been faked. I criticise the attitude of those who declared there is something supernatural in the circumstances attending to the taking of these pictures because, as a medical man, I believe that the inculcation of such absurd ideas into the minds of children will result in later life in manifestations and nervous disorder and mental disturbances...'

The *Manchester City News* reported: 'We must either believe in the almost incredible mystery of the fairies, or in the almost incredible wonder of faked photographs.' The magazine *Truth* was more blunt. It said: 'For a true explanation of the fairy photographs, what is wanted is not a knowledge of the occult phenomena but a knowledge of children.' None of this deterred Sir Arthur from pursuing his supernatural discovery, embarking on a round of lectures and even devoting an entire book to the subject. Published in 1922, *The Coming of the Fairies* recounted the story of the photographs and their supposed provenance.

Despite criticism, Conan Doyle remained utterly convinced of the existence of the tiny sprites. He even arranged for a medium, Geoffrey Hodson, to visit the girls in Cottingley in the hope that they could 'spirit up' fresh fairies. He returned from Yorkshire and faithfully reported what his sponsor no doubt wanted to hear. He said he had seen prancing fairies in a field and wood elves under some beech trees. Hodson also wrote a book on the subject, *Fairies at Work and Play*, in which he averred: 'I am personally convinced of the bona fides of the two girls who took these photographs. I spent some weeks with them and their family, and became assured of the genuineness of their clairvoyance, of the presence of fairies, exactly like those photographed, in the glen at Cottingley, and of the complete honesty of all parties concerned.'

Yet more fairy pictures were produced by Elsie and Frances. Their quality was poor but helped convince a growing number of people who were becoming intrigued by the whole affair. Sir Arthur was delighted that he was at last being 'proved right'. In one of his lecture papers, he wrote: 'If I am myself asked whether the case is to be absolutely and finally proved, I should answer that in order to remove the last faint shred of doubt, I should wish to see the result repeated before a disinterested witness.'

It was not to be. Interest in the Cottingley fairies waned until, more than half a century later, modern technology and a belated confession by Elsie revealed the fairy story for what it really was... a great big hoax.

Close examination of the photographs with computerised equipment showed that the fairies were 'dancing' at the end of a thread. They had, in fact, been copied by Elsie from the *Princess Mary Gift Book*, which was so popular at the time that it is incredible no one noticed. The girls had used hat pins to attach the fairy figures onto leaves and twigs. They themselves found it hard to believe anyone could have been fooled.

The story of the Cottingley Fairies, just like the photographs, slowly faded. But the girls' lives continued in a very normal way. Frances married solder Sydney Way in 1928 and settled in Ramsgate, Kent. The couple went on to have two children. Frances died in 1988 aged seventy-eight. Elsie married an engineer and emigrated to India. During the Second World War, she was a captain in the WRVS working in military hospitals in Calcutta. She and her husband had a daughter and Elsie returned to England after the 1947 Declaration of Independence.

The first, oblique admission that the pictures were faked finally came in 1976. 'As for the photographs,' said Elsie, 'let's say they are figments of our imagination, mine and Frances's, and leave it at that.'

Throughout most of her life Frances remained tight-lipped about the fairies. But five years before her death aged eighty-seven in 1988, Elsie decided to come clean. 'I felt that we couldn't tell Sir Arthur Conan Doyle they were fakes because it might have upset him dreadfully,' she said. 'When we cut our fairies out, Frances had rather podgy hands and couldn't cut the fingers properly. So her fairies had thick-looking hands, and some of the experts got excited and said the fairies had fins. Fins, I ask you! I forgot to put wings on one fairy and that caused a great to-do as well.'

Speaking on the BBC television programme *Nationwide* in 1983, Elsie further explained: 'At that time women wore great big pinwheel hats, you know, with great big crowns and they have to take their hat pins about this long.' So, if fashions had been different then, there may well have been no Cottingley fairies.

By the time of their deaths, Elsie and Frances had both admitted that neither of them had ever believed in fairies and never would. Apart from being given £20 each from a grateful Sir Arthur, the girls had received no great financial reward for their hoax – but they did find immortality of a kind. Their story became known around the world. Frances and Elsie's story was told in a Warner Bros film, *Fairy Tale – A True Story*; which held its British premiere in Yorkshire in 1998.

In a rare confession, Frances Wright once proudly remarked: 'It is perhaps every hoaxer's dream: the immortality that follows the perpetration of some well-staged and well-publicised piece of hocus-pocus.'

Chapter 16

'A Sucker Born Every Minute'

Phineas is a Biblical name, in Hebrew meaning 'Brazen Mouth'. How fitting, then, that an austere Puritan couple living in Bethel, Connecticut, should have chosen it for the son born to them on July 5, 1810. For Phineas Taylor Barnum grew up to be not only 'brazen' but a big-mouthed huckster whose fantastic fakery brought him fame and fortune.

Barnum's ingenuity and his ability to tell the most outrageous lies to lure an audience made him the most famous showman in the entire world. He is also considered the father of modern advertising because of his remarkable talent for grabbing the attention of the public. He is credited with coining the phrases 'Never give a sucker an even break' and 'There's a sucker born every minute'. He lived his entire life by following these two adages, and made two fortunes on the backs of his gullible customers.

The garrulous trickster was not always so successful. A discontented jack-of-all-trades, Phineas was a store clerk, ran lotteries, sold men's hats, edited a newspaper and was joint owner of a grocery store. Despite this modest success, however, he saw himself as a failure and determined to become an entrepreneur at any cost.

In the first real surge of his adventurous spirit, he sold his interest in the grocery store and embarked on a bizarre adventure into showmanship. He had learned the most elementary lessons while working in a barter store in Bethel. Here, goods were paid for not in cash but in kind. Because so much suspect merchandise was being offered, the store's policy was always to offer faulty goods in return. As Barnum recalled: 'Everything in that store was different from what was represented.' Burnt peas, for instance, were offered as coffee beans and cotton in place of wool.

With this insight into fair trading, thirty-three-year-old Phineas, now married to Charity Hallett and the father of two children, took his family to New York and opened a Broadway sideshow. His first exhibit was an ugly and withered black lady named Joice Heth whom he had come across in a similar sideshow in Philadelphia. Joice, blind and partly paralysed, assured him that she was 160 years old and had once been George Washington's nursemaid. Barnum bought her on the spot for a pittance. Then he plastered Manhattan with posters:

'The greatest curiosity in the world and the most interesting, particularly to Americans, is now exhibiting at the saloon fronting on Broadway; Joice Heth, nurse to General George Washington, the father of our country, who has arrived at the astonishing age of 161 years, as authentic documents will prove,and in full possession of her mental faculties. She is cheerful and healthy though she weighs but forty-nine pounds. She relates many anecdotes of her younger master.'

Displaying his great flare for publicity, Barnum dreamed up incredible tales for the press and learned the lesson that free editorial space is much more cost-effective than expensive advertising. So astute was Barnum that he even wrote anonymous letters to the newspapers calling into question the claims about Joice. He reasoned that it was better to have people talking about you than not and, as many confidence tricksters have reaffirmed since, bad publicity is better than no publicity. Crowds queued along the sidewalks of Broadway to see the 'female Methuselah'. And they certainly got their money's worth with her phoney memories of Washington, the many errors in her narratives being excused because of her extreme antiquity.

When initial interest in his 'Methuselah' died down, Barnum took an advertisement in a newspaper to announce that Joice Heth was not a real person at all — but a robot. The crowds flocked back when he proclaimed: 'What purports to be a remarkable old woman is simply a curiously constructed automaton, made up of whalebone, india-rubber and numberless springs ingeniously put together and made to move at the slightest touch.'

Long after she retired through ill health, Barnum took great care of her. On her death in 1836, however, he found a new way of making money out of the old hag. He hired a surgeon to perform an autopsy on Joice in front of an invited audience. Barnum had long known that Joice was nothing like her advertised age, but he roared with laughter when it was revealed that the old lady had fooled even him. The surgeon pronounced Joice to be no more than eighty years of age. 'I, like you, have been duped,' said the irrepressible Barnum, and his name remained in the news for another few weeks.

Joice Heth had not been Barnum's only exhibit, of course. There was his 'Feejee Mermaid' which he claimed had been fished out of the Pacific in 1817. In fact it was, in Barnum's own words, 'an ugly, dried-up, black-looking and diminutive specimen' which he had bought from a Boston showman in 1842. He kept his acquisition secret at first while he distributed 10,000 leaflets arguing that mermaids existed and displaying engravings of beautiful specimens disporting themselves on rocks. No mention was made of Barnum's own ugly specimen until, public interest having been awakened, he announced its arrival at the museum. Thousands of people handed over their ten cents to see what was nothing more than a monkey's torso attached by amateurish taxidermy to the tail of a large fish.

There were even more blatant frauds. Barnum persuaded spectators to pay to view 'the horse with its tail where its head should be' — only to encounter an ordinary horse tethered in its stall back to front, with its tail in the feeding trough. Barnum even exhibited an ordinary black alley cat, advertising it as 'the world's only cherry coloured cat'. When his customers complained, they were told that the animal was the colour of black cherries!

Richer from displaying Joice Heth and his other fraudulent acts, Barnum took to the road in the late 1830s with the country's first canvas-top circus.

When love of his family drew him back to New York, he found the showbusiness game tougher than ever. A string of short, theatrical ventures led him finally to a go-for-broke gamble that would have frightened other men.

Scudder's American Museum was up for sale, a five-storey shell of a building that had been a money loser for years. With nothing for collateral but his dreams, Barnum convinced the owners that he could ride their white elephant into fields of glory. And he did.

From the date of its opening, Barnum's American Museum was destined to become the new wonder of the Western World. He displayed educated dogs and jumping fleas, fat boys and giant, dwarfs and rope dancers, performing Indians and the first Punch and Judy Show ever seen in New York.

Being Barnum, however, the virtues of every act were wildly exaggerated. The fleas were advertised as 'insects that can draw carriages and carts' and it was only when the punters had paid their money that they discovered that the conveyances were suitably minuscule. At the other end of the scale, a live hippopotamus was also exhibited in the American Museum. It would have been a big enough draw in its own right but Barnum could not resist billing it as 'the great behemoth of the Scriptures'.

In three years, Barnum paid for his museum and expanded it beyond even his wildest dreams. With his incredible imagination and sense of the bizarre, he entertained millions. Still seeking fresh phenomena to tempt, tantalise and astonish audiences, the super-showman then made a find that would turn out to be one of his greatest — tiny Tom Thumb. Barnum's half-brother, Philo, tipped him off that a remarkable midget was being exhibited at Bridgeport, Connecticut. Barnum dropped everything, raced north and examined him. He discovered a bright, five-year-old boy of amazingly minute proportions. The boy had been born on 4 January 1838 weighing nine pounds and had developed normally until the age of six months. Since then, however, he had not grown another inch. Barnum signed up the little fellow on the spot for $3 a week.

The midget was called Charles Stratton. With his showman's flair, Barnum renamed him General Tom Thumb and made him his Number One attraction. Not content with the truth, Barnum billed the child as 'a dwarf of eleven years of age just arrived from England'. He taught him to act 'autocratic, impudent and regal' and dressed him in various guises, from a mini-Cupid to a Roman gladiator to Napoleon Bonaparte. The partnership between the six-foot showman and tiny Tom was a remarkable one which developed into an enduring friendship. As Tom Thumb grew into adulthood, he remained a perfectly formed midget, two feet tall and weighing fifteen pounds. What he lacked in size, the brilliant little man made up for in personality. With patter, songs and dances devised by Barnum, he made theatrical history — and enough money to ensure his and Barnum's passport to even greater fame abroad.

There were overflow crowds when Tom Thumb and his supporting cast appeared at a London theatre, and a command performance was given at Buckingham Palace, where even Queen Victoria was amused. There were audiences with King Louis-Philippe of France, Queen Isabella of Spain, Belgium's King Leopold and other European royals. With sell-out performances, and with gifts from the crowned heads, the three-year European tour made Thumb and Barnum very rich. Their association would continue for thirty years, and it was the warm-hearted midget who came to Barnum's aid when fate dealt the entrepreneur a flurry of blows.

Back in the United States, Barnum had grown richer still with his sponsorship of Jenny Lind, the 'Swedish Nightingale'. But in 1855 disaster befell him. Always a soft touch for his friends, Barnum had underwritten a dying enterprise, the Jerome Clock Company. When his friends plummeted into bankruptcy, they took Barnum with them. The next blow was the burning down of Barnum's home, 'Iranistan'. The palatial mansion and international showplace exploded into flames after a painter dropped a lighted cigarette.

The greatest blow, however, came in 1865 when Barnum's precious American Museum was also destroyed by fire. Wild animals escaped onto the streets of New York, an orang-utan being recaptured in an office block. A gallant fireman single-handedly carried the 400-pound Fat Lady to safety but the 7ft 11inch World's Tallest Woman had to be lifted free with the aid of a derrick. It all made huge headlines; Barnum saw to that.

One was killed in the museum blaze but the loss of the half a million cherished exhibits was heartbreaking for Barnum. The damage was put at $500,000 but the insurance covered only a fraction of it. Phineas faced ruin. At this point Tom Thumb stepped in and revealed himself as big of heart as he was small of frame. He helped finance a new European tour which was the beginning of

Barnum's second fortune. By 1870 he had repaid his creditors, rebuilt his museum and opened his newest, bigger, better-than-ever circus.

When Barnum formed a partnership with James Anthony Bailey in 1871, the Barnum & Bailey Circus reached its zenith with the three-ring spectacle that became circus tradition. 'The Greatest Show On Earth' travelled across North America in its own railroad cars, adding new words and phrases to the English language — such as jumbo, ballyhoo and white elephant.

Barnum's white elephant was called 'Toung Taloung' and had to be repainted every time it rained. More enduring, however, was a mighty elephant which Barnum purchased from London Zoo in 1882 and inspirationally renamed 'Jumbo'. The animal was advertised as 'the only mastodon on Earth, whose like the world will never see again — a feature crushing all attempts at fraud'. Thereafter the creature gave its name to everything from jumbo-sized burgers to jumbo jets. On one occasion, Jumbo seemingly felt so overworked that he embarked on a sit-down strike. Unwilling to leave England, the pachyderm refused to enter his van until Barnum bribed him with a barrel of beer. Jumbo died in 1885 after being hit by a train during a tour of Canada.

Meanwhile, Barnum's beloved wife Charity had become an invalid, and she died in 1873 after a series of strokes. Sick with loneliness, Phineas took a new wife ten months later: a lovely young English girl named Nancy Fish. Barnum was sixty-four and Nancy forty years younger but she remained a devoted wife and friend until his own death at the age of eighty-one.

When it became evident that his death was near, the *New York Evening News* did a remarkable thing. With Barnum's permission, they published his obituary in advance so that the showman could read it. 'Great And Only Barnum,' the headline said. 'He Wanted To Read His Obituary And Here It Is!' Laughing, Phineas and Nancy read it together, and it was close to his bedside when the 'Great And Only' died. He left a fortune of $5million – finally proving the Barnum adage: 'There's a sucker born every minute.'

Rogue Romanov… Claiming to be a Russian royal who escaped assassination, Anna Anderson fooled historians and scientists alike – until modern-day science proved her to be a fraud.

The royal and the rogue… Grand Duchess Anastasia as a young girl (left) and Anna Anderson who spent a lifetime trying to convince the world that she was Anastasia, the only survivor of the massacred imperial royal family.

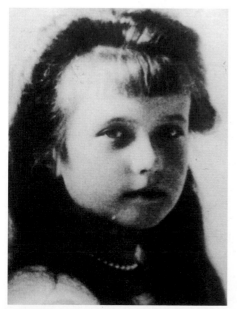

Anna Anderson in her youth (left)… She was committed to a mental institution in 1920 after a failed suicide bid. Two years later, she announced for the first time that she was the Tsar's youngest daughter, the Grand Duchess Anastasia.

Anna Anderson in frail old age (right)… She died in hospital in Charlottesville, Virginia, in 1984. By the end of her life, it is clear that she really believed her own wildest claims to be the last of the Romanovs.

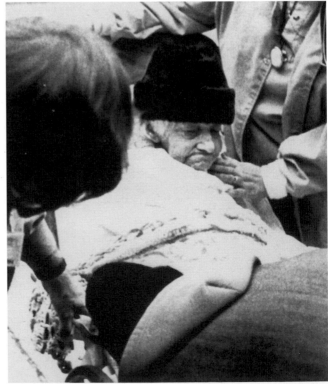

Art faker… Tom Keating exposed the phoney values of the art world by painting hundreds of fakes – or 'Sexton Blakes' as he called them in Cockney rhyming slang.

Wild West tales… Cowboy Frank T. Hopkins rode into the annals of horse-racing history – until it was revealed that he had saddled his admirers with a galloping great lie.

Giant hoax… George Hull thought big and pulled off one of the most over-sized hoaxes in history – by creating a giant 'prehistoric petrified man'.

'Count Cagliostro'...
Sicilian peasant
Giuseppe Balsamo
reinvented himself as
a phoney nobleman
and fooled the courts
of Europe.

The 'Missing
Link'... Charles
Dawson created
this skull to
convince the
world he had
discovered the
secret of how ape
became man –
and made a
monkey out of
the experts.

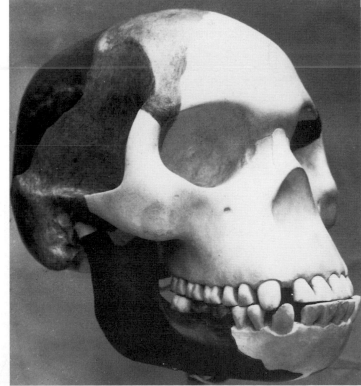

Fake self-portrait …
This scribble was
passed off as a self-
portait of William
Shakespeare – but was
drawn by a young
faker named William
Ireland.

From Bard to worse! …
Ireland created 'lost'
masterpieces in the style
of the Bard. They fooled
some experts but,
unfortunately for him, not
his 18th-century audiences.

To the Reader.
This Figure, that thou here feeft put,
    It was for gentle Shakefpeare cut;
Wherein the Grauer had a ftrife
    with Nature, to out-doo the life:
O,could he but haue drawne his wit
    As well in braffe, as he hath hit
Hisface ; the Print would then furpaffe
    All,that was euer writ in braffe.
But,fince he cannot, Reader, looke
    Not on his Picture, but his Booke.
                                    B. I.

Just a fairy tale… Two young girls convinced the world that there really were fairies at the bottom of their garden – and kept their secret for almost a lifetime.

Boastful Barnum… Phineas Taylor Barnum was the most famous showman in history – and his outrageous claims to lure an audience came 'Jumbo' sized, as this poster shows.

JUMBO GOES BACK TO EUROPE.

JUMBO The ONLY MASTODON on EARTH
Whose Like the World will never See Again

LEADS far the LARGEST HERD of ELEPHANTS

THE GENTLE and HISTORIC LORD of BEASTS
The Prodigious Pet of both England and America.
A Colossus of International Character.

WELCOME JUMBO

A FEATURE CRUSHING ALL ATTEMPTS AT FRAUD
There is but one JUMBO–The Admired of Millions
The Towering Monarch of His Mighty Race.

JUMBO, THE UNIVERSAL SYNONYM FOR ALL STUPENDOUS THINGS.
Steadily GROWING IN TREMENDOUS HEIGHT and WEIGHT
GIVE THE LITTLE ONES A LAST RIDE ON THEIR GIANT, DOCILE FRIEND.

'There's a sucker born every minute'… that was the motto of Barnum, whose fantastic fakery brought him fame and fortune. One genuine exhibit, however, was Tom Thumb, pictured with him here.

Lying through their lenses… Conning cameramen like William Mumler (left) convinced his American customers that he had captured long-gone relatives on film. It was a cruel deception.

Snapshots 'of the dead'… English spirit photographer Frederick Hudson took advantage of the vulnerable, who were desperate to see their dead loved ones again (above right, left and below).

Cruel trickery…
Frenchman Edouard
Buguet was a 'spirit
photographer' who made
his reputation – and pots
of money – by producing
likenesses of deceased
relatives of his sitters.

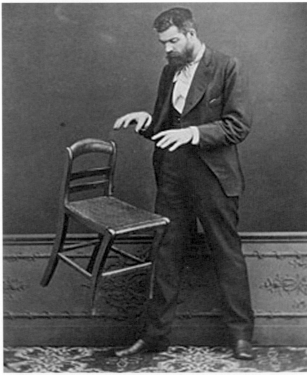

Phoney sailor... Donald Crowhurst could not face the humiliation of being uncovered as a cheat. His dream of glory in a round-the-world yacht race ended with his death at sea.

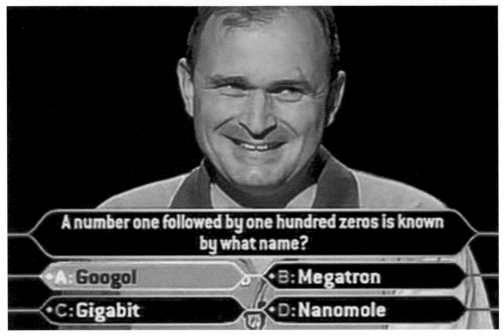

A number one followed by one hundred zeros is known by what name?

A: Googol

B: Megatron

C: Gigabit

D: Nanomole

Cheating major… Charles Ingram (pictured below with his wife) entered the TV quiz *Who Wants To Be A Millionaire?* and got his hands on a cheque for £1million – but only fleetingly.

Quiz king quizzed… Charles Van Doren's brilliant mind gained him fleeting fame as a contestant on America's top TV quiz show – until he was exposed as a cheat.

Upper-class pranksters… This group of 'Abyssinian royalty' (below), famously feted by the Royal Navy, were all outrageous hoaxers, one of whom was famed novelist Virginia Woolf (seated left).

'Honest, I really am a forger!'… Han Van Meegeren painted fakes that made him a fortune – but which also almost got him hanged as a traitor because he had sold them to the Nazis.

Puzzling patterns…At one time believed to be freaks of nature or even the works of aliens, crop circles like this one were simply the result of funsters having a field day.

Dodgy diaries… The
'private papers' of Adolf
Hitler were about to be
published worldwide
before the real author
was revealed to be a man
whose forte was forging
luncheon vouchers!

Chapter 17

Weird World of Princess Caraboo

She arrived from foreign shores, telling tales in a strange tongue about pirates and kidnap. The appearance of such an exotic stranger caused much excitement in the town. Local gentry could not wait to be introduced to the princess, and the more charitable among the townspeople did all they could to make the enchanting visitor feel at home. But 'Princess Caraboo', as she called herself, was a fake, the romantic invention of a poor servant girl. She fooled everyone she met and, even though she was a fraud, one had to admire her play-acting – right down to the strange language she used and the bizarre behaviour she adopted.

The story of the make-believe princess began in April 1817 in the bucolic setting of the small English West Country town of Almondsbury, near Bristol. A clergyman answered a knock on the door and encountered a young woman who immediately started babbling away in a language he could not understand. Noting her plain black dress, ruffles around her neck and a black turban wrapped around her head, the clergyman did not know what to make of her.

She was obviously exhausted from her travels and the kindly man knew he could not turn her away. After letting her rest a while, he took her to the Overseer of the Poor, a Mr Hill. Even he was at a loss as to what to do when the stranger refused his offer of a shilling to find herself a bed for the night. So the two men put the girl into a carriage and took her to Knole Park, the grand home of Bristol town clerk Samuel Worrall and his wife Elizabeth. The sight of the house seemed to frighten the girl, and it was only with Mrs Worrall's gentle persuasion that she went inside.

The learned couple were baffled when the girl failed to

understand what they were saying. Instead, her black eyes would look at them in puzzlement, her full lips every so often breaking into a broad smile. After studying the girl for a while, Mrs Worrall announced that she must be a foreign gypsy. It was only after some effort that the good lady managed to extricate a name from her house guest. Mrs Worrall repeatedly pointed to herself, saying 'Elizabeth, Elizabeth'. The girl finally responded, pointing at herself and saying gravely, 'Caraboo, Caraboo'.

Caraboo, accompanied by one of the Worrall's maids, was sent to a local inn to spend the night. There she refused to touch the supper laid out on a table for her. But she greedily grabbed a cup of tea, covered her eyes, gabbled some sort of prayer and noisily devoured the contents. The sight of a bed mystified her and she curled up on the floor instead. The landlord's daughter showed her what the bed was for, and only then did Caraboo lie down on it and drift off to sleep. When Mrs Worrall arrived at the inn the next morning, Caraboo ran to her, squealing and holding tightly onto her hand. Mrs Worrall felt obliged to take the girl back to Knole Park.

Word quickly spread about the enchanting visitor staying at the 'big house'. There were strange stories, too, such as how the girl had cut the cross from a hot cross bun and stuffed it inside her dress. And how she performed peculiar war dances, swam naked and darted up trees like a wild animal.

Yet she showed bewilderment when anyone tried to talk to her and she still uttered odd sounding words. Even when someone tried to catch her out, running into her bedroom and shouting 'Fire!', Caraboo stared blankly at them. The Worrall's family doctor voiced his suspicions, saying Caraboo's skin was too white to be from any exotic continent. Her features, he said, were European. Mrs Worrall, however, refused to accept the doctor's verdict and continued to humour the poor girl.

It was the arrival in the village of a Portuguese traveller which seemed to solve the mystery. He was Signor Manuel Eynesso, who had spent some time in the Far East and supposedly knew the Malay language. He was invited to the Worralls' home, where he spoke to Caraboo at length before declaring that she was a princess from an island called Javasu. Her language, he said, was a mixture of dialects used on the coast of Sumatra. This surprised even Caraboo, since the language she was speaking was totally made up!

Eynesso described how Caraboo had been kidnapped by pirates and had escaped overboard in the Bristol Channel. The Worralls seemed satisfied with the explanation, not realising that Eynesso was almost as great a charlatan as Caraboo herself. In fact, it was later suggested that the two of them had been in cahoots all along, the Portuguese visitor hoping to cash in on a share of the phoney princess's fame and fortune.

Princess Caraboo was then introduced to a friend of the Worralls. A retired naval captain, he used sign language and a smattering of words she seemed to understand. An even more remarkable story emerged. Not only did she come from Javasu in the East Indies, but her father, Jessu Mandu, was a high-caste Chinese, so revered that people fell to their knees in his presence. Lowly men carried him around on their shoulders and he wore a headdress made of peacock feathers. One of his four wives was Caraboo's mother, a beautiful Malay who blackened her teeth and wore jewels in her nose.

The story continued of how Caraboo was in her garden when she was seized by pirates, bound hand and foot and carried off to sea. After more than a week, the pirate chief sold her to the captain of a brig who, because of his huge whiskers and evil eyes, so terrified Princess Caraboo that she jumped overboard. It just so happened that the brig was off the coast of England at the time, so she could safely swim ashore.

At the time of her escape, Princess Caraboo had been wearing a fine silk dress, spun with gold. However, this was given to a peasant girl in exchange for more simple clothes, and she used a shawl as a turban to wrap around her head. The princess then roamed the countryside, lost and frightened in the strange land. She slept in barns and survived by begging until she eventually found herself in Almondsbury.

When the naval captain who was relaying this fantastic story showed Caraboo a book on Java, she reacted with delight, pointing animatedly at the pictures. It appeared obvious that this was the princess's homeland.

Yet another visitor came to inspect Princess Caraboo. Dr Charles Wilkinson was considered an intellectual and an expert on foreign affairs. After meeting the princess, he announced: 'Her manners are extremely graceful, her countenance surprisingly fascinating. If before suspected as an impostor, the sight of her removes all doubt.'

The Worralls and their friends could not help but be impressed with their 'royal' guest and it was agreed that she should make Knole Park her home for as long as she wished. Having Princess Caraboo living with them, however, meant the Worralls had to get used to her strange habits. Princess Caraboo would stalk around with a bow and arrow. She prepared her own food, showing a particular love of rice and spicy vegetable curries. She ate little meat and drank only water and tea. Once, after stalking a pigeon, she caught it with one hand, cut its head off and buried it together with the bird's entrails in a strange ceremony. She then plucked the rest of the pigeon, curried it and ate it. The princess was also very religious. When shown the drawing of an idol from the South Seas, she threw it to the ground, declaring Allah-Tallah as the only god she would worship. She set up a temple in the Worralls' shrubbery, saying her prayers there every morning and evening.

All was going well until Dr Wilkinson began writing about Princess Caraboo in journals and newspapers. Then the princess disappeared. Feeling he was responsible for scaring her away, Wilkinson tracked her down in Bath, where she had made new friends among the fashionable spa guests. The women wanted to touch her; the men offered her generous gifts of up to £20 a time to help towards her passage back home to Javasu. The princess did not take the money, apparently ignorant as to what to do with it.

It was one of Dr Wilkinson's newspaper reports, however, that revealed the princess for what she really was. A Mrs Neale recognised the girl's description and told friends that she was the same person who had stayed at her lodging house in Bristol. The girl had amused herself by wearing a turban and making up her own language. Word got back to Mrs Worrall, who was obviously shaken at the news. She confronted Princess Caraboo on her return to Almondsbury and made the imposter come face to face with Mrs Neale who shrieked: 'Yes, that's her. That's Mary Baker!' Instantly dropping her regal facade, Mary Baker burst into tears and – in a strong North Devon accent – begged Mrs Worrall to forgive her.

That same year, what was claimed at last to be the true story of Mary Baker was published in a pamphlet called *Caraboo: A Narrative Of A Singular Imposition Practised Upon the Benevolence Of A Lady*. The fact that Mary herself had provided the information to author John Matthew Gutch made it somewhat implausible but it was nevertheless colourful reading. The pamphlet told how she was born Mary Willcocks, one of many children of a poor but respectable couple in the village of Witheridge, near Crediton, Devon. She received little education and ran wild until she was eight years old. Then, to supplement the family's meagre income, she was taught to spin. When she was sixteen, her parents found her a job at a nearby farmhouse, doing manual work and looking after the farmer's children.

Rural life as a humble domestic servant was not good enough for Mary, who was already dreaming her wild dreams and making up fantastic stories about herself. Sometimes she pretended she was Spanish or French. On other occasions she was a gypsy. After two years at the farm, Mary asked for a pay rise and, when the farmer refused, she returned home. Furious that she had so readily left gainful employment, Mary's father thrashed her, so she ran away. Then, so Mary's story went, she really did live with a band of gypsies until becoming ill and being admitted to St Giles Hospital in London. Eventually she found a good position with a Mr and Mrs Matthews at their house in Clapham. Mr Williams taught Mary to read and write, even allowing her to use his library. She spent her leisure time with her head buried in books about far-off lands, weird and wonderful customs and romantic tales.

After three years, Mary was dismissed and took to the road again, sometimes dressing as a man to deter robbers. She then became servant to a fishmonger's wife in Billingsgate, her only recreation being occasional afternoons off to browse in bookshops. In one of these she met a well-travelled gentleman who introduced himself as Herr Bakerstendht. Mary said she married him, shortening her surname to Baker. It is more likely that the couple simply lived together and that he deserted her when she had a child. The baby was apparently handed over to a foundling hospital.

It was around this time that Mary decided to become 'Princess Caraboo'. She practised mannerisms, rehearsed strange behaviour and wove a fantastic story around herself. It was incredible that the Worralls and everyone else who came into contact with Mary could have been so easily taken in. But her charade was greatly enhanced by the 'language' she spoke. It comprised mainly Malay and Arabic words which she had picked up from Herr Bakerstendht, together with a smattering of Romany from the gypsies. Her knowledge of foreign parts had come from the books she had so eagerly devoured.

It was even more remarkable that when Princess Caraboo was revealed as a fraud, no one turned against her. Instead, the forgiving Mrs Worrall helped Mary fulfill her dreams of going to America. She gave her money and clothes and paid for her passage aboard a ship from Bristol to Philadelphia. In return, Mary was to be in charge of a group of missionaries. It is believed that Mary's dreams of an exciting new life in America were not fulfilled, however. Although she was treated as a curiosity when she arrived, she was disappointed when she failed to get the enduring recognition she felt she deserved, and so set off on her travels once again.

But that was not the last anyone heard of Mary Baker, the fake princess. A report appeared in the *Bristol Journal* in September 1817, supposedly from Sir Hudson Lowe, governor of Napoleon's prison island, St Helena. The tale it related is almost certainly apocryphal (and may even have been fabricated by a newspaper reporter) but, given the astonishing life story of Mary Baker thus far, it is worth repeating. Apparently, watching one day from the harbour during a fierce storm, Sir Hudson saw a ship in trouble a short way offshore. Later he witnessed a small boat enter the bay and, going down to the beach to investigate, he found a woman disembarking. She told him her name was Princess Caraboo and that she desperately wanted to see Napoleon. Was Mary Baker up to her old tricks again? The story goes that Napoleon was so captivated by this pretty creature that he asked if she might be allowed an apartment in his house. The story may well have been intended as a joke, but the pairing of Napoleon and Caraboo proved so appealing that many of the accounts that have since appeared have reported the fanciful tale as fact.

The fake princess made two subsequent appearances. Mary Baker paid a return visit to London and assumed the character of Princess Caraboo while attending a Bond Street gallery. She then disappeared again, re-emerging back in Bristol – a full seven years after she had left the city for America – where she tried to exhibit herself as Princess Caraboo for 'a shilling a peep'.

Mary's fantasy life had now run its full course, however. She spent the next twenty years collecting and selling leeches to the Infirmary Hospital in Bristol. She died, aged seventy-five, on January 4, 1865, and was buried in an unmarked grave in the city's Hebron Road cemetery. However, in death she found the fleeting recognition she had so craved – with an obituary on her colourful life in the top people's newspaper, *The Times*.

Chapter 18

Snapshots of the Dead

American William H. Mumler was a photographer who specialised in taking pictures of people who weren't there – but whom others wanted to see. One of the first so-called spirit photographers, Mumler took advantage not only of a time when belief in Spiritualism was high, but also of the vulnerable who were desperate to see their dead loved ones again.

Formerly an engraver for a Boston jewellery company, William Mumler first came to the public eye after announcing that he had not only made a successful photograph of a spirit but that he had been able to repeat their capture on camera. He once declared that he was 'an instrument in the hands of the invisible host that surrounds us for disseminating this beautiful truth of spirit-communication'.

He charged ten dollars a time for his spirit pictures, quite a mark-up when normal portrait photographs could be obtained for a few cents. In fact, the way Mumler worked was not much different from a normal portrait sitting. The person wanting a picture of a deceased friend or relative would simply pose in the studio. The ghostly image of their loved one would then appear on the negative and subsequent print.

Mumler, who narrowly escaped prosecution for fraud, initiated a tradition of spirit photography which continued to thrive well into the Twentieth Century, despite the efforts of critics – including the great Harry Houdini who himself knew a trick or two.

Said one commentator: 'The existence within the period of a spirit of genuine inquiry, however, does not absolve Mumler and his colleagues from the charge of charlatanism. They were crooks. Using a combination of technical and psychological tricks, they exploited the Nineteenth Century's desire to see documentary proof of the immaterial world. Many of these images were produced with deliberate sloppiness – a cracked negative here, flecks and specks there – in the hope that such artless errors would imply the absence of complex technical deceit.'

We now know that the psychic effects were achieved with clever double-exposure techniques and the use of dummies. But to the believers at the time, American president Abraham Lincoln really was caught on camera flying over the head of his widow; the dead of the First World War looked down from the Armistice Day clouds and the face of Sir Arthur Conan Doyle did actually manifest itself in a glob of ectoplasm protruding from Mumler's nose.

It is laughable nowadays but the serious side was that so-called spirit photographers like Mumler preyed on the grief-stricken and gullible. One of his victims was magazine editor Moses A. Dow. He was distraught when one of his staff, a young woman called Mabel Warren fell ill and died after just nine days. The woman had been like a daughter to him. Said Mr Dow: 'She peacefully and quietly passed to the spirit land. I will not attempt to give language to the grief which I felt at her death. She seemed like a dearly-beloved daughter, her natural father having died in her infancy. Her funeral was attended by a large circle of weeping friends who felt that a vacuum had been made in their circle which could not be again filled.'

A week after Mabel's funeral, however, that void was filled with her spiritual presence. In a series of séances held at Dow's home using a medium – an associate of Mumler – Mabel sent messages written on slate and paper. One of these was particularly specific and gave the order to Mr Dow to go to 170 West Springfield Street, Boston, where Mabel promised to show herself wearing a wreath of lilies. The address was that of Mumler's studio and, not surprisingly, Mabel did make an appearance there.

It was in 1869 when Mumler moved his highly-lucrative spirit photography business from Boston to New York – and got arrested. He was charged with public fraud, larceny and obtaining money under false pretences. The arguments of the defence and prosecuting attorneys during the highly-publicised trial matched the two attitudes towards the whole issue of spirit photography. Mumler's defence attorney argued that Mumler was using ordinary photographic methods and his success in obtaining spirit figures was not subject to his control. He also stressed that Mumler's procedures had been scrutinised with no evidence of deception being found and that many customers had recognised the features of departed loved ones in his pictures – even in cases where no likenesses of those people existed.

The fact that many of the spirit 'extras' in Mumler's pictures had been identified was the central feature of the defence attorney's argument. How, he asked, could identifiable spirit portraits be produced by fraudulent means?

The prosecutor offered a simple explanation, however. He suggested that the vagueness of the spirit forms in Mumler's photographs left most of the matter of identification to the imagination, and that the sitters credulously imagined they saw what they wished to see. In his words: 'Those who went to him prepared to believe, of course did believe on very slight proof... that is all this evidence proves. It proves the existence of belief in the prisoner's statements, not the truth of those statements.'

Though all this was perfectly true, spiritual believers felt they had a firm case, too. In all, both sides, believers and non-believers, were convinced photographs could not lie. Though the weight of public opinion was on the prosecution side, neither they nor the defence team could prove their case, and the judge dismissed all charges against Mumler through lack of evidence.

The next spirit photographer to receive wide attention was the first to make his mark in England in the early 1870s. Frederick Hudson used drapes to obscure the 'spirit' faces and, just like his fellow fraudulent photographers, made a very good living out of his art.

He used an ingenious camera made by a man whose normal expertise lay in manufacturing conjuring apparatus. The camera was of the old square wooden type and contained a light metal frame that, in its normal position, rested on the bottom of the smaller of the camera's two telescopic portions. This frame held a waxed paper positive of the desired ghostly image. When the dark side was pushed into the camera, it activated a lever, raising the frame to a vertical position in contact with the photographic plate. When the plate was drawn out of the camera, the frame automatically fell back to its hidden position.

Hudson's reputation grew after a visit by Samuel Guppy and his wife Agnes Guppy-Volckman. The couple went to him after several unsuccessful attempts to obtain psychic photographs in their own home. Another client, famed naturalist Alfred Russel Wallace, went from cynic to believer after Hudson purportedly took two different portraits of his dead mother, representing two different periods in her life and unlike any photographs taken during her life.

Yet another customer, William Howitt, obtained the likeness of two deceased sons. A Dr Thomson obtained an image of a lady whom his uncle in Scotland identified as the likeness of Thompson's mother. She had died in childbirth and no picture of her remained.

One of his most regular clients was Miss Georgina Houghton, who wrote the first book on spirit photography. A committed believer, Miss Houghton lived her life under her own personal band of seventy archangels who not only chose her home and the wallpaper and carpets to go in it, but who even directed her feet when she went for a walk. It was no wonder she was such a follower of Hudson, not even expressing doubt when Hudson's associate, a well-known medium, sat behind a backdrop curtain at the very same place from which emerged a white-robed figure.

Sometimes Hudson played the ghost himself by dressing up. Close examination of his psychic pictures revealed duplications in carpet patterns or parts of the background showing through the legs of the sitter and the 'ghost'. Hudson explained this away as 'refraction', saying the spirits had told him that the spirit aura differs in density and refracting power from the ordinary terrestrial atmosphere. Such resourceful explanations, together with the belief that Hudson actually did take some genuine spirit photographs, helped rebuild his tarnished reputation as a spirit photographer.

Edouard Buguet was another 'spirit photographer' making his reputation – and an awful lot of money – by producing remarkable likenesses of deceased relatives of his sitters. If you looked at one of the French photographer's pictures, you would not only see his living subjects, but the ghostly form of their dead family members too!

Today, of course, we would know that this was all just a clever ruse combined with simple trickery to fleece the gullible of their money. But back in the Victorian age, at a time when much faith was put in all things spiritual, people wanted to believe in the presence of guests from 'the other side'. To get himself in the right mood, Buguet would put himself into a trance before taking his psychic picture. His greatest coup was photographing the Rev Stainton Moses in Paris – while sitting in a trance in London.

Buguet's career was profitable but short. He set up in 1873 and was forced to close in 1875 after being arrested on charges of swindling. The trial was one of the most sensational of its day, especially when Buguet immediately confessed that he had never taken a genuine spirit photograph, stating that he used the technique of double exposure. First he dressed up his assistant to play the part of the ghost and then later constructed a doll to replace the human assistant for the body of the ghost.

Amazingly, this did not turn his loyal Spiritualists away from him. In court, witness after witness – including a journalist, photographic expert, musician, merchant, 'man of letters', optician, ex-professor of history and a colonel of the artillery – testified that they were satisfied his pictures were authentic and they recognised the spirit figures as departed ones. They largely stuck to their evidence even when confronted in the courtroom with the dummy heads, false beards, cheesecloth and other equipment with which it was claimed Buguet had achieved his photographic results. One picture caused a huge stir when it was discovered that the spirit face, positively identified as belonging to a man dead for twelve years, actually belonged to someone else's father-in-law, a man very much alive and very much annoyed to be a spirit before his time!

Still the Spiritualists stayed on Buguet's side, claiming that he had made a false confession under duress or to gain a more lenient punishment. His photography was definitely genuine, they stated, even if he had occasionally had to resort to trickery when his powers were a little weak, and there was no way they would accept his statement of guilt. The Rev Stainton Moses was one of Buguet's stalwart supporters. He said he believed at least some of the photographer's spirit pictures were genuine and that the persecution had its basis in an over-enthusiastic Christian attack. He also said Buguet must have been bribed or terrorised to confess and been forced to manufacture a collection of trick photography equipment. In an article in the journal *Human Nature* in May 1875, Moses stated that out of 120 photographs produced by Buguet, evidence of recognition or of the operation being produced under test conditions was available in forty cases.

Everyone, it seemed, had an opinion on Buguet and his spirit pictures. The editor of one newspaper said that Buguet was under the influence of bad spirits. Buguet eventually retracted his confession after the trial but never attempted to set up as a spirit photographer again. Perhaps that had something to do with his year's imprisonment and 500 franc fine.

Buguet was in good company. There were many self-proclaimed mediums who could conjure up the ghostly form of those who had passed on into the next world. One was English physician Dr d'Aute Hooper, whose most famous picture was that of a small spirit girl taken in 1905. It came about when Dr Hooper had a patient staying with him to receive spiritual healing. The doctor recalled it all: 'My patient had been out for a walk and when he came back he said "Doctor, I feel so queer. I feel as if there is someone with me. Will you get your camera and take a snapshot of me?" I got the camera and before I exposed the plate, I told him I saw a beautiful child with him.

'I put a dark tablecloth over the door in the drawing room to form a background and then exposed the plate. The gentleman himself took the plate to the darkroom and developed it. And there appeared the beautiful spirit form of a little girl with a bouquet of flowers in one hand and a roll of paper in the other. The exclamation of the gentleman was "Good heavens! It's my daughter who died thirty years ago".'

There were many cynics, of course, especially amongst legitimate photographers. An editorial in the *American Journal of Photography* stated: 'How wonderful is the recent progress of our art! We now in the usual way, go through the process of having our picture taken but when the finished photograph is present, lo! Beside our lovely image is the attendant spirit, a babe, a grandfather or an unknown! Spirit photographs show that the spirits dress in clothes of earthly fashion, that they sit in chairs and that in sitting for their pictures they put on smirks which some have supposed peculiar to mortals.'

Whatever the arguments, it was all a particularly cruel way to treat those who had lost loved ones. As Bill Becker, a modern- day collector of these psychic photographs, says: 'Spirit photography is the manipulation of photographic material and the human psyche. The people who were producing spirit photographs had to know they were faking it. It's not a victimless crime. You can see the hope on the subjects' faces. It's hope for proof that they'll soon be able to make daily contact with the dead.'

Chapter 19

Sad Fate of the Phoney Sailor

is last words showed the despair of a man who wanted to impress the world but who paid the ultimate price. 'It is finished, it is finished. It is the mercy. It is the end of my game. The truth has been revealed.'

After scribbling this note in his boat as he tossed around the South Atlantic, one can only imagine the feelings experienced by feted but fraudulent yachtsman Donald Crowhurst. One can only imagine, too, that Crowhurst's body sunk deep into the waters that day, together with his unachievable dream of yachting glory.

Crowhurst had wanted to be part of the challenging, round-the-world Golden Globe Race, to join such legendary names as Robert Knox-Johnson and Chay Blyth and, above all, to be hailed a hero. All this was far beyond his grasp, however, for Crowhurst was not even an able yachtsman and his vessel, a trimaran called *Teignmouth Electron*, was not up to the gruelling task of spending ten months at sea and sailing the 27,000 miles of a race considered to be the ultimate test of daring.

And when his plan to simply drift aimlessly around the South Atlantic and create false log books in a bid to scoop the prize money proved less than watertight, Crowhurst had no choice but to disappear. His desire to be known as a brilliant navigator and sailor ended instead with notoriety as a conman.

Born in India in 1932 to a railway superintendent and a schoolteacher, Donald Crowhurst returned to Britain at the age of fifteen after the death of his father and lived in Reading, Berkshire. But all the money saved in India was worth considerably less than in England and family life in their new home was difficult. Crowhurst was forced to leave school early and started a five-year apprenticeship at the Royal Aircraft Establishment in Farnborough. He later received a commission as a pilot but his

RAF days ended when a prank, during which he rode a motorcycle through a barrack room, went wrong. There was also talk that he had been caught in a compromising position with a senior officer's daughter. Later, he was compelled to resign from the Army after crashing an uninsured car.

Crowhurst met his wife Clare at a party in Reading when he was twenty-three. His family's finances were more settled and he was about to take up a place at Cambridge University. Clare was later to describe their meeting as 'love at first sight. I thought he was a lot older than me, although the age gap was only two years and he was incredibly interesting and charming.' The couple married in October 1957, just six months after that first meeting. Their first son John was born in 1959 and three other children followed, Simon, Roger and Rachel.

The family moved to Bridgwater in Somerset and Crowhurst started a business called Electron Utilisation Ltd. This led on from his interest in inventing new electronic gadgets and amongst his successes was a sleep-inducing machine and a hand-held navigational device he called the Navicator, which allowed the user to take bearings on marine and aviation beacons. It was snapped up by Pye Radio. Crowhurst, determined to better himself all round, was active in his local community as a member of the Liberal Party and in 1967 was elected to represent the Central Ward of Bridgwater Town Council. He also developed a passion for sailing and bought a small sloop to take out around the coast at weekend.

To outsiders, the Crowhursts were the epitome of an affluent and go-getting family. They were also considered to be social climbers, cultivating a tight knit of regular dinner party guests at their large £7,000 white-washed house. In reality, Crowhurst's business was ailing and he took out a big mortgage.

The chance to win the recognition he felt he deserved as well as securing the money he desperately needed, came with the announcement in 1968 of the Golden Globe, the race inspired by Francis Chichester's successful single-handed round-the-world voyage, stopping in Sydney. The considerable publicity this race attracted promoted a number of sailors to plan a non-stop single-handed, round-the-world trip. *The Sunday Times* newspaper, which had sponsored Chichester with highly profitable results, now wanted to get involved with this latest venture but did not know which sailor to sponsor. So it declared the race open to all-comers, with noone needing to demonstrate their single-handed sailing ability to enter.

On reflection, anyone without proven sailing abilities would be mad to attempt the race. It involved circumnavigating the earth non-stop using the old tea-clipper route between Britain and Australia which runs south of the Atlantic, around the Cape of Good Hope, east across the Indian and Pacific Oceans, round Cape Horn and northwards back home. But Crowhurst saw the race as an excellent way to publicise his Navicator, looking forward to it proving its worth on the first solo round-the-world race. Word quickly got round that an amateur adventurer wanted to join the 'big boys' in the race.

Noone loves a sportsman with a sense of spirit more than England, and so what was perhaps once just a crazy idea, snowballed into reality. Wealthy retired businessman Stanley Best offered £8,000 to fund the project and Crowhurst hired Rodney Hallworth a crime reporter who had worked for the *Daily Mail* and *Daily Express,* as his public relations officer. Hallworth had left Fleet Street and set up a news agency in Teignmouth, Devon. He promised Crowhurst he would broker lucrative news, film and publishing deals if Crowhurst named his boat after the seaside resort. With the deal struck, the whole country was soon reading about the 'plucky, old-fashioned adventurer'.

Entrants for the Golden Globe were required to start between June 1 and October 31 so that they would pass through the Southern Ocean in the summer. Crowhurst had to move fast as other contestants were already well on their way. He decided that the quickest boat would be a trimaran which he commissioned from a firm in Norwich. At the time, the trimaran was an unproven type of sailing boat for a voyage of such length and is virtually impossible to right if capsized. So to improve the safety of the boat, Crowhurst had planned to add an inflatable buoyancy bag on top of the mast to prevent capsizing. But with a race against time, all safety devices were left uncompleted and it was already early October by the time the boat was finished.

Perhaps the champagne bottle failing to smash as the vessel was named was an omen Crowhurst should have taken notice of. For right from the start, things went wrong. Sailing around the coast from Norfolk to the Devon starting line, the boat was becalmed and a three-day journey took two weeks with Crowhurst suffering severe seasickness. The trimaran was not up to the job of a short trip in the English Channel let alone the South Atlantic, for several reasons. The boat-builders had failed to fit the bilge-pump - perhaps the most vital piece of equipment - and the watertight hatches leaked. There was also excessive vibration when the boat got up to speed. A group of fishermen at Teignmouth could not believe Crowhurst actually planned to take this boat out. One declared it a 'right load of plywood'.

And such was Crowhurst's haste to beat the race deadline for entrants on October 31, 1968, that he left a valuable box of spares on the quayside, not to mention the piping needed to pump out the flooded hatches. Telling his wife 'I'll be back when the spring daffodils are sprouting', Crowhurst set off. Although deep in his heart he knew he was destined for failure – just nine other yachtsmen, all far more experienced than Crowhurst, had risen to the challenge – he knew there was no turning back. Indeed, he believed that the terms of the sponsorship deals he had agreed to would mean that his house would have to be mortgaged if the boat was lost or he gave up the race. Crowhurst feared that failure could even leave his wife and four children homeless.

His wife was to later confess this was the moment she should have begged him to stop. 'I still feel so incredibly guilty about it. I think if I had just said "This is barmy – stop it!" he would have listened,' she said. 'But I was scared that in five years' time he'd have regretted not going and I would have stopped him fulfilling his dream. That last night together was frightful. We were both in a terrible state. I had never seen Donald crying before except when his friend was killed in a car crash but he was really weeping. I held him in my arms and comforted him. Neither of us slept at all. To Donald, taking care of the family was everything and he was desperately worried.'

Crowhurst was plagued with mishap upon disaster as he

progressed at a painfully slow pace. His biggest problem was to keep out water. Soon he was forced to revise his early estimates that it would take him a mere 243 days to complete the course. As early as November 15, Crowhurst knew he could have and should have turned back. But foolish pride together with lingering ambition and the need for money, made him go on in the face of mounting odds.

There was only one thing left to do – *pretend* to take part in the Golden Globe. Within six weeks he began to complete a second, false log book glamourising his pace. Falsifying the entries took many hours and ironically was harder to complete than real ones due to the celestial navigation research required. He stopped radio contact with race organisers for months at a time to maintain his cover. He tape-recorded his impressions of phoney sightings and sailed to the Falklands to film the coastal view he would have enjoyed had he been sailing north past them towards home. He even put ashore in Argentina to make some repairs, strictly against the rules of the event but Crowhurst told the coastguard he was in a regatta. This misdemeanour wasn't discovered until much later.

Instead of rounding the treacherous Cape Horn, Crowhurst lingered in the South Atlantic before doubling back on himself, monitoring the progress of his rivals on radio. Robin Knox-Johnston was in the lead position set to scoop the Golden Globe as first past the post. But the £5,000 prize money for the fastest competitor was still up for grabs as all the yachts had set sail on different dates. Crowhurst pitched himself back into the race when the second-placed Nigel Tetley was homeward bound.

Suddenly, he realised that if he won, his log books would be scrutinised and his falsifications would shine out. He decided to settle as runner-up to the first two genuine competitors, happy that it would bring him valuable kudos. But disaster struck when Nigel Tetley was forced to abandon his sinking boat 1,200 miles from home. Donald Crowhurst could not help but win the first prize for the fastest passage – until the judges surveyed his concocted log books.

Crowhurst was acutely aware of the shame and dishonour that would follow. His feelings of guilt were compounded when congratulatory messages began pouring across the radio waves. It was then that his nerve broke and his fragile emotions lay in tatters. Together with the loneliness of life on the open sea which he had endured for nearly seven months, it was enough to drive him mad.

Entries in his log book which were later found and examined prove his agitated state of mind in those last few months. The final entry in the log was on July 1, 1969, at 11.20 am. No one knows precisely what happened to the tortured Crowhurst. It is thought he jumped overboard to meet a watery end in the Sargasso Sea, close to the Caribbean. He was probably clutching the bogus log book which would have illustrated his deception beyond all doubt. His body was never recovered.

Nine days later the Royal Mail ship *Picardy* found the *Teignmouth Electron* adrift in the Atlantic. Aboard, crewmen found three log books, plenty of food and fresh water but no sign of sailor Crowhurst. The log books revealed how panicked Crowhurst was when he thought he stood a chance of winning the race. There were poems, quotations and random thoughts, which together with the fake entries, amounted to more than 25,000 words.

The discovery was hailed as a tragedy at home. But doubts had already been raised by race judges chairman Sir Francis Chichester about Crowhurst's apparent bursts of incredible speed and his long lapses of radio silence. It was enough to put two *Sunday Times* reporters, Nicholas Tomalin and Ron Hall, on the trail of a scandal. They probed the log books and pieced together the sad story of Donald Crowhurst's blighted bid for fame. In the books, Crowhurst had given himself a fifty-fifty chance of surviving the trip.

The news of the fraud sent shockwaves through the world of sailing, hitherto known for its good repute and high codes of ethics. Still, there were many who stopped short of outright condemnation out of respect for the man who paid the ultimate price for his sham. Robin Knox-Johnston, who finally won both the Golden Globe trophy and the prize for the fastest passage, handed over the cash to an appeal fund for Crowhurst's wife and four children. 'None of us should judge him too harshly,' the victorious sailor remarked.

In 2006, the film *Deep Water* documented Crowhurst's ill-fated trip. It opened old wounds for Clare Crowhurst, who later moved to Seaton in South Devon. She knew her husband's reputation would never be redeemed but to her, he would always remain someone special.

'The man who went to sea would never have thought of cheating. But who knows what somebody goes through when they can't reach out and touch someone and receive human warmth?' she said. 'Whatever happened to my husband out there at sea, I believe that Donald really made an effort to do something extraordinary. To me he will always be a hero.'

To the world, however, Donald Crowhurst will forever be known as the man who 'sailed around the world' without ever leaving the South Atlantic.

Chapter 20

Missed Clues to the Fake 'Missing Link'

t was just a collection of fragments of a skull and jawbone but the discovery set the archaeological world alight. For nothing excites archaeologists more than a breathtaking 'find' – the unearthing of evidence that yields something magical and mystical from a time fascinating but long forgotten, or a clue that promises to solve the mystery of man's early days on Earth. Thus it was with hysterical delight that one particular discovery was greeted in 1912: that of 'Piltdown Man', so-called because his remains were found in a gravel pit near Piltdown Common, Sussex.

Here, it was claimed, was crucial proof of Charles Darwin's controversial Theory of Evolution. When Darwin had published his *Origin of Species* in 1859, he had been denounced as a crank and even a heretic. How dare he suggest that man originated from apes? What evidence did he have? But now, over sixty years later, here was that vital evidence. Piltdown Man was the famous Missing Link between ape and man.

It was a shame it all had to end the way it did ... with the discovery finding fame not for its importance to evolution but for being one of history's most famous hoaxes.

The world was alerted to the existence of Piltdown Man by a respected lawyer, Charles Dawson. He had been informed by workmen of bones in the Sussex gravel pit after a labourer had found an object there when digging in 1908. The workman had smashed it with his pick but kept a piece to give to Dawson, whom he knew to be a keen amateur geologist. Dawson identified the fragment as a piece of bone from a human skull and remarked that it looked very old indeed. The enthusiastic amateur then began a painstaking search for further pieces, but it was not until 1911 that he found four more fragments which appeared to be from the same skull.

Dawson wrote to Dr Arthur Smith Woodward, keeper of the geology department at the British Museum in London: 'I have come across a very old Pleistocene bed overlying the Hastings beds between Uckfield and Crowborough which I think is going to be interesting.'

At Woodward's behest, Dawson then carefully parcelled the pieces up and took his finds to London. When he saw them, Woodward could not contain himself. Could this at last be the Missing Link? The two men returned to Piltdown to continue their dig. They found more fragments and called in other experts for advice. It was agreed that the pieces of bone made up a tiny brain area, an ape-like jaw and teeth, ground away just as human teeth would have been. From the British Museum reconstruction, Woodward proposed that Piltdown Man represented an evolutionary missing link between ape and man, since the combination of a human-like cranium with an ape-like jaw tended to support the notion then prevailing in England that human evolution was brain-led. And this is what he announced to a meeting of the Geological Society of London on December 18, 1912. The group agreed. They could come to only one conclusion. They had unearthed a creature that was half-man, half-ape and which had lived no less than 500,000 years ago. And although the skull was that of a woman, the find was officially named *Eoanthropus Dawsoni* — Dawson's Dawn Man.

The announcement threw archaeological experts into a frenzy. Piltdown was scheduled to be named a National Monument. Dawson was hailed a hero. Woodward wrote a book about the discovery of 'the earliest Englishman'. The British Museum displayed the skull to excited public hoards. A pub in Piltdown changed its name from The Lamb Inn to The Piltdown Man. Visitors arrived by the coachload to view the site of the find.

Not everyone was as excited about the discovery. Woodward's reconstruction of the Piltdown fragments was strongly challenged at the Royal College of Surgeons where students pieced together their own model using copies of the fragments used by the British Museum. And in 1915, French palaeontologist Marcellin Boule concluded that Piltdown Man's jaw came from a fossil ape. In 1915, a scientist, G. S. Miller, observed that 'deliberate malice could hardly have been more successful than the hazards of deposition in so breaking the fossils as to give free scope to individual judgment in fitting the parts together.'

None of this held back Dawson's great enthusiasm and he continued his excavation. Over the next few years he pieced together parts of a second skull. The finds ceased only when Dawson died in 1916, at the age of fifty-two. After his death, and despite exhaustive digging, no other fossilised fragments were ever found again. This was hardly surprising ... considering that Dawson had placed every one of them there himself.

The drying up of these revolutionary anthropological discoveries raised cautious suspicion but it was not until 1948 that practical steps were taken to investigate further the mystery of Piltdown Man. Since Dawson's first discovery back in 1912, sophisticated scientific testing had been developed to decide the authenticity of such finds. Dr Kenneth Page Oakley, Woodward's successor at the British Museum, subjected the skull fragments to fluorine analysis, a form of test he had developed himself to determine the age of bones. He quickly realised the skull was only 50,000 years old, not 500,000. This news made scientists sit up and listen but did little to shake the faith of the general public; to them, the scientific debate seemed little more than nit-picking. And in 1923, anatomist Franz Weidenreich examined the remains and correctly surmised that they consisted of a modern human cranium and an orang-utan jaw with filed-down teeth. It was to be another thirty years before the scientific community conceded Weidenreich was correct.

On July 23, 1938, a memorial was unveiled to mark the site where Piltdown Man was discovered by Charles Dawson. At the ceremony, archaeologist Sir Arthur Keith concluded his speech by saying: 'So long as man is interested in his long past history, in the vicissitudes which our early forerunners passed through and the varying fate which overtook them, the name of Charles Dawson is certain of remembrance. We do well to link his name to this picturesque corner of Sussex – the scene of his discovery.'

The inscription on the memorial stone reads: 'Here in the old river gravel Mr Charles Dawson FSA found the fossil skull of Piltdown Man, 1912-1913. The discovery was described by Mr Charles Dawson and Sir Arthur Smith Woodward in the Quarterly Journal of the Geological Society 1913-15.'

Eventually, in 1953, a further series of tests were carried out on the now infamous skull. It was these that finally proved Dawson had been the perpetrator of the greatest archaeological hoax ever. First they revealed that even Oakley had been wrong. It was not just a question of the dubious age of Piltdown Man. The skull was quite simply a fake, a relatively 'new' skull that had been planted in the gravel in recent time. The jaw teeth had come from a modern orang-utan and had been filed to make them look human. They had even been stained with oil paint to 'age' them. There had also been a smell of burning when scientists drilled a hole in the jaw. This would not have happened with ancient bone. The same newspapers that had earlier reported on the discovery of the century now boasted other headlines, such as: 'Great Missing Link Hoax Rocks Scientists', 'Experts Were Spoofed By Monkey's Jaw' and 'All the World Laughs At The Piltdown Man'.

In November 1953, *The Times* published the evidence gathered by Page Oakley demonstrating that the fossil was a composite of three distinct species. It consisted of a human skull of medieval age, the 500-year-old lower jaw of a Sarawak orang-utan and chimpanzee fossil teeth. The appearance of age had been created by staining the bones with an iron solution and chromic acid. Microscopic examination revealed file-marks on the teeth and it was deduced from this that someone had modified the teeth to give them a shape more suited to a human diet.

Dawson, of course, was no longer around to answer any charges about his monumental hoax. But all the evidence pointed at him. Such an archaeological coup would have set him down in history for ever. The temptation of such international and timeless kudos would have been enormous. However, there were other names put forward as potential hoaxers, including Sir Grafton Elliot Smith, one of the British Museum's leading experts who had been called in to advise on the bones. This Australian-born scientist was known as a practical joker who had initiated a number of hoaxes, seemingly for no better reason than to enliven the museum's stuffy atmosphere.

Another name put forward was that of William Johnson Sollas, professor of geology at Oxford University, who, it was suggested, might have wanted to have some fun at the expense of his old enemy Dr Arthur Smith Woodward. A further suspect was Sussex fossil collector Lewis Abbot, who thought pompous paleontologists needed to be taken down a peg or two. Yet another was a man called Pierre

Teilhard de Chardin who had travelled to regions of Africa where one of the anomalous finds originated and was residing in the Wealden area from the date of the earliest Piltdown finds. Added to this list was a Martin A. C. Hinton who once left a trunk in storage at the Natural History Museum in London and which was later found to contain animal bones and teeth carved and stained in a manner similar to that of Piltdown Man. Yet another name put forward as being behind the hoax was none other than Sir Arthur Conan Doyle, author of the Sherlock Holmes stories. He had been present when Dawson wrote that first excited letter to the British Museum.

One convincing clue to the true perpetrator of the Piltdown hoax, however, followed the bequest of Dawson's private collection of geological specimens to a museum in Hastings, Sussex. When tested in 1954, most of the life's work of the creator of the Piltdown Man were also found to be painstakingly created forgeries. It transpired that from 1895, he made dozens of minor 'discoveries' including the first evidence of cast-iron figure-casting in Roman Britain, a medieval clock face, a flint arrowhead and shaft and a number of other remarkable finds that weren't as he declared. On one occasion a collection of flints Dawson exchanged with another collector, Hugh Morris, turned out to have been aged with chemicals.

It turned out that there were numerous individuals in the Surrey area well-acquainted with Dawson who had long-held doubts about Piltdown and Dawson's role in the whole affair. But given the sheer weight of scholarly affirmation for the find, few were willing to speak publicly for fear of being ridiculed. It is believed that sometimes Dawson had appropriated the finds made by workman and reported them to scientific journals as if they were his own discoveries. Most of his written works proved to be uncredited collations of others' work, material that could have drawn outright accusations of plagiarism.

As one scholar who studied Dawson's work commented: 'His initial motivations may well have lain along the lines of gaining further fame and notoriety in his native Surrey but it is clear that his increasingly successful early frauds may well have emboldened him to pull off the master-stroke that would have landed him his most cherished goal, that of a fellowship in the prestigious Royal Society. It was a long ambition that ultimately went unfulfilled.'

Chapter 21

Fantasy 'Friend of the Stars'

He broached security at Windsor Castle and caused a royal scare that left police red-faced with both anger and embarrassment. He claimed to be a friend of Princes William and Harry. He was linked in the gossip columns with stars and models. He posed as a playboy, a detective and a top surgeon. But reality finally caught up with the serial fantasist when he was hauled into court and revealed to be humble Michael Hammond, the son of working-class parents from east London.

Hammond honed his master conman skills in the Sussex seaside town of Bexhill, where his family then lived – and where teenager Michael collected for bogus charities and pocketed the cash. After a spell at a youth custody centre in Dover, he returned to Bexhill where one example of his ingenuity is almost breathtaking in terms of sheer cheek…

The young trickster tried to buy a businessman's Porsche on sale for £10,000. The owner insisted on cash or a banker's draft. As they talked, Hammond stole headed notepaper from the businessman's office. Then he turned up at a bank in the town with a letter introducing himself as a director and trustee of the company on the notepaper. He was allowed to open an account with borrowing facilities and days later returned to the businessman and handed him a bank draft for £10,000. It was weeks before the bank discovered they had been duped.

One man who knew him in those early days said: 'Michael Hammond makes Walter Mitty look a novice. He could walk into an office and take over in a matter of minutes. He has an air of confidence about him. I've lost count of the strokes he has pulled. He is well educated, well spoken and totally believable.'

Hammond's tale is a chilling lesson in just how far a conman can ply his trade. He has posed as a millionaire property developer, duped banks, claimed to be a confidant of royalty, a boyfriend of actress Renee Zellweger, models Jordan and Catalina Guirado and singer Dannii Minogue. He even claimed to be the lover of Prince Andrew's ex-girlfriend Caroline Stanbury.

In 2000, at the age of thirty-two, he was first caught impersonating a policeman and spent ten weeks in Wandsworth prison. By then, he was living in the Kent Village of Brasted with Oxford-educated Lucy Bloomfield, the mother of their child Rupert, born in 1998. His family home life did not, however, deter him from claiming that he and Prince Andrew were sharing the affections of the prince's girlfriend Caroline Stanbury. The blonde PR executive was stunned to read stories about how Hammond had showered her with gifts and even bought her a Mercedes SLK.

Pictures of the 'millionaire' and Caroline together were supposed proof of their relationship. Hammond was quoted bragging that he and the Duke of York were close pals. 'Prince Andrew is a friend. We hang out together,' he claimed. Hammond even told a tabloid newspaper that Miss Stanbury was a 'fantastic, sexy lover'. She, of course, denied there was a romance. True, they did meet at a polo match at Cirencester, where Hammond always did his best to make sure he stood beside well-known figures when photographs were being taken. But Miss Hammond said: 'I met him at the match in the company of a lot of other people. I never liked him, never went out with him and knew him simply as a very little man with a very large imagination.' She admitted that he did visit her home in Chelsea once as a dinner guest and acknowledged that he helped her choose a car. But she added: 'He likes the attention and says all kinds of things that aren't true.'

Singer Dannii Minogue made the mistake of being photographed with him at a celebrity party. Very soon afterwards, he sold stories about how he was going out with the Australian songstress, who was starring in a West End musical at the time. Angry Dannii said: 'I did know him when I was in *Notre Dame De Paris*. He hung around with a few people I knew but I have never gone out with him, not even on one date. I have never slept with him. That's completely ludicrous — I never had any interest in him like that at all. For people to think I was his girlfriend was absolutely astonishing to me and, I have to say, a bit embarrassing.'

He did the same with model Jordan (real name Katie Price), model Catalina Guirado and *Bridget Jones* star Renee Zellweger, who all dismissed his claims of being lovers as ludicrous.

It might be thought that Hammond's falsehoods were harmless enough, the fantasies of many young men. But any thoughts of grudging admiration for his brazenness should be balanced by the evidence given by police when they finally caught up with him. For Hammond was proved to be a Walter Mitty with menace – a fantasist maybe, but a very dangerous one.

Among those who would concur with that view were three young men caught up in a police swoop in central London in February 2004. It happened after a 'Detective Sergeant Hughes' telephoned New Scotland Yard and convinced switchboard operators he was attached to the Serious Organised Crime Group. What he told officers alerted a team from the Diplomatic Protection Squad to stake out busy Whitehall.

In the resulting operation, one undercover policeman sat in his car directing operations from a mobile phone as high-powered patrol cars screeched to a halt. Officers in flak jackets brandishing MP5 sub-machine guns spilled out and surrounded three suspects. The men froze as torches strapped to the guns shone in their faces.

The three men stopped so dramatically were totally innocent and simply on a night out. They were merely the latest victims of one of the most dangerous fantasists loose in Britain at the time.

Detectives finally caught up with Hammond in May 2004 at Windsor Castle as he sought to pull off his boldest scam. He had used his mobile phone to con his way into the castle, claiming to be a high-ranking cop who was looking after friends of Princes William and Harry. The story made headlines all over the world.

What was not revealed at the time, however, was the sheer scale of Hammond's deceptions. For when police analysed his mobile phone, they discovered that within the past few months he had made a staggering 18,000 calls on it, more than 100 of them to police.

For months, police all over the country had been swamped by hoaxes – fingering 'murder suspects' and pinpointing 'armed criminals' – but no one had ever pieced together who was behind the calls. The phone from which they were made was registered to a respectable financial advice company that had employed Hammond for four months before his contract was terminated because he failed to bring in business. He had hung onto the phone and had begun making his bogus calls to the police in September 2003. He had called Scotland Yard four times claiming men with guns were breaking into his apartment. Each time an armed response unit was called. Then the deceptions became more bizarre.

Just after noon on February 23, 2004, Hammond called Scotland Yard claiming to be Dr Eli De Silva, a surgeon at London's St Thomas's Hospital. He said he was stuck in traffic and needed a police escort to get him to the hospital where he had to carry out a life-or-death operation on a six-year-old. He was told the Met did not escort private cars but, undaunted, surgeon at another famous London hospital, Guy's.

The force, who were dealing with a fatal road accident, dispatched a car to meet Dr De Silva. Hammond, in his black Mercedes, followed the police patrol, often on the wrong side of the road, as they sped to the hospital. An officer was even sent to stop traffic at a busy junction. The conman called the police the next day to thank them and say the girl's life had been saved – and then tried the sick trick twice more that day.

Hammond was also making hoax calls to police in Kent, Sussex, Manchester and Cambridgeshire and starting to impersonate policemen. He began posing as Detective Chief Superintendent Simon Morgan after seeing him on TV – Morgan then being head of Britain's biggest manhunt, for a serial rapist who preyed on elderly women. The bogus officer called London City Airport claiming he was tailing a murder suspect boarding a flight to Edinburgh. He asked for support from two armed policemen on a balcony inside the terminal. One passenger on the flight that morning was Hammond himself.

A week later, he entered Windsor Castle through a staff entrance, creating a major security scare only ten days after an extensive review of royal security. He duped officers in the castle's control room into letting him through the Henry VIII gate, which is normally reserved for members of the royal family and staff.

He then rang a police number pretending to be Morgan. But the call was taken by a particularly sharp-eyed officer who at the time was watching a shabbily-dressed man on closed-circuit TV. It was Hammond – who was on a mobile phone at the same time as 'Morgan' was calling in. Mr Connell said: 'The officer could see the mouth movements of the man in the camera picture and concluded it was the same man he was speaking to on the phone!'

Hammond was arrested but while out on bail he sold the story of his arrest to a newspaper, claiming he had seen the Queen and that he was 'testing' security. In fact, the Queen was not even at Windsor at the time.

The cons Hammond admitted to may well have been merely the tip of the iceberg. Detective Sergeant Neil John, who led the investigation into Hammond, said: 'Not one thing he told me was the truth. I don't think he knows what the truth is. Hammond is just like Frank Abagnale, the real-life con-artist played by Leonardo Di Caprio in the film *Catch Me If You Can*. He's certainly very intelligent and, like many conmen, has a good memory for names. But he's a wannabe. He's not happy with being a nobody. He desperately wants to be famous.'

After his arrest, Hammond feigned illness and was taken to hospital to avoid being quizzed. But being arrested didn't stop him posing as a policeman. Two months after being caught at Windsor, Hammond was on a cross-Channel ferry arriving in Dover when he posed as an Interpol officer with a fake identity card and tried to have an Iraqi family arrested 'for being members of Al Qaeda'. The totally innocent family were stopped but their papers were found to be in perfect order. Hammond soon skipped bail and fled to Switzerland where he supposedly underwent 'medical treatment'. When he returned to the UK, he booked into Guy's Hospital where police arrested him. Among his belongings in a bedside cabinet was a badge from the Los Angeles Police Department.

Another identity he was assuming at the time was that of 'Michael

Edwards-Hammond', a millionaire property developer living in a £3,000-a-month penthouse in one of London's prestigious Docklands developments. He drove a £110,000 black Mercedes SL convertible. The truth, however, was that he was deep in debt, and after his arrest was booted out of the apartment. Credit companies began reclaiming, and the Mercedes was returned to its rightful owner.

Hammond, aged thirty-six, was finally brought before Isleworth Crown Court, in West London, where he admitted one count of being a public nuisance, incorporating eleven separate instances of impersonating a police officer and one of wasting police time. He heard himself described by Tony Connell, the lawyer who was leading the prosecution, as 'wicked and despicable'. Of the Whitehall police swoop, he said: 'What happened to those three totally innocent lads is truly horrifying. In all my time as a prosecuting lawyer, I've never come across another case like this.'

On February 4, 2005, Judge Richard McGregor-Johnson sentenced Hammond to four and a half years in jail, telling him: 'On three occasions, innocent people were stopped at gunpoint because of what you said and pretended to be. Quite apart from the stress and fear that must have caused those people, you created the risk of something much worse. You could not possibly know how those being searched would behave or react and, however well trained and disciplined armed officers are, carrying or producing loaded weapons in such circumstances inevitably carries with it the risk that an action or reaction could be misunderstood, with tragic consequences. Fortunately that didn't happen – but you had no way of knowing whether that might or not.'

Chapter 22

Deeds of the Dastardly Digger

T*he Times* of London dated March 19, 1867, had no sympathy for the man who had duped Victorian Britain's antique collectors. The story read: 'Flint Jack, a notorious Yorkshireman, one of the greatest imposters of our times, was last week sentenced to twelve months imprisonment for felony at Bedford. The prisoner gave the name of Edward Jackson, but his real name is Edward Simpson, of Sleights, Whitby, although he is equally well known as John Wilson of Burlington and Jerry Taylor of Billery-Dale, Yorkshire Moors. Probably no man is wider known than Simpson under his aliases in various districts – viz "Old Antiquarian", "Fossil Willy", "Bones", "Shirtless", "Cockney Bill" and "Flint Jack", the latter name universally. Under one or other of these designations, Edward Simpson is known throughout England, Scotland and Ireland – in fact, wherever geologists or achaeologists resided, or wherever a museum was established, there did Flint Jack assuredly pass off his forged fossils and antiquities.'

Indeed, it was the name Flint Jack which now grated on the ears of the antique collectors, a typically upper-crust bunch, with servants, starched collars and waxed moustaches who had, to their great humiliation fallen foul of a trickster. Dabbling in ancient history was the height of fashion for the moneyed gentlefolk of high society. Yet somehow a man who looked and smelled no better than a tramp; wore holed corduroys, a cloth coat worn through at the elbows, a yellowing shirt and a scrap of a neck tie, rubbed shoulders with the elite and won their trust.

Despite his tatty appearance, this odd fellow was made welcome at the most noted archaeological events across the nation. His currency was an apparently boundless supply of aged artefacts, coupled with a specialist knowledge that set him head and shoulders above many. Only after the shabby itinerant melted away into the countryside did the well-heeled historians realise they had been duped by none other than Flint Jack, one of the most successful forgers of all time.

Jack had received a basic training in the identification and collection of fossils and had a genuine love of ancient archaeology. However, the prospect of easy money to finance a costly drinking habit lured him into the shadowy world of fraud. By the end of the Victorian era, examples of Flint Jack's expert handiwork appeared in many of the country's leading collections. Even the British Museum was taken in and displayed some of his work.

Flint Jack was born Edward Simpson in 1815 at Sleights, a village in North Yorkshire. As a teenager, he found work with two eminent historians, acquiring skills that would serve him well in later life. When his second employer died, Flint Jack decided to make a living by scouring the country for fossils in which to trade. He soon discovered a new talent, however. He found he could make copies of old flint arrowheads using just a few basic tools. At the request of a local dealer, and with the use of a home-made kiln, he produced a range of much sought-after items of 'ancient' pottery. For a while, collectors did not suspect that the oddments they purchased were freshly sculpted. When their suspicions were aroused, Flint Jack left Yorkshire and embarked on a tour of Britain, taking his craftsmanship to new and different markets.

Encouraged by his success, he expanded his range. There was a Roman breastplate made from an old tin tray which he found on a roadside. Milestones, urns, seals and stones were all turned out with his magic touch. By 1846 he was moving from town to city selling sufficient amounts to finance the next leg of his tour. He visited Peterborough, Birmingham, Liverpool, Sheffield, Colchester, Hadrian's Wall, the Lake District, the West Country and Ireland. Word of his antics spread slowly. During the 1860s more and more collectors realised they had been fooled and warnings about him were published in specialist journals.

Yet there was much more to Flint Jack than plain scallywag. He would join archaeological digs and happily impart his voluminous knowledge to the experts. In 1862 he demonstrated his skills before a meeting of the Geologists' Association in Cavendish Square, London. His ragged appearance caused ripples of mirth and some consternation in the eminent audience. *The People's Magazine* gave us a graphic account of what this roving fraudster looked like:

'He was a weather-beaten man of about 45 years of age and he came in dirty, tattered clothes and heavy navvy's boots, to take precedence of the whole assemblage. He wore a dark cloth coat, hanging in not unpicturesque rags about the elbows. It was unbuttoned over a cotton shirt which might once have been white but which had degenerated to a yellow brown. About his neck was a fragment of a blue cotton handkerchief. His skin was of a gypsy brown, his hair hung in lank black locks about a forehead and face that was not altogether unprepossessing, except for the furtive and cunning glances which he occasionally cast around him from eyes that did not correspond with each other in size and expression. His corduroys, which were in a very sorry condition, had been turned up, and their owner had evidently travelled through heavy clay, the dry remains of which bedaubed his boots.'

The quizzical glances of the eminent audience turned to looks of awe, however, when Flint Jack was introduced by the vice-president of the Geologists' Association. He explained that their guest, with only a bent iron rod, could produce the most amazingly realistic artefacts. The assembly then watched in total silence as he went to work, casually turning out replicas of arrowheads one after the other.

By now, he was notorious among serious collectors, many of whom could not forgive him for making fools of them. But the public loved him, particularly as he was disarmingly honest. If confronted, he always admitted he was a forger. In 1866 the story of Flint Jack's life appeared in the *Malton Messenger* and was so popular that it was published as a pamphlet and distributed nationwide. That's how author Charles Dickens seized on the character for his story *All The Year Round*.

By 1867, Flint Jack's notoriety eventually forced him out of the forgery business. In January of that year, the destitute itinerant paid a visit to an old acquaintance, James Wyatt, a journalist and archaeologist. The details are recorded in Wyatt's diary. Flint Jack explained to him: 'When some species are scarce and people don't know them well, you must do your best.' Jack borrowed sixpence from Wyatt to tide him over until his next 'commission'. However, as the diary recalls:

'It appears that he proceeded to the last house on the London Road, but unfortunately that is a public house and he could not resist the temptation of entering. The consequence was that he got drunk and as the craving increased after his money was gone he came back to the town, opened the front door of a house near mine and took a barometer, but having been seen by a man outside, he bolted and threw the barometer away. Later in the evening, finding a light in the schoolroom attached to the Methodist Chapel he entered and stole a clock, which he tried to sell to the keeper of a public house, and finally left him with it as a deposit. The police got on the scent and ran him down to a low lodging house, and then removed him to the lock-up.'

For the crime, Flint Jack was tried on March 12, 1867, and sentenced to a year's imprisonment in Bedford Jail. *The Times* report of his downfall, continued thus: 'For nearly 30 years this extraordinary man has led a life of imposture. During that period he has "tramped" the kingdom through repeatedly vending spurious fossils. Roman and British urns, fibulae, coins, flint arrow-heads, stone celts, stone hammers, adzes etc, flint hatchets, seals, rings, leaden antiquities, manuscripts, Roman armour, Roman milestones, jet seals and necklaces and numerous other forged antitquities.

'His great field was the North and East Ridings of Yorkshire – Whitby, Scarborough, Burlington, Malton and York being the chief places where he obtained his flint or made his pottery. Thirty years ago he was an occasional servant to the late Dr Young, the historian of Whitby, from whom he acquired his knowledge of geology and archaeology and for some years after the doctor's death he led an honest life as a collector of fossils and a helper in archaeological investigations.

'He imbibed, however, a liking for drink and he admits that from that cause his life for 20 years past has been one of great misery. To supply his cravings for liquor he set about the forging of both fossils and antiquities about 23 years ago when he "squatted" in the clay cliffs of Bridlington Bay but subsequently removed to the woods of Staintin-dale where he set up a pottery for the manufacture of British and other urns and flint and stone implements, with which he gutted the antiquaries of the three kingdoms.

'In 1859, during one of his trips to London, Flint Jack was charged by Professor Tennant with the forgery of antiquities. He confessed and was introduced on the platform of various societies and exhibited the simple mode of his manufacture of spurious flints. From that time, his trade became precarious and Jack sunk deeper and deeper into habits of dissipation until at length he became a thief and was last week convicted on two counts and sent to prison for 12 months.'

Such was his standing in society that an archaeological magazine, The Reliquary, organised an appeal on Flint Jack's behalf. The journal's plea ended: 'The man possesses more real practical antiquarian knowledge than many of the leading antiquarian writers of the day, and he is a good geologist and palaeontologist. Is it meet, then, that he should be allowed to starve when a few mites from those that he may have duped but whom, at all events, he has ultimately benefited by his open disclosure and by his indomitable skill, would materially assist him, and perhaps turn his talents into a better and more honourable channel?'

The appeal fell on deaf ears. On his release from prison, Flint Jack continued his gypsy lifestyle and faded from public gaze. It is thought he died in a workhouse in Yorkshire.

Chapter 23

The Woman Who Cried 'Wolf'

There are many, many amazing stories of survival during inhumane times of war. They highlight just how far one a person will go to keep alive, beating all the odds and pushing himself or herself to the most gruelling of mental and physical limits. The survival of Misha Defonseca was one of those extraordinary stories.

Misha had been forced to wander 3,000 miles across Nazi-occupied Europe searching for her deported parents. Aged just eight, yet having the resolve to forage for food, eat mud to stay alive and live off her wits while under constant threat of discovery and death, Defonseca was testimony that in punishing times, fact is more incredible than fiction.

It was no wonder that when she wrote about her harrowing trek as a Jewish child dodging the Nazis and eventually spending two harsh winters under the protection of a pack of wolves, Defonseca was writing herself into the annals of war-time history. Her book *Misha – A Memoir of the Holocaust Years* was a bestseller, earning her £10million and translated into eighteen languages. Defonseca's story was told in an equally high-profile way with the release of the film *Survivre Avec les Loups* (Surviving with the Wolves). Everyone agreed the story was just unbelievable... Literally so, as it turned out.

For in 2008, just over ten years after her book was published, Defonseca admitted she had made the whole thing up. Defonseca was not even her real name. And she wasn't Jewish. The only truth in her tale seemed to be the disappearance of her parents, who were deported for their membership of the Belgian resistance movement. This all left a very sour taste, particularly for those who actually had endured horrific treatment at the hands of the Nazis or whose lives had been torn apart forever by World War Two.

In retrospect, this particular Holocaust survivor story did stretch belief. It started in the autumn of 1941 when the little Belgian Jewish girl ran away from the family that took her in when her parents were arrested by the Germans. In the truly illogical mind of one so young, it was simply a case of starting to walk until she found them, she later told those fascinated by her tale. Over the next four years, she wandered through Germany, Poland and the Ukraine, turning south through Romania and the Balkans, hitching a boat ride to Italy then walking back to Belgium via France. Some feat for one so young.

During her travels, Defonseca slept alone in forests – until being taken in by her wolf friends, of course. Her bleak and lonely existence was not without other extraordinary trials and challenges. She joined bands of partisans, sneaked in and out of the Warsaw ghetto, witnessed the execution of children and killed a German soldier with a pocket knife.

By the late 1980s, Defonseca was living in the US, in Massachusetts, and regularly telling of her experiences – including an address to the congregation of a synagogue on Holocaust Memorial Day. Her story was then taken up by Jane Daniel who, working in public relations, realised it had the makings of a best-selling book. Daniel's neighbour and French specialist Vera Lee was recruited to co-write it. Lee took the job very seriously, even eating mud as Defonseca claimed she had done, to see what it tasted like.

Said Lee: 'We did a lot of talking. It was over fifty years ago, and she had some very vivid recollections of certain episodes and scenes, but naturally there were certain loopholes. I was trying to piece it together in a way that was as true to life as possible. In other words, there had to be transitions. She went to a country; we had to know how did she get to the next one? How did she do her travelling? So I would write and bring it back to Misha and very often it would jog her memory of every single thing that happened. You had to make a book. And it had to be true to Misha.'

However, the three women fell out over the way the book should be written and Lee and Defonseca later took Daniel to court, claiming they were owed overseas royalties. Meanwhile, doubts about Misha's story were already being raised. At least two people who were asked by Daniel to contribute blurbs for the book warned her that it was not true. Yet a third, Bette Green, asked for her blurb to be removed because she found the book unbelievable.

One of the dissenters, Lawrence L. Langer, winner of the 1991 National Book Critics Circle Award for his book *Holocaust Testimonies: The Ruins of Memory*, consulted a Holocaust scholar who also thought the story impossible. He said: 'The story was sketched to me and I said, "Don't do it because it isn't true. Ask her how she crossed the Rhine in the middle of the war when the SS is guarding the bridges at both ends. Find the Elbe on a map and ask how a little girl goes across the river. She speaks no German, she's Jewish, poorly dressed and no one asks her, "Who are you, little girl?" I said, "It's a bad idea, don't do it".'

The book was published in April 1997 and, although it sold only 5,000 copies in America, was optioned for a film by The Walt Disney Company. This idea was dropped because of the legal problems between Daniel, Lee and Defonseca, which became public in 1998. In 2001, a jury awarded Defonseca and Lee over £5million. A judge's decision later tripled this amount to over £15million, and rights to the book were also awarded to Defonseca.

The European print and film rights were separate from Defonseca's contract with Daniel and her company, Mt Ivy Press, and the book went on to be a best-seller in France, selling over 30,000 copies. Over 37,000 copies were sold in Italy. In all, *Misha – A Memoir of the Holocaust Years* was translated into eighteen languages. French film rights were sold to French Jewish film-maker Vera Belmont, with *Survivre Avec Les Loups* opening in Belgium in late 2007.

In February 2008, Misha Defonseca was forced to admit the whole story was made up. A genealogist, Sharon Sergeant, noticed an internet 'blog' posted by Jane Daniel, through which she aimed to challenge the court judgement against her by discrediting Defonseca. Using clues from the various versions of the book's manuscript – including the use of a Defonseca 'pseudonym', Monique de Wael – Sergeant turned up some damning early documents. These included baptismal and school records for a real-life Monique de Wael – which showed that when 'Misha' was supposed to be wandering through Europe in 1943, she was actually enrolled in elementary school.

After Daniel published these documents on the blog in late February 2008, Belgian newspaper *Le Soir* took up the story, unearthing and publishing more detail on de Wael's parents. Within a week, Defonseca had acknowledged that every aspect of her story was untrue and that her real name was Monique De Wael, born in 1937 to Robert De Wael and Josephine Donvil.

She was not the daughter of Jewish parents but had been brought up a strict Catholic. Her parents had been members of the Belgian Resistance, which led to them being arrested by the Nazis on September 23, 1941. Nazi records indicated that Robert de Wael was executed on May 3 or 4, 1944, and that Donvil died sometime between February 1 and December 31, 1945.

In her own 'confession', de Wael, now aged seventy-one and living in the small town of Dudley, fifty miles southwest of Boston, said her guardianship had first gone to her grandfather, Ernest de Wael, and then to her uncle, Maurice de Wael. She said that apart from her grandfather, those who took her in treated her badly, including calling her 'the traitor's daughter' because her father was suspected of having given information under torture. She remained with her uncle's family and did not go off in search of her missing parents as 'Misha' did. It was during this time, de Wael said, that she began to 'feel Jewish' and to fantasise about living with the wolves.

Interviewed by *Le Soir*, de Wael said: 'My name is Monique de Wael and since the age of four I have wanted to forget. It's true that, since the beginning, I have felt Jewish and that later in life I was able to come to terms with myself by being taken in by that community. So it's true that I have always recounted to myself a life, another life... That's also why I fell in love with wolves and why I entered into their universe. It's my story. It's not the real reality, but it's my reality, my way of surviving.'

De Wael's co-author, Vera Lee, and publisher, Jane Daniel, said they had always had doubts about the extraordinary story. Lee admitted she had had reservations from the start and had consulted a group called Facing History and Ourselves which helps to guide how the Holocaust is studied in schools. 'There were doubts but so much seemed credible that I couldn't just throw doubt on the whole thing,' she said.

Daniel said she became worried in 1999 when another prize-winning Holocaust memoir, *Fragments: Memories of a Wartime Childhood 1939-1948* by Binjamin Wilkomirski, was proved to be a fake. She recalled: 'It sent a shudder through the industry. Up until then, publishers had never been called upon to vet their stories.'

Daniel even put a defensive memo 'from the publisher' on the Mt Ivy website. It listed several reasons why Defonseca's story could be true but then added: 'Is Misha's story fact or invention? Without hard evidence one way or the other, questions will always remain.' Some time later, Daniel said: 'I have no idea whether it is true or not. My experience is that all Holocaust stories are far-fetched. All survivor stories are miracles.'

Issuing a statement on de Wael's behalf, her lawyer Marc Uyttendaele said: 'It matters little whether the account is real or partly allegorical. It is the product of absolute good faith, a cry of suffering and an act of courage.'

Many did not see de Wael's deceit that way, however. Speaking on behalf of all Holocaust victims – those who died and those who survived – Lawrence L. Langer said: 'Truth matters where the Holocaust is concerned. I have spent years interviewing Holocaust survivors. If people start making up stories, it may make real witnesses doubt their memories. It feeds ammunition to the sceptical that everyone exaggerates. But that's not true.'

Chapter 24

The Fake from Fantasy Island

George Psalmanazar (no one knows his real name) was a Frenchman with an uncanny command of languages. He arrived in Britain at the start of the Eighteenth Century claiming to be from Formosa, a country about which conveniently little was known at the time. Over the next few years, he was able, without detection, to publish *An Historical and Geographical Description of Formosa*, to invent a complete 'Formosan' language, and to instruct Oxford students in the use of it. He had, of course, never been near the place.

Psalmanazar introduced himself to London society in 1703, labelling himself 'Native of Formosa' (present-day Taiwan) and said he had been converted to Christianity by English missionaries. Explaining his very Western looks, he said it was a simple fact that Formosans appeared more European than Oriental. Noone questioned his story. For these were years of great exploration, and people were eager to meet those from far-off, exotic lands. Foreign travellers always had such fascinating tales to tell. And Psalmanazar's tales were not only fascinating but pure fantastic.

The newcomer was introduced to the Bishop of London who was so impressed by the educated 'Formosan' that he obtained a grant for him to study at Christ Church College of prestigious Oxford University. The idea was that Psalmanazar would train missionaries to be sent out to his heathen homeland. He also set himself a challenging task: the 'translation' of the Church of England Catechism into his native Formosan tongue. Being a complete and utter fraud, Psalmanazar could not actually do this, of course, but he burned candles in his window at night to convince people he was working on this important project.

It is not surprising that Psalmanazar declined an invitation to perform a similar translation of the English Bible. However, he fooled everyone with his Catechism 'translation', for there was no reason for anyone to doubt Psalmanazar's work. The language he produced was regular and his. The alphabet he supplied looked suitably intricate and mysterious. Most of all, the language was so different from any heard in England before that no one was in a position to challenge it.

Creating a new language was not at all difficult for him. The one genuine talent he had was a fluency in languages and his knowledge of Latin. In fact it was in Latin that Psalmanazar wrote *An Historical and Geographical Description of Formosa* in 1704. It was an immediate success, full of colourful tales about the Formosan way of life.

Most Formosans, he wrote, lived to be a hundred years old because they ate raw meat and drank snake's blood. He said the religion in Formosa was more bloodthirsty than that of the Aztecs. Indeed, 18,000 boys, all under the age of nine, were offered as human sacrifices to the pagan gods every year. They were ritually slaughtered and their hearts burned out to appease the gods. This practice naturally led to a great shortage of males on the island and polygamy was rife. Drawing on his fantastic imagination, Psalmanazar wrote:

'The husband sends for one of his wives whom he has a mind to lie with that night. And in the daytime he sometimes visits one of them, sometimes another, according to his fancy. This kind of life is sweet and pleasant enough, as long as every one of them is of an agreeable humour. But if the husband begins to love one wife more than another, then arises envy and emulation.'

Laws were harsh, wrote Psalmanazar. Robbers and murderers were hanged head down and then shot to death with arrows. Other offences were punished in ways which made mediaeval hanging, drawing and quartering, mild by comparison. Describing the island itself, he said it was inhabited by huge wildlife including elephant, giraffe and rhinoceros. It was no wonder that his work of fantasy – a second edition of his book was published in 1705—made him a celebrity. He was lionised by London society, including Dr Samuel Johnson who described him as 'a saved exotic'.

There was one man who was not taken in by Psalmanazar, however. A Dutch Jesuit, George Candidus, had actually been to Formosa and knew it well. So he was shocked when he sat down to read Psalmanazar's history of the island. Candidus did his best to explain what Formosa was really like. He wrote that, far from being a bloodthirsty society, the laws on the island were so lenient as to be almost non-existent. Robbery usually went unpunished. And if adultery or murder was committed, the gift of a few hogs to the offended party was considered adequate compensation.

Incredibly, it was Psalmanazar's version that everyone chose to believe. There were two reasons for this. One was that Jesuits were discriminated against in Protestant England at this time. The other was that during these years of exploration, Psalmanazar's romantic account of bloodthirsty savages and untold riches was more appealing to an adventure-hungry public than poor old Candidus's true story. Even more incredible was the fact that belief in Psalmanazar's version of the Formosan island survived for twenty-five years. This was despite the loss of his credibility as his tales became ever more fantastic. Eventually, however, the interloper was treated as a figure of fun. Once handsomely supported and much sought after as an expert on the mysterious East, he was forced to take humble employment as a clerk to an army regiment.

In 1728, then in his fifties, Psalmanazar fell ill. Perhaps fearing punishment by a Christian God who would bar him from heaven, he decided to repent and confess his sins as an impostor. In his confession, accompanied by much weeping, wailing and wringing of hands, he begged for forgiveness for leading a life of 'shameless idleness, vanity and extravagance'. Such a soul-bearing act did not, however, prevent him from going on to commit another act of fraud. He contributed chapters on China and Japan to a book called *Complete System of Geography*. This contribution was almost entirely based on earlier writings of George Candidus.

In 1752 Psalmanazar wrote his memoirs, but they were published only after his death in 1766. His last years were not unhappy ones. For once in his life, he undertook honest work, carrying out genuine research and submitting his own original articles to reference books. His only vice in his declining years was the drug opium, 'taken in a pint of punch' after long stints at his writing desk. Now greatly humbled, Psalmanazar refused to have his name ascribed to any of the books he wrote. And when putting his affairs in order, he instructed that upon his death his body should be buried in some obscure corner of a common graveyard, 'in a shell of the lowest value, without lid or other covering to hinder the natural earth from entirely surrounding it'.

Even after being revealed as a hoaxer, Psalmanazar kept his friends, who enjoyed his witty conversation and knowledge. He was also revered for his piety. Samuel Johnson once even remarked: 'I would as soon have thought of contradicting a bishop.' But even Johnson, Psalmanazar's long-term drinking companion, never really learned the truth of his friend's origins.

His real name is lost forever, but it is now believed that the French fraudster was born near Avignon around 1680 and was educated in a Jesuit school. A master of languages, he travelled through France posing first as an Irish pilgrim on his way to Rome and then as a Japanese adventurer. In Holland, he encountered a Scottish army chaplain whom he allowed to 'convert' him to Christianity. Newly christened as George Psalmanazar (apparently after Biblical Assyrian king Shalmaneser), he left for England with a glowing introduction to the Bishop of London. The secret of his real name and identity, however, was taken to his grave when the old fraud was finally laid to rest, as requested, in a common burial ground.

Chapter 25

Ahem! It's the Cheating Major

Mixed with the 'Ooohs' and 'Aahs', the applause and the groans of the studio audience was another, more ominous sound – a persistent bout of annoying coughing. It had been a background noise throughout the recording of an episode of the highly successful TV quiz, *Who Wants To Be A Millionaire?* And although quizmaster Chris Tarrant was unaware of it as he concentrated on hosting the hit show, behind-the-scenes production staff were treating the coughing fits, first as an annoyance, then with deep suspicion. Finally they realised that the coughs were a secret code between someone in the audience and the contestant who at that very moment, by a string of 'intuitive' quiz answers, was heading inexorably towards his goal of winning the quiz's £1 million top prize.

That fortunate contestant was British Army officer Charles Ingram. His challenge to reach the magic million was a series of fifteen multiple-choice questions. Each correct answer doubled his prize money. One incorrect answer would cost him dear. Naturally, the questions became more and more difficult but the major did not fail on any of them.

Tension in the studio reached fever pitch when Ingram arrived at the half-million pound question. Chris Tarrant asked him: 'Baron Haussmann is best known for the planning of which city?' Ingram correctly answered: 'Paris'. Which brought him to the magic million-pound question: 'A number 1 followed by 100 zeros is known by what name?' The four alternative answers offered were: (a) Googol, (b) Megatron, (c) Gigabit and (d) Nanomol.

Major Ingram took his time as the audience held its collective breath – all but one or two members of it, from whom continued to emanate the mysterious coughs. At this stage, the lucky contestant could have stopped right there and walked away with £500,000 – or he could risk a wrong response which would lose him all but £32,000 of his gains so far. Ingram puzzled aloud, evaluating each option. Finally, he offered his answer: 'Googol'. To build up the tension for the millions of viewers whom he assumed would shortly be watching the pre-recorded show, Tarrant delayed confirming whether the answer was right or wrong. But after a dramatic silence, his face lit up with a broad grin, he gave Ingram a big hug and, to the riotous applause of the studio audience, he handed him his seven-figure cheque.

Off-camera, however, panic reigned. Tarrant was called away by the producer and, out of the hearing of the audience, was told that suspicions had been raised that coughs from the audience were a secretly coded series of prompts to help Ingram reach his goal. The major was asked to hand back his cheque – and his fleeting fame and fortune were replaced by ignominy and ruin.

The man who became a millionaire for only a fleeting few minutes had never looked destined for the limelight. The son of an RAF wing commander and a successful theatre designer, he had watched his elder brother become a commander in the Royal Navy and his sister a high-flying accountant, but he himself had shown only moderate academic ability. He followed his father and brother into the armed forces, joining the Royal Engineers, then in 1989 married a former college girlfriend, Diana Pollock.

Diana seemed to give her husband the resolve that the affable but fairly directionless Charles seemed to have lacked. She was ambitious for his career but Army pay gave them little chance to better their circumstances and, after giving birth to three daughters, the couple found themselves £50,000 in debt and without a home of their own, since they had always been housed in service quarters. The ambitious Diana decided that if they couldn't earn their way to a grander lifestyle, they would simply have to win one.

Diana Ingram, along with her brother Adrian, bid to become TV contestants on *Who Wants To Be A Millionaire?*, the success of which had seen its game-show format exported all over the world. They bombarded the TV company's premium-rate phone lines to gain a place on the show and even practised on a mock keyboard to maximise their chances of getting through the preliminary 'fastest finger first' round. Their perseverance paid off and in 2001 Adrian and then Diana appeared as contestants and won £32,000 each.

It was not enough to pay the Ingrams' debts or satisfy their greed. Diana came up with the idea of writing a book titled *Win A Million*, containing tips for getting onto the show, strategies for winning and typical quiz questions to learn by heart. She found a publisher but, before the book could be completed, Diana's husband got himself a place on the show – and in September 2001 he won the chance to sit in the same seat that his wife had occupied earlier in the year.

The genial major was in many ways a perfect contestant. Chatty and ebullient, he laughed and joked with quizmaster Tarrant as he correctly answered the early, simpler questions, doubling his money from £100 to £200 and ever upwards. By the time he got to the £8,000 question, however, floor managers working for the programme makers, Celador, were already warning senior executives that 'something strange was going on'. A camera was kept trained on Diana Ingram, seated high in the audience. By the £32,000 question, unaware that her every move was being recorded on videotape, she coughed twice to signal the answer to the £32,000 question: 'Who had a hit with *Born To Do It*?' The major had initially indicated his belief that it was boy band A1 before changing his mind when his wife coughed twice at the correct answer 'Craig David'.

The next bout of coughing came from a different quarter, however – a fellow contestant awaiting his turn in the hot seat just 10ft away. This time, the person with a tickly throat was a bespectacled college lecturer named Tecwen Whittock, sitting in the front row. Whittock seemed to be prompting Ingram when the correct answers to the £64,000 and £125,000 questions were mentioned by Tarrant. As the audience held their breath, Ingram correctly attributed the painting *The Ambassadors* to Holbein and won himself £125,000. The next question was: 'What type of garment is an Anthony Eden?' As Ingram pondered the answer, Whittock coughed three times to signal that an 'Anthony Eden' was a type of hat. Ingram then became £250,000 richer when he correctly answered: 'A hat'.

By this time, the production team were watching both Tecwen Whittock and Diana Ingram like hawks. The camera trained on Mrs Ingram revealed some extraordinary reactions. She appeared to be fuming that her husband was overplaying his hand and that he had gone on beyond the £125,000 question. And, as he launched himself into the £1 million question, she was heard to mutter: 'Oh God, don't start'.

So intent was Chris Tarrant on doing his job that he was wholly unaware of the drama being played out around him. When Ingram correctly responded to the final question with the answer 'Googol', the TV host hugged the major and beamed: 'You are the most amazing contestant we have ever, ever had. I have no idea how you got there.' Urging the audience into rapturous applause, he added: 'I have no idea what your strategy was; you were so brave. I am so proud to have met you. You are just an amazing human being.'

Fortunes have been won and lost with alacrity in the murky world of crime but none so fleetingly as that bestowed that day upon Charles Ingram. His loss of fortune led to sudden shame and a summons to court where, in March 2003, thirty-nine-year-old Ingram, his thirty-eight-year-old wife and Tecwen Whittock, aged fifty-three, all denied that they had 'procured a valuable security by deception' by dishonestly getting Tarrant to sign the £1 million cheque on September 10, 2001. The winning cheque is a genuine one, the court was told, because Tarrant is a signatory to the show's bank account.

Prosecutor Nicholas Hilliard told the jury: 'You may think it inevitable, human nature being what it is, that where a million pounds is regularly on offer someone, somewhere might have thought about how it might be possible to improve their chances of getting their hands on money by cheating. There is a saying that two heads are better than one and two people's general knowledge is likely to be better than one person's. After all, they won't know exactly the same things.'

Mr Hilliard said there was a clear connection between Tecwen Whittock and the Ingrams family in the run-up to the major's TV appearance. The lecturer insisted that his only contact had been a few telephone calls to Diana seeking tips on how to secure a place on the show. But the court was told that no fewer than thirty-eight calls had been made between Whittock and the Ingrams, the last being just hours before the second part of the programme was recorded when Whittock was already at the studios awaiting his own turn on the programme.

When the recording of that dramatic studio session was replayed in court, Whittock was heard to cough nineteen times, many of them just after Ingram, musing aloud about the four suggested options, had repeated the correct answer to the questions. The plan, said Mr Hilliard was that a cough would immediately follow when the contestant voiced a correct answer. The court heard that Whittock had told the production crew that he had a cough before the show started – yet when he got his own turn in the hot seat immediately after the major, his cough disappeared. So, it seems, did his skill at answering the questions, for after risking all for Ingram, he himself walked away with only £1,000. The jury's attention was also drawn to the timely coughing of Diana Ingram when, as in the case of the £32,000 pop music question, she apparently knew the answer whereas Whittock did not.

The prosecution suggested that the coughing ploy was a back-up to another, more sophisticated plot that had gone wrong. The Ingrams, it was alleged, had practised a high-tech scheme in which the correct answers would be sent to the major via four vibrating pagers hidden about his person. The prosecution suggested that the Ingrams' intended scam involved planting a stooge in the audience who would have a mobile phone with the line permanently open to another accomplice outside the studio. This fourth person could hear the questions, look up the answers and send the right responses to the pagers: one bleeper for each of the four multiple-choice answers. Just hours before he went into the hot seat, messages were being sent from the major's mobile to the four pagers, but by the time Ingram appeared on the show, the plan had been abandoned as being too risky.

After twenty-two days in court and still protesting their innocence, Charles and Diana Ingram and Tecwen Whittock were all found guilty but were spared the ignominy of being sent to prison. Whittock was given a suspended jail sentence of one year and was fined £10,000 with £7,500 costs. He subsequently resigned from his job as head of business studies at Pontypridd College in South Wales. The Ingrams each received eighteen-month suspended jail sentences and were fined a total of £30,000 with £20,000 costs.

Passing sentence, Judge Geoffrey Rivlin described the pair as quiz show addicts and said it was this obsession that had caused them to be overcome with the idea of cheating the system. 'You, Tecwen Whittock, were only too prepared to go along with it,' said the judge. 'As to the shabby schoolboy trick you two men ultimately played, you certainly had no notion that it would result in you, Charles Ingram, going on to win £1 million. But somehow, more by good luck than good management, it did.'

Turning to Diana, the judge added: 'You might be well advised to thank your lucky stars you are not going to prison today, and put aside any childish wishes of bravado that you are entitled to this money.' The judge's entreaty went unheeded, however. Immediately following their court ordeal, the major and his wife made a further string of television appearances, this time legitimately, to proclaim the unfairness of the verdict.

Diana Ingram countered press portrayals of her as a 'Lady Macbeth' character, saying she was no evil schemer leading her husband on but, as a lifelong fan of Chris Tarrant, was simply someone who had seen an opportunity to get her family out of financial difficulties. Her husband told a newspaper that he had considered suicide after the court verdict, knowing that it would mean the end of his Army career. He accused TV company Celador of 'ruining our lives', adding that they were now so in debt that they would have to leave their rented home in Easterton, Wiltshire, and find more humble lodgings.

There was a brief fillip in the Ingrams' fortunes immediately after the trial when the canned episode of *Who Wants To Be A Millionaire?* was finally shown and seventeen million viewers tuned in to watch it in Britain alone. The couple gained brief celebrity status across the Atlantic, where they were invited onto TV talk shows. A movie about the case was even considered. The Ingrams believed they stood to make a mint from after-dinner speaking and thought that, with their image glamourised by Hollywood, their earning power could be boosted further. But the film project came to nought, and so did their ambitious plans to reinvent themselves as international celebrities. They returned home again as deeply in debt as before.

In October 2003, Ingram was convicted at Bournemouth Crown Court of another bit of cheating: an insurance fraud. He had duped one company into insuring his house by failing to declare past claims with another firm, and had then claimed £30,000 for a burglary at his home. He narrowly escaped jail and was given a conditional discharge because Judge Samuel Wiggs said he had 'reflected on the punishment you have brought upon yourself and your dire financial state'. It had been revealed during the case that Ingram, the man who had been a millionaire for a moment, was now £400,000 in debt.

As he left court, Major Ingram complained: 'I am an honourable man who has always been willing to put my life on the line for Queen and country. But I would have faced less humiliation if I had mugged an old lady.'

He later mourned his lot by telling a newspaper: 'The dishonour is just too much to bear. Everywhere we go, people know who we are. The downside is that if I buy something and it's broken, I no longer feel able to take it back. People recognise us and think we would cheat on everything.'

Chapter 26

The TV 'Wasp' Who Stung!

Major Charles Ingram was not the first TV quiz show contestant to cheat – and almost beat – the system. For a brief period in the late 1950s, a respectable, clean-cut, all-American academic named Charles Van Doren was the most popular star in the United States. 'Charles Who?' would be the question today. Yet for ten months in 1957, Mr Van Doren got higher ratings than even the King of Rock, Elvis Presley.

Van Doren certainly had the brains to be successful. He was the son of poet Mark Van Doren and mother Dorothy, a novelist and editor of a political magazine. His uncle, Carl, was a Pulitzer Prize-winning biographer. Young Charles did them all proud. At the age of thirty, he was a respected lecturer at Columbia University. But that was not enough for the ambitious egghead who got hooked on fame and fortune. Van Doren's brilliant mind gained him an invitation to become a contestant on the popular television quiz show of the time, *Twenty One*. In a formula that has been often emulated, contestants on the programme would be placed in a sound-proofed box to isolate them from the studio audience. The hopeful entrants would then be bombarded with quiz questions, the answers to which became increasingly and nail-bitingly difficult.

Van Doren started out in January 1957 as just another contestant – most lasting only a few weeks before flunking too many of the questions. But week after week, Van Doren came up trumps. His reign seemed to go on and on, as he accumulated an ever-growing mountain of cash. More importantly to the television company bosses, he also accumulated a vast fan following. A weekly audience of millions were hooked on *Twenty One*. Van Doren's happy smile shone out from the cover of every magazine, from fanzines to *Time*. His phenomenal power of recall was studied by psychologists. His brilliant intellect was the envy of educators and the bane of college dunces.

Van Doren did not make his role look easy, however. After quizmaster Jack Barry had asked him a particularly difficult question, his brow would furrow. Beads of sweat would build on his temple as he stared intently at the floor, trying to pluck the answer from his whirring brain cells. Seconds would pass and seem like minutes. These moments of seemingly mental torture made the TV show the astounding success that it became. Every week the same team of Jack Barry and Charles Van Doren would have the audience at home and in the studio perched on the edge of their seats as the tension built to its inexorable climax. Every week, as the last crucial question was correctly answered, the quizmaster would shout 'Correct' and the audience would howl with delight. Yes folks, every week would end with Van Doren victorious.

At the end of an incredible fifteen-week run, Charles Van Doren had won more than $129,000 worth of prizes, a small fortune in those days. Which was not such a feat after all... because before going on air, the producers had supplied Van Doren with every answer! Even his nail-biting responses had all been carefully rehearsed. Charles Van Doren, the all-American hero, was a cheat.

It had not always been so. When he was first invited onto the show, Van Doren greeted with disdain the suggestion that he be given clues to the answers. The producer was persuasive, however. He pandered to Van Doren's vanity and told him that, by 'helping glamorise intellectualism', he could do a great service to the youth of America. Like a drug addict, once he had begun to cheat, Van Doren found that there was no turning back. After all, it was a scam in which no one was getting hurt. Everyone made money and the public were ecstatic.

Van Doren's synthetic reactions to the questions put to him were so well acted that he almost got away with the fraud. It wasn't a television watchdog that caught him out, however; it was one of his fellow contestants. Joseph Stempel had been invited onto the show before Van Doren's premier appearance and had been equally successful. That was because Stempel, a thirty-year-old New Yorker, had also been supplied with the answers.

However, when Stempel was joined on the show by Van Doren, the producers and advertisers found that the latter's clean-cut image was more popular with the audience. Stempel was told his time was up – that he would have to give a wrong answer and bow out. Astonishingly, he agreed. But as he watched his former rival stashing away a small fortune week after week, Joseph Stempel changed his mind. He reported the quiz show's shameful secret. He said: 'I was so depressed and disgusted. I just didn't want to have anything to do with the show. I got tired of being in the shadows. Once I saw Van Doren, I knew my days on the show were numbered. He was tall, thin and "waspy". I was this Bronx Jewish kid. It was as simple as that.'

Van Doren's *Twenty One* run ended when he lost to Vivienne Nearing, a lawyer whose husband he had previously beaten. But because of his celebrity status, he was offered a three-year contract with NBC News as a special 'cultural correspondent' for the flagship *Today* programme. His career in television was short-lived, however. When the *Twenty One* fraud was exposed by Stempel and others, Van Doren at first attempted to lie his way out of trouble. He denied any wrongdoing, saying, 'It's silly and distressing to think that people don't have more faith in quiz shows.'

His weasel words failed to convince. The press, the public and, of course, rival television stations were outraged. Even President Dwight D. Eisenhower publicly condemned the cynical deception. He ordered an investigation by the Justice Department and Van Doren was interrogated by a grand jury. But when faced with the might of a Congressional sub-committee on November 2, 1959, he broke down and confessed all. He said that, as time went on, the show had 'ballooned beyond my wildest dreams' and that 'this went to my head'. His full explanation and apology for his deception was eloquently put:

'I was involved, deeply involved, in a deception. The fact that I, too, was very much deceived cannot keep me from being the principal victim of that deception, because I was its principal symbol. There may be a kind of justice in that. I don't know. I do know, and I can say it proudly to this committee, that since Friday, October 16, when I finally came to a full understanding of what I had done and of what I must do, I have taken a number of steps toward trying to make up for it.

'I have a long way to go. I have deceived my friends, and I had millions of them. Whatever their feeling for me now, my affection for them is stronger today than ever before. I am making this statement because of them. I hope my being here will serve them well and lastingly.

'I asked producer Albert Freedman to let me go on *Twenty One* honestly, without receiving help. He said that was impossible. He told me that I would not have a chance to defeat Stempel because he was too knowledgeable. He also told me that the show was merely entertainment and that giving help to quiz contests was a common practice and merely a part of show business. This of course was not true, but perhaps I wanted to believe him.

'He also stressed the fact that by appearing on a nationally televised programme, I would be doing a great service to the intellectual life, to teachers and to education in general, by increasing public respect for the work of the mind through my performances. In fact, I think I have done a disservice to all of them. I deeply regret this, since I believe nothing is of more vital importance to our civilization than education.'

Charles Van Doren's reputation was utterly ruined. Congress passed the so-called 'Stempel Laws', making fraud by television a criminal offence. Van Doren escaped a prison sentence but he lost his post with Columbia University and found himself snubbed by other leading institutions. He got a job as a researcher-writer for Encyclopaedia Britannica, where he remained for twenty-eight years. As a reclusive author, he initially produced books under a pseudonym but from the mid-1980s, he once again used his own name, writing and editing numerous books, including *The Idea of Progress* (1967), *The Joy of Reading* (1985) and *A History of Knowledge* (1991).

He never again spoke of the *Twenty One* scam, although one man who tried to make him talk was movie actor and director Robert Redford. As a twenty-year-old student at the American Academy of Dramatic Art in New York, Redford was one of the TV show's enthralled millions — not because he enjoyed quiz shows but because he was convinced Van Doren was a second-rate actor. In a telling reflection of what the Van Doren story meant to him, Redford eloquently explained:

'As I watched him come up with these incredible answers, the actor in me said, "I don't buy it". But what is weird is that I never doubted the integrity of the show. I merely accepted that Van Doren was guilty of a poor performance. That's no crime. I did not ask myself why he was doing it. He might have been hamming it up but he was giving education a good name, setting a fine example to the nation's youth. Elvis Presley was the dark-haired nightmare that every respectable parent prayed their daughter would not bring home. Charles Van Doren was the fair-haired and clean-cut man of their dreams. It did not occur to any of us that this paragon was cheating. The producers were feeding him the answers and rehearsing his tortured appearances. That scandal marks the moment when America began its slow journey towards scepticism and distrust, especially of politicians and the media. As long as we kept being entertained, who cared about decency and morality. Van Doren suffered public humiliation while everyone else connected with the show moved merrily on to their next project. He was only as bad as the people feeding him the answers.'

Twenty-five years after watching *Twenty One* on his black-and-white TV set, Robert Redford decided to make a movie about the scam. Titled *Quiz Show*, it was released in 1994 and won four Oscar nominations. But its making was not all plain sailing. English actor Ralph Fiennes was given the leading part and Van Doren himself was offered a role as consultant. The aged academic turned the proposal down flat. Frustrated that he could not study the character he was to portray, Fiennes travelled to Cornwall, Connecticut, and knocked on the door of the retirement home of Charles Van Doren. Posing as a lost tourist, the actor managed to have a five-minute chat with the reclusive ex-contestant.

He found him to be still the charming, smiling intellectual with the Ivy League accent. And despite his disgrace, he did not seem to have suffered financially through his twenty-five years in the wilderness. For after his brief but celebrated career as a television star, no one had ever asked the flawed quiz king to hand back his prize money.

Chapter 27

Hail the 'Emperor of Abyssinia'!

The urgent telegram that was delivered to the battleship HMS *Dreadnought*, pride of the British Navy, at anchor in Weymouth Bay, Dorset, on February 7, 1910, sent its officers into a frenzy of activity. Addressed by the Foreign Office to Admiral Sir William May, Commander-in-Chief of the Home Fleet, the missive warned of an imminent visit to the ship by the Emperor of Abyssinia and his entourage.

There was barely enough time to send a greeting party to Weymouth railway station before the dignitaries arrived, accompanied by an interpreter and a Foreign Office official. Despite the short notice, their reception was impressive. A red carpet stretched from the train down the platform and through the station concourse. Beyond was a guard of honour which they graciously inspected. A launch then took them to the *Dreadnought* which was bedecked with bunting.

There was a slight hiccup when the national anthem of Zanzibar was played instead of that of Abyssinia but no one took umbrage. Equally unfortunately, a gun salute had to be cancelled at the last moment because no one knew the number of rounds protocol dictated to honour a foreign Emperor. Nevertheless, the party was ceremoniously piped aboard and senior officers donned full dress uniform to accompany them on a tour of the mighty ship.

The guests were delighted. Indeed, they could hardly contain their glee. For they had achieved the purpose of their visit with unforeseen ease ... and made utter fools of the Royal Navy. The 'Emperor of Abyssinia' and his entourage were a group of London high society dilettantes led by Horace de Vere Cole and his cousin, novelist Virginia Woolf.

In retrospect, it seems incredible that anyone could have been taken in by the motley party. They overacted their roles to a ludicrous degree. Their faces were stained with make-up, they had false moustaches and spoke in a made-up language. They shouted 'Bunga Bunga' to one another whenever anything of interest caught their eye. Despite the banquet laid before them, none of the hoaxers ate. Cole explained that their religion precluded them breaking bread at sea. The real reason, however, was a warning by one of the group, theatrical make-up expert Willy Clarkson, that eating or drinking would ruin their disguises.

Clarkson had done a good job. The costumes and make-up fooled everyone. Their first test had been at London's Paddington Station when Cole, in top hat and morning coat, announced himself as Herbert Cholmondesley of the Foreign Office and imperiously demanded that the stationmaster lay on a special train to convey his royal guests to Weymouth. It was Cole who had sent the telegram to HMS *Dreadnought* and it was he who had persuaded six of his friends – Clarkson, Woolf, her brother Adrian, artist Duncan Grant, sportsman Anthony Buxton and judge's son Guy Ridley – to perpetrate the elaborate hoax.

They feared exposure only twice during their day's visit to Weymouth, ostensibly to join celebrations for the fourth anniversary of the launching of *Dreadnought*. The first occasion was when they were introduced to an officer who was related to Virginia Woolf and who had met Horace Cole on several occasions. The officer looked them both in the eye but recognised neither. The second crisis was when Buxton sneezed and half his moustache blew off. He stuck it back on again before anyone noticed.

At the end of their visit, the hoaxers tipped the ordinary seamen who had carried their bags and posed for photographs before reboarding their train for the return journey to London. Even then, they did not let their guise slip. Before dinner was allowed to be served on the train, Cole demanded that it stop at Reading so that white gloves could be purchased for the waiters.

Unfortunately for the impostors, word of their exploits was leaked to the newspapers. Questions were asked in the House of Commons about this appalling breach of security by the Royal

Navy. The hoax was described as 'an insult to His Majesty's flag'. Sir William May had to suffer children shouting 'Bunga bunga' at him in the streets of Weymouth. There was even talk of jailing the perpetrators of this ambitious confidence trick.

Horace Cole was indeed sought out for summary punishment. Two naval officers armed with canes arrived at his house threatening to avenge the honour of the Navy by giving him a sound beating in front of his household. Ever the smooth talker, however, Cole persuaded them that they could beat him only if he could beat them back. In a bizarre ritual, the three men then crept off to a backstreet where Cole and the officers ceremoniously but gently caned each other in a display of Edwardian drama. They then shook hands and went their merry ways.

The *Dreadnought* hoax would never again be equalled by Cole, but it was neither his first nor his last. As a Cambridge University student, Cole and Virginia Woolf's brother Adrian Stephen had enjoyed a successful 'dry run' for their later adventure when they read that the Sultan of Zanzibar was touring England. The pair had themselves made up in oriental garb and sent a telegram to the mayor of Cambridge announcing the sultan's imminent arrival. The city's dignitaries met their train and escorted the royal party, with full pomp, to the Guildhall, where they were honoured with a formal reception. Stephen, who played the sultan, and Cole, posing as the sovereign's bilingual uncle, spent the day touring the town and its colleges before, in a fit of giggles, dashing away into the crowd.

The visit of the 'Sultan of Zanzibar' became a rehearsal for the far more risky visit by the 'Emperor of Abyssinia' to *Dreadnought* – at a time when Britain and Germany were engaged in an arms race that would soon flare into the Great War. Although Cole would never again match that ambitious hoax, he nevertheless continued to prick the pomposity of London society.

He once strode into Piccadilly Circus wearing workman's garb, erected barriers across the thoroughfare and tore up the road, having persuaded policemen to reroute the traffic. He bought tickets for a row of seats at the theatre and paid a number of bald men to sit in them. Each of them had a letter painted on his pate, which together spelled out an expletive that shocked the audience in the front rows of the balcony above. On another occasion, he held a party at which every one of the guests realised, upon introducing one another, that they all had surnames which included the word 'bottom'.

On his honeymoon in Venice, Cole left his new wife in the middle of the night to collect bags of horse manure, which he then spread around the famous Piazza San Marco. The next morning, which just happened to be April 1, the residents were confused to find evidence that horses had been visiting their island city for the first time in history.

But it is the stunt Cole and his friends perfected at the expense of the Royal Navy that February day in 1910 for which the arch hoaxer will be best remembered. The *Dreadnought* stunt had cost him and his pals £4,000, a tidy sum in those days. But they declared it money well spent to expose the gullibility of the officialdom and to prick the pomposity of the military hierarchy.

Virginia Woolf felt she had another reason to look down her nose at mankind and she ultimately used the hoax in a 1921 short story, *The Society.* According to Woolf, when the real Emperor of Abyssinia arrived in London weeks later, wherever he went, 'the street boys ran after him calling out, Bunga bunga!' And when the emperor asked if he could look at the British fleet, the First Lord of the Admiralty replied that he 'regretted to inform his majesty that it was quite impossible'.

Chapter 28

Genius Who Proved Himself
a Forger

Perhaps the most famous art forger of all time is Han van Meegeren, a Dutchman addicted to alcohol, morphine and prostitutes, but who, through his amazing mastery of brushwork, proved himself to be a genius. His creation of gems supposedly from the Seventeenth Century Golden Age of Dutch painting made him a fortune – and almost had him hanged as a traitor. It was only an amazing series of events after the fall of Nazi Germany in 1945 that exposed van Meegeren. Until then, the master forger really did believe he had got away with it...

Henricus ('Han' being the diminutive) Antonius van Meegeren was born in Deventer, in the Netherlands, about fifty miles east of Amsterdam, in 1889, the second of five children. His mother was some fifteen years younger than his strict, schoolteacher father and it was from her that he inherited his artistic talents. But while his delicate, sensitive mother praised his drawings and painting, his father would tear them up scornfully. This cruel behaviour did not deter the budding artist, however. Referring to those childhood days, van Meegeren once said: 'I invented a world where I was king and my subjects were lions.'

In his teens, van Meegeren took up a place at the Institute of Technology in Delft, where he was a highly regarded student and gained the institute's gold medal for the best painting by a student. At the age of twenty-three, he married Anna de Voogt, the Sumatran daughter of a Dutch government official serving in the East Indies, who soon became pregnant. Perhaps his sudden responsibilities affected his work because he was bitterly disappointed when he failed his final exams.

Van Meegeren and Anna moved to Scheveningen, then a small

seaside town, where, during a lull in his painting, van Meegeren produced his first fake, a copy of the watercolour for which he had won the gold medal. (Later, during one of his leaner periods, he sold the prize-winning painting for £100.) Anna refused to let him pass it off as the original and the couple argued fiercely. It was the first of their frequent rows, many brought on by van Meegeren's series of mistresses. The marriage fell apart and Anna returned to Rijswijk to live with her grandmother. So in 1917 the artist was alone again, struggling at his easel but not producing any acclaimed work. His paintings were described as being of high technical standard but lacking in richness and quality. One major exhibition in the Hague in 1922 received harsh reviews. The fiercest came from revered critic Dr Abraham Bredius – and van Meegeren was never to forget him, for one thing he could not stand was ridicule.

For many unrewarding years, the increasingly disillusioned painter was forced to design Christmas cards to make a living. He added to his income by doing some restoration work and selling portraits to tourists. Van Meegeren was now no longer an aspiring, young genius but a broken, frustrated artist aged forty-three. It was at this particularly low point in his life that he decided to become a professional forger, choosing the great Dutch master Johannes Vermeer as the first artist to imitate. Van Meegeren could not help but smile as he realised the fun he could have at the expense of the critics and art experts he so despised.

His choice of Vermeer had been deliberate: the Seventeenth Century Dutch painter was the one most admired by Dr Bredius. There was another reason: one of van Meegeren's close friends, Theo Wijngaarden, had been victim of Dr Bredius's bullying. Wijngaarden had sincerely believed that he had discovered a Frans Hals painting and had even had it authenticated by art experts, but the picture was dismissed out of hand by Bredius. This was not the end of Wijngaarden's dealings with Bredius, however. Seeking revenge, Wijngaarden painted a 'Rembrandt' and four months later was again standing before the self-important art expert. Dr Bredius examined the pictured and pronounced it as genuine. Wijngaarden then gleefully took hold of the painting and slashed it top to bottom with a palette knife just to witness the look of horror on his adversary's face.

Van Meegeren, meanwhile, had moved from Holland to a villa in the south of France to set about his secret work with great determination, application and patience. It was important that the materials he chose fooled everyone. And so anxious was he to make his masterplan work that he spent four years hunting down the very same pigments that Vermeer himself would have used. This was by no means an easy task, for Vermeer obtained his characteristic blue colour from the semi-precious stone lapis lazuli which had been powdered. Van Meegeren did the same, paying extraordinary attention to detail, even grinding the pigments by hand so that the particles would look irregular when examined under a microscope. After great trial and error, he found that mixing phenol resin and oil of lilacs with the paints gave them the correct viscosity and fast drying properties.

Providing the right canvas, too, was crucial. It had to look old. Van Meegeren simply bought old, genuine ones and either cleaned them or painted over the original pictures. And finally, not a detail overlooked, he even prepared special brushes which would reproduce the smooth texture of Vermeer's brush strokes. Even before he started on his first 'Vermeer', van Meegeren had the ageing of the work down to a fine art. The process was completed in a specially-built oven with electric elements. Again much patience was needed to obtain the right temperature and time – 105 degrees centigrade for two hours – to bake the picture and harden the paint without causing any damage to the canvas. At last, everything was perfect. Was it the lilac oil he could scent... or the sweet smell of revenge?

It took van Meegeren seven months to complete the great religious work *The Disciples at Emmaus*, his first and most brilliant forgery. In keeping with Vermeer's style, it was a strong, simple composition. Christ and his disciples were seated at a table near a window through which light poured in upon the scene.

Van Meegeren had thought long and hard about the challenging subject, for only one genuine 'religious' Vermeer existed for comparison. The forger concentrated on every detail of the phoney work, collecting as many Seventeenth Century items as he could find, such as pots, plates and chairs, to ensure he was copying authentic articles for his picture. And having spent so many years trying to recreate the great master's work, van Meegeren had become not only obsessed with Vermeer, but virtually possessed by him too.

'It was the most thrilling, the most inspiring experience of my whole life,' he recalled later. 'I was positive that good old Vermeer would be satisfied with my job. He was keeping me company, you know. He was always with me during that whole period. I sensed his presence; he encouraged me. He liked what I was doing. Yes, he really did!' However, what Vermeer would have thought of van Meegeren using a passing Italian tramp as a model for Jesus in his religious work, we shall never know.

When *The Disciples at Emmaus* was finished, it underwent van Meegeren's intricate, perfected ageing process. After applying a coat of varnish, he then had to set about 'cracking' it. As with all his other forgery techniques, van Meegeren had painstakingly practised this one over many weeks. Previous tests had proved that a genuine but worthless Seventeenth Century oil painting could be stripped down to the last layer of paint. The last thin layer had the authentic cracks and van Meegeren had found that, as he painted the new picture over an old one, these original cracks came through. For good measure, he used a cylinder around which he rolled the painting, and then he filled in all the cracks with black Indian ink to give the appearance of the accumulated dust of three centuries. The final touch was another coat of varnish, this time in a brownish colour. Only when he was certain the picture would stand up to detailed scientific examination was he ready to make the public aware of this great 'missing Vermeer'.

Van Meegeren first paid a visit to a member of the Dutch Parliament and explained how a Vermeer had come into his possession. It belonged to a Dutch family now living in Italy, he said. The owners wished to remain anonymous for personal reasons and had asked him to make the necessary approaches to determine the painting's authenticity. Naturally, van Meegeren continued, an expert would have to be called. Perhaps – and he could barely bring himself to say the name – that famous Dr Bredius might like to cast an eye over this mysterious work. The parliamentarian agreed to act as mediator and took the painting to Dr Bredius. The art expert made great play of first holding the painting at arm's length and then peering at it so closely that his nose almost brushed the canvas. With a final examination of the signature, Bredius was happy to agree the painting was indeed a Vermeer and to issue a certificate of authenticity.

The discovery soon became big news in the art world and the prestigious Boymans Museum in Rotterdam bought the picture for £58,000. When the 'Vermeer' went on show in 1937 it caused further excitement in the newspapers, one hailing it as 'The art find of the Century'. Dr Bredius naturally enough took all the glory for discovering a Vermeer masterpiece. He went as far as to announce the discovery in the *Burlington Magazine* in 1937: 'It is a wonderful moment in the life of a lover of art when he finds himself suddenly confronted with a hitherto unknown painting by a great master, untouched on the original canvas and without any restoration, just as it left the painter's studio. We have here a – I am inclined to say, *the* – masterpiece of Johannes Vermeer of Delft.'

Van Meegeren, who had quite wisely not made his involvement in the matter too public, nevertheless paid a visit to the museum on a day he knew Dr Bredius and fellow experts would be there. The master forger took one look at the 'Vermeer' and pronounced it a fake. He was ignored. This was the reaction van Meegeren wanted. He now knew the money he had received for the painting was quite safe. And any intention he originally may have had about admitting the forgery and returning the money had disappeared. He would instead have further fun at the expense of the pompous elite of the art world.

With the same precise attention to detail, van Meegeren painted two 'de Hooghs' which he sold for £46,000 each. Returning to the artist who had helped him wreak such satisfying revenge, van Meegeren then painted no fewer than five further Vermeer forgeries. They sold for fantastic prices. Among the purchasers were the fabulously wealthy collectors D. G. van Beuningen and W. van der Vorm.

Van Meegeren received the equivalent of £20million or more for his works at today's prices, his ill-gotten gains enabling him to lead a very fine life. He had artist's models more than willing to become artist's mistresses; he became a regular diner at nightclubs and, although reports vary, he was the proud owner of up to fifty properties throughout the world. Rather ironically, he also owned many fine and original works of art.

It does seem incredible that his sudden, not inconsiderable wealth was not challenged. The artist told many tales about where the money had come from, including winning the state lottery no less than three times. Sadly, however, van Meegeren was not enjoying life to the full. He was sliding into alcohol and drug addiction, and he was a prolific user of prostitutes.

With the outbreak of the Second World War, and the German invasion of Holland, a more sinister suggestion for van Meegeren's riches began to surface. Could he perhaps be involved with the Nazi regime? In fact, van Meegeren had already made a dangerous mistake in this direction. He had sold one of his Vermeer forgeries, *The Woman Taken in Adultery*, to Nazi leader Reichsmarschall Hermann Goering for almost £200,000.

After the Nazi collapse in 1945, Luftwaffe chief Goering's priceless art collection was uncovered at his Bavarian mansion. Most of it had been looted from churches, galleries and private collections as the Nazis swept through Europe. But among the collection was, of course, *The Woman Taken in Adultery*. Investigating agents soon discovered it had been purchased from a dealer in Amsterdam – van Meegeren. The artist was to be arrested, not for the crime of forgery, but for being a collaborator. He was accused of selling a national treasure to the enemy.

It presented the forger with a bitter dilemma. The idea of being thought a collaborator both offended and terrified him. If found guilty, he could face the death penalty. The alternative was to confess to his faked works of art and risk ruin. For several weeks, he maintained that he had bought the painting from a family and then sold it. He had had no idea it would end up in Nazi hands, he told his accusers.

Eventually, however, he admitted the painting in Goering's possession was not only a fake but a fake painted by him. At first, his astonished interrogators refused to believe him. Then a novel solution to the claim was devised. Van Meegeren was ordered to paint a copy of *The Woman Taken in Adultery*. He refused to do this, saying he didn't copy works; he created them. To prove his innocence as a collaborator but his guilt as a forger, van Meegeren would paint a new 'Vermeer' before the very eyes of witnesses.

Thus *Christ Teaching at the Temple* came to be. Undertaken in the somewhat stressful conditions of custody, it was not one of van Meegeren's better forgeries but it was convincing enough. Upon its completion, the faker declared to anyone who would listen: 'I had been so belittled by the critics that I could no longer exhibit my work. I was systematically and maliciously damaged by the critics, who don't know the first thing about painting.' The experts, he added, were 'arrogant scum'.

A commission was set up to evaluate other paintings Meegeren said he had forged. Such an inquiry was sorely needed, for van Meegeren claimed to have faked no fewer than fourteen paintings which had all been declared genuine and sold at prices reflecting their 'authenticity'. Van Meegeren's work had been so skilful that even ultra-violet and infra-red photography revealed no clues. The pictures also stood up well to chemical tests. And all the pigments, thanks to van Meegeren's fastidious care, were genuine. Well, all except one. When he painted *The Woman Taken in Adultery*, he used cobalt blue for Christ's robe. It was unbelievable that after such methodical and painstaking research and experimentation, the counterfeiter could have made such a grave and basic error. For that particular pigment was not used until the Nineteenth Century.

This mistake alone may not have cleared van Meegeren of treason and the forger was desperate, above all else, to clear his name as a traitor. His argument was that, far from collaborating with the Nazis, he had courageously forced Goering to strike a bargain. The Reichsmarschall had been allowed to take possession of the fake Vermeer only if 200 works of art looted from Holland by the Germans were returned. Incredibly, because he was so anxious to get his hands on the Vermeer, Goering had agreed.

Unconvinced, one of the investigating officers told van Meegeren: 'You may have saved 200 minor works, but in exchange Goering acquired one of only a handful of paintings by Vermeer.' The forger's rejoinder was fiery: 'Fools! You're like the rest of them. I sold no Vermeer to the Germans – only a van Meegeren, painted to look like a Vermeer. I have not collaborated with the Germans. I have duped them.'

Van Meegeren's court hearing, in November 1947, lasted just one day. It cleared his name of the stigma of treason but exposed him as a master forger who had 'corrupted' the art world. He was found guilty of deception and forging signatures but, mercifully, he was given the minimum possible sentence: one year in prison.

Han van Meegeren never served his time. Neither did he ever paint again. For before starting his sentence he suffered a heart attack and died six weeks later, on December 30, 1947. Shortly before his death, he explained why he had devoted his latter years to reproducing the work of other artists in a bid to fool art experts and dealers. He said: 'I had to prove, once and for all, their utter incompetence, their shocking lack of knowledge and understanding.'

Chapter 29

Puzzling Patterns or Just a Corny Con?

It was always a fascinating notion. Some strange beings came in the night and literally left their mark in fields of crops. Sometimes the patterns would be simple, sometimes intricate, but because of their lack of obvious human intrusion, always intriguing. It was no wonder the phenomena opened up much debate, provoked research papers and books and caused many words to be exchanged between the cynics and the believers.

Crop circles, as the overnight art form was called, first seized public imagination in England in the 1980s. Dozens of photographs appeared showing perfect circles of flattened crops clearing defined against the upstanding cereal around them. There were no signs of footprints, no damage outside the circles, and apparently no reason for their creation.

It looked for all the world as though some alien spacecraft had hovered above the smoothed area, left its mark and then simply returned to whence it had come. Of course, the UFO lobbyists were more than happy to put forward this as an obvious explanation. Who else but visitors from space could leave such perfect signs without any trace of actually being there? Supporters of the UFO theory backed this up with the fact that the circles sometimes appeared in conjunction with a UFO sighting. They claimed some of the early, simpler forms of crop circles suggested fields might have been flattened by the weight of a grounded flying saucer. When the shapes became more complex, it was said that the marks were left due to the strange effect on plants of the craft's drive force. Others argued that the patterns were messages deliberately left by the flying saucer's crew.

Other theories ranged from the eccentric to the more down-to-earth, with crop circles being the work of the Devil, fairies, ancient earth power lines, whirlwinds or the activities of wild animals such as hedgehogs and rabbits.

Rather more believable theories put forward at the time were that the crop circles were the result of purely physical phenomena. A consultant meteorologist, George Terence Meaden , who was head of the Tornado and Storm Research Organisation, reckoned that unusual air vortexes were a factor behind many of the patterns. He called it the 'plasma vortex phenomenon' and described it as 'a spinning mass of air which has accumulated a significant fraction of electrically charged matter'. He said the effect was similar to that of ball lightning but larger and longer lasting.

This theory was strongly backed up by a couple out walking along the edge of a corn field in the Hampshire countryside. It was a still August day in 1991, yet suddenly Gary and Vivienne Tomlinson of Guildford, Surrey, saw the crops around them begin to move. They were caught up in the middle of a forming circle. Vivienne recalled: 'There was a tremendous noise. We looked up to see if it was caused by a helicopter but there was nothing. We felt a strong wind pushing us from the side and above. It was forcing down on our heads, yet incredibly my husband's hair was standing on end. Then the whirling air seemed to branch into two and zig-zag off into the distance. We could still see it like a light mist or fog, shimmering as it moved. As it disappeared, we were left standing in a corn circle with the corn flattened all around us. Everything became very still again and we were left with a tingly feeling. It all happened so quickly that it seemed to be over in a split second.'

Dr Meaden later interviewed the couple and was impressed by their power of recall. 'The story these people told is so detailed they cannot have made it up,' he said. 'They had no knowledge of corn circles yet they described a scientific process that could easily cause them. This really is a magnificent eyewitness account – much better than any we have had previously.'

Throughout the Eighties, reports of crop circles became more widespread. Although southern England was still very much the epicentre, examples were found in Australia, North America and

Japan. Scientists from these countries were soon clamouring for the chance to spend a summer in the UK to conduct in-depth scientific studies. Theories on crop circles abounded. It got to the point that, so absorbed in their subject were the crop circle enthusiasts, that they earned themselves a special name: cereologists. The word comes from the name of the Roman goddess for vegetation, Ceres.

At the height of the appearance of crop circles – in 1990, more than 700 appeared throughout Britain – someone, somewhere dared to suggest that perhaps crop circles owed their existence to something much closer to home... humans who had tricked the world with elaborate hoaxes. And the finger of blame began to be pointed at certain groups of people who displayed their fiendish sense of fun by leaving their names at the sites of their work. Among them were 'Merlin & Co', 'The Bill Bailey Gang', 'The Wessex Skeptics' and 'Spiderman and Catwoman'.

The next step in the crop circle saga was that farmers became increasingly irritated by the damage caused to their crops – at the time, upwards of £60 for each night's work. So it was no surprise when they, too, decided to cash in on the crop circle cult. That meant using their own creativity – and then charging sightseers to come and see the mysterious markings.

One perceptive cereologist, Lee Krystek, said: 'Several factors argue in favour of the complete hoax theory. First, there is a lack of historical precedent for crop circles. Crop circles as they are seen today are a recent phenomenon only twenty or thirty years old. Secondly, the number and complexity of the circles have grown in proportion to the media coverage of them, suggesting that people are more apt to make circles if the circles get in the news. Finally, there are almost no credible reports of someone actually seeing a circle being made by either a UFO or weather phenomena, suggesting that the hoaxers are purposefully keeping out of sight.'

None of this brought an end to crop circle controversy, with some cereologists now claiming that the plants in hoaxed circles had broken stems, while those in 'real' circles were bent. Their argument was that the bending was the result of the condition of the plant rather than the type of force used in flattening. During the summer, green, moist wheat is easily bent and can only be broken with great difficulty.

In short, there were still those who kept an open mind about 'genuine' crop circles and hoax ones. One commentator observed: 'The fact that a few country bumpkins managed to trick scientists and car-loads of gullible townies is one thing. To conclude from this that all crop circles are hoaxes is quite another. It is tantamount to saying that because art experts are often fooled by forgers, all old masters are fakes.'

As the patterns of crop circles increased in intricacy, a letter writer to the authoritative magazine *New Scientist* questioned how long it would take before a recognisable mathematic symbol, such as a Mandelbrot Set, appeared. A Mandelbrot Set is a bulbous circular pattern named after the mathematician Benoit Mandelbrot who pioneered research into fractal geometry. As if in answer to this question, a Mandelbrot Set circle was found on August 12, 1991, in a field near Cambridge University. To the cynics, its appearance was an obvious hoax, a cheeky reference to the fractal research pursued at the university. Serious cereologists had another explanation – that the thought patterns of the university researchers had somehow been detected and mirrored in the neighbouring field by the alien crop-circle makers!

The plain fact is that there is nothing new about crop circles. They have manifested themselves in Britain for at least 4,000 years. And while the modern-day farmer is mostly able to shrug off crop damage, his Bronze Age counterpart struggling to survive may have taken a dimmer view. Any circle prankster around 2,000 BC could probably expect to get an axe through his head.

A study of the circles' history shows that in many cases the theories behind their creation have a strikingly familiar ring. In 1686, Doctor Robert Plot, of Oxford University's Faculty of Science and a fellow of the Royal Society, published a book called *The Natural History of Staffordshire,* in which he told of his desire to identify a 'higher principle' which might explain crop circles other than the then fashionable claims of rutting dear, over-active moles, urinating cattle and fairies. One pamphlet, published eight years earlier told of a field 'neatly mowed by the devil or some infernal spirit'.

Dr Plot did not dismiss these ideas but his own conclusion was that equally bizarre ball lightning was to blame. 'They must needs

RUTTING
EXPENSIVE

be the effects of lightning, exploded from the clouds most times in a circular manner,' he said. As we have said earlier, this theory was to be put forward again in the Twentieth Century by Dr Meaden.

It is far from clear why there seemed to be a 300-year gap in the study of crop circles. Perhaps it is because 'genuine' cases are extremely rare. But for the labours of modern-day hoaxers, the phenomena night never have been brought to the attention of a wider audience. Despite jokers being blamed for at least half of the crop creations, there were those who continued to look for other plausible explanations.

One serious study was carried out by electrical expert Colin Andrews at a cost of £50,000 in 1983. It concentrated on central-southern England. Mr Andrews' twelve-strong team concluded that the circles were somehow linked to disturbances in the earth's magnetic fields, disturbances which in turn stemmed from a 'hole' in the ozone layer of the atmosphere. Sensors had picked up violence fluctuations in the force field around areas where a plethora of circles had appeared.

Mr Andrews reported: 'One of the circles that appeared recently in Hampshire amazed us even more than the others because the flattened crops grew back in dartboard formation. There were seven concentric rings of crops with a series of perfect spokes going out from the centre.'

The Andrews team even claimed that the molecular structure of the crops might have been damaged. Later, they returned to the fray, asserting that circles were being created by 'some sort of high energy, but we don't know what... The shapes are becoming more and more complex and I believe that what we are heading for is circles in the form of snowflakes and flowers. The shapes we have seen recently are just the start of what is to come.'

In the summer of 1990, Mr Andrews led another group of researchers determined to solve the mystery once and for all. They camped out on a hillside in Wiltshire – a focus for the crop circle phenomena – and waited with banks of recording equipment for something to happen. 'Operation Blackbird', as it was called, was a high-tech affair sponsored by British and Japanese television networks and aided by the British army. On July 25 the operation seemed to meet with success. Mr Andrews excitedly announced to the waiting media that a circle had formed during the night in an adjacent field. He spoke too soon. When the researchers examined the circle more closely, they found a hoaxer had left a board game called Horoscope and a wooden crucifix in the middle of the swirled stalks.

So how exactly does one go about making a crop circle? American academic and author Lee Krystek, who founded the 'Museum of Unnatural Mystery', said the tools needed were simple. 'A stake, a chain or rope, some boards, and a few people. The stake is pounded into the ground at the centre of the soon-to-be-circle and the rope attached to it. The rope is then stretched out and someone standing at the end marches around the stake to make a perimeter. The boards can then be used to easily flatten the plants within the circle. Rings can be made through the same technique simply by leaving some sections undamaged.'

Whether all crop circle artists use the same technique, we don't know. But we do know they became a worldwide feature on the landscape – and were never quite what they seemed. In August 1991 three giant circles were discovered in a hay field near Inman Park, in Atlanta, Georgia. The three patterns ranged from 24 ft to 48 ft in diameter and were perfectly in line with a prominent radio tower. They also happened to be in the same area as a 'Harmonic Convergence Gathering of Tribes' campground several years before.

A report in *The Georgia Skeptic* newsletter said the circles had all the trademarks of being genuine, including bent, unbroken stalks, perfect circularity, outward-spiralled grain and the lack of footprints or walkways into the patterns. In fact, the circles were the *Skeptic*'s own invention to prove just how easy creating crop circles really was! Two of the newsletter's staff, Becky Long and Larry Johnson, were behind the ruse. 'We used a rope and our feet,' said Long. 'It was real easy to make. Someone held one end of the rope and I stood in the middle and they just ran around in a circle.' Johnson then kept watch on the circles for several days, noting that the crops remained bent despite heavy rains and that they continued to grow in the bent condition – both phenomena that circle enthusiasts claim are paranormal. Said Long: 'Every type of grain we walked on bent and didn't break. I can't imagine why everyone thinks it's so remarkable that the crop circle grain is bent and not broken.'

Early in February 1993, a circle appeared in a field of rye outside Johannesburg, South Africa. The media speculated over whether it was the work of a UFO, with newspapers, TV and radio all discussing the phenomenon. The discussion went on until February 14, when a small detail, incredibly overlooked in all the excitement, was pointed out. The circle formed a BMW logo. The rye field artwork turned out to be that of the Hunt Lascaris agency working on behalf of BMW. Television commercials soon followed, showing aerial views of the circle accompanied by the catchline: 'Perhaps there is intelligent life out there after all.' Hunt Lascaris claimed it won something approaching £1million worth of free publicity for the stunt. In July 1997, in Warwickshire, a similar trick was pulled. A circle appeared in a field displaying the logo of a band *Sneaker Pumps* who were playing in a nearby festival.

In the summer of 1991, with the corn circle debate raging at its height, two sixty-year-old British artists dropped a bombshell on the cereologists. Dave Chorley and Doug Bower claimed responsibility for many circles over the previous thirteen years. Their motive was to see how many so-called experts and New Age followers they could embarrass. They were also intrigued to know how long the hoax would last. They said they used a simple gun-sight mounted on a baseball cap to align prominent objects in the distance for their straight lines. A rope formed the radius of their circular patterns and they demonstrated how easy it was to enter and exit fields via tractor ruts. They said they always chose remote, sparsely-populated regions and, as they became more expert in their technique, drew more elaborate designs.

An interesting aspect of the two men's story was that their wives and friends backed up their claims of where they were on particular crop circle-making forays. The wives became so suspicious of their night-time excursions that they checked the mileage of their cars. The two men always had a ready cover story but the two women had had enough, guessed what they were up to and begged them to stop the silly stunts.

Chorley and Bower claimed to have fooled leading British investigators, including a team of Japanese scientists, farming groups, several government departments and Colin Andrews who had led the costly research in 1983. The hoaxers told how they had met in the late Sixties with a common interest in art and UFOs. A few years later, inspired by a famous 'flying saucer circle' in northeast Australia, they made their first attempt in Strawberry Field, near Cheesefoot Head, Winchester. These early circles attracted no media attention and the pair were on the brink of giving up, but when they suddenly started getting publicity, their enthusiasm was rekindled. Media hype became so great that Chorley and Bower were credited with creating the bulk of British crop circles.

The now defunct British newspaper *Today* reported how the two men had come forward with their story on the eve of the first-ever United Kingdom Corn Circle Conference, when 300 circle-watchers gathered in Glastonbury. Bower and Chorley carried out an experiment for the newspaper, creating a crop pattern and then inviting pro-circle investigator and author Pat Delgado to view it without knowing the background to its creation. Delgado inspected the circle and declared: 'No human could have done this.' When the hoax was pointed out to him, Delgado was forced to admit: 'I was taken for a ride like so many other people.' Bower shrugged his shoulders and later told a television news programme: 'How on earth can intelligent people of that sort – professors etc – just walk into a field, see flattened corn and make all this out of it over the years? We're just as astonished as anyone else?'

Gradually, the number of crop circles sightings have diminished over the years. The complete truth about the creation of some of them may never be known. But what is certain is that the hoaxers have had a field day – literally! And it is a fact that when interest in the circles began to disappear, so too did they.

Chapter 30

A Charlatan's Greek Myth

Helen of Troy, Greek King Agamemnon, Ulysses ... all are known to schoolboys who have swatted up on the ancient Trojan War. Yet no one knows for sure the full extent of fact and fable that surrounds this classic piece of Greek history. Indeed, what poetic licence did Homer use in *The Iliad*? And who can say exactly where and how the Siege of Troy took place?

Normally, one can rely on the discoveries of archaeologists to help unravel the mysteries of an age long gone. Sites have become hallowed historical havens as they yield artefacts which can tell us so much about those who lived before. And so it should have been in the case of Victorian archaeologist Heinrich Schliemann. The excavations he carried out in that age of discovery looked set to put him on record forever as the man who unearthed not only the city of Troy, but also its wealth of lost riches, all of great historical significance.

For a while, Schliemann did earn himself a formidable reputation as archaeologist extraordinaire. From the moment he set foot on the plain of Troy, in Turkish Asia Minor, his excavations went from strength to strength. He again disputed the beliefs of earlier scholars that Troy was sited three hours from the sea near a place called Bunarbashbi. Instead, he chose a huge mound near Hissarlik, an hour from the sea, for his excavations. The mound contained several cities and Schliemann decided Troy must be the lowest. Here, a wealth of ancient, hidden artifacts seemed to have been awaiting discovery by Schliemann.

Furthermore, he was fortunate to fall upon the treasures of Trojan King Priam: a fabulous hoard of gold and silver cups, shields, vases, daggers, copper spears, gold diadems, earrings and ornaments. Completing his success as a world renowned archaeologist, Schliemann was also able proudly to boast of the discovery of the grave of Greek King Agamemnon. But while no one can deny that Schliemann uncovered city walls and the remains of an ancient

Greek community, the authenticity of his other discoveries was to prove doubtful indeed. Every Greek legend became historical 'fact', borne out by Schliemann's amazing on-site finds.

Schliemann's own colourful past began with his birth in Neu Buckow, Germany, in 1822. He was one of seven sons of a minister. His mother died when he was very young, and his father scandalised local society by taking a maid as a mistress. Heinrich had a fiery relationship with his father but he soon became fiercely ambitious. Although his first job was as a grocer's assistant, by the age of twenty he had progressed to the post of book-keeper for a prestigious international trading company. Heinrich taught himself nine foreign languages (at the end of his life, he spoke twenty-two) and within two years he so impressed his employers that he was sent as company agent to St Petersburg. Here Schliemann established his own business almost immediately. It became so successful so quickly that he was able to enjoy a more leisurely lifestyle, finding time on his hands to study Greek, and thus fulfil a boyhood desire.

Schliemann visited Greece for the first time when he was thirty-seven and then travelled to Paris to take up his studies in archaeology. Later he returned to Greece and visited Mycenae. Schliemann's startling theory that the home of Agamemnon was to be found not outside the ruined walls of the citadel, as had always been believed, but inside, earned him his doctorate by the University of Rostock. He claimed he actually wrote his thesis in classical Greek but this was later disproved.

Schliemann's curiosity about the Greek language, lifestyle and legend became an obsession. He was so ruled by all things Greek that, having divorced his first wife, a Russian, he was adamant that her replacement should be a Greek – and enlisted the help of a Greek archbishop who supplied him with photographs of suitable candidates. Out of these came wife Sophia Engastonmenos, chosen for her innocence and her knowledge of Homer. She was sixteen and Schliemann was forty-seven. The couple had two children, Andromache and Agamemnon.

The archaeologist made his home in a palace in Athens, and from this base launched expeditions throughout Greece and Turkey in search of ancient relics. It was in 1870 that Schleimann arrived at Hisarlik Hill, near Truva, with his young wife and a copy of *The Iliad*. His personal goal was to locate the city of Troy, that mystical place so magically described in Homer's epic poem. The site had already been tentatively explored by Englishman Frank Calvert, but Schliemann was impatient and believed he could make more astounding discoveries much quicker. He gathered together eighty workers – many without any of the crucial archaeological skills needed for such a significant task – who were soon hacking their way underground. Around three years later, treasures were finally unearthed, including necklaces, rings, bracelets, swords, spearheads, earrings and coins.

Schliemann paid reviewers to comment favourably on his work, so contemporary reports cannot be relied upon. These were to the effect that the flamboyant excavator had uncovered a copper shield, a gold bottle and a golden cup in the shape of a ship. He also allegedly found mummified bodies with golden death masks. Most impressive of all was a golden headdress made up of 1,353 intricately worked pieces. Schliemann had no doubt – he had uncovered the Mask of Agamemnon, the treasure of Troy's King Priam and the fabled Nestor's cup. 'I have gazed on the face of Agamemnon,' he declared to all those gathered at the site.

Schliemann's seemingly single-handed discovery of every aspect of Greek life and legend meant he was lionised when he visited London in 1877. Victorian England revered him. Society gasped at photographs of his wife decked out in the gold jewellery he had so expertly unearthed. All agreed that she made a splendid 'Helen of Troy' adorned in necklaces with 12,000 links of gold bearing 4,000 gold leaves. The treasures were part of what Schliemann claimed was the Priam hoard he had uncovered in 1873.

Sigmund Freud said Schliemann was the man whose life he most envied. Gladstone attended his lectures, spoke highly of him and wrote the introduction for one of Schliemann's archaeological books – although Gladstone did draw the line at agreeing to be Agamemnon's godfather.

However, others acquainted with Schliemann had differing opinions about his archaeological exploits. Some said his finds were authentic but that they had no connection with King Priam or indeed any other famous Greek. Others said Schliemann planted the artefacts at the Troy site, having 'imported' them from elsewhere. Yet others believed Schliemann was not even a proper archaeologist but simply a spinner of stories to win enduring fame.

Schliemann would fly into a rage if anyone dared question his declarations. But slowly the truth about him began to filter through. There was doubt about whether the site he had been excavating was that of Troy at all. The palaces he claimed to have discovered were rumoured to have been pigsties. It also seemed remarkable that historically significant finds were made only by Schliemann. Most damning of all, it was said that he may even have paid to have his legendary artefacts made to order.

Even this news did not entirely shake the faith of Schliemann's devout followers. Perhaps he was just overenthusiastic in his bid to piece history together, they said. But what could not be dismissed was the obvious fakery of Schliemann's own autobiography – a complete fantasy tale from start to finish.

One touching extract relates how Schliemann dreamed of excavating Troy when he was just eight years old, yet no mention of this is made in the hundreds of letters and diaries he had painstakingly kept throughout his youth. His tales of meeting American Presidents were also proved false. And Schliemann, who had worked so hard to make his autobiography exciting, was further proved a fraud over his graphic eyewitness description of the great fire of San Francisco of June 1851. The conflagration he spoke of had broken out a month before Schliemann arrived.

Accounts of his discoveries no longer rang true. People questioned why Schliemann had always seemed to be alone when making his major finds. For instance, he had claimed that wife Sophia had been by his side when he made the significant Priam treasure discovery. Yet the truth was that she was nowhere near Troy at the time, having left the site weeks before. And it seemed odd that the most significant finds were always made at the end of a dig.

Entries in the diaries Schliemann kept on his archaeological work were less than reliable. Following one discovery, the word 'Athens' was crossed out and 'Troy' was written in. It was also strange that Schliemann had written no actual description of any of the wonderful finds he claimed to have unearthed. Moreover, Schliemann appeared to have been bribing local workers on his Turkish digs to keep quiet about any finds they made. He would promise them payment if the authorities were not told. It all helped him build up a secret store of artefacts which he could later 'discover' en masse at the site of his choice – and link to whichever bit of Trojan history he chose.

Even more damning to Schliemann's credibility was one discovery he wished had never been made: that before he took up archaeology, he had been sued for fraud while trading in St Petersburg. The dishonesty centred on his dealings in gold with miners. It was this particular line of business which had helped him amass his early fortune.

Further disgrace followed. Although the site still belonged to Frank Calvert, the archaeologist who had found it, Schliemann did not keep his promise to hand over his finds to the Turks but stole all the jewellery he had discovered, hiding it in his wife's shawl and smuggling it out of the country. He even gave the ornate headdress to Sophia.

After wary museums refused to buy his artefacts, Schliemann finally bequeathed his Trojan treasures to a Berlin museum. They disappeared in 1945 in the closing days of the Second World War, and some ended up in Moscow's Pushkin Museum in Moscow. Schliemann himself died in 1890 and, of course, ended up just like the treasure he found – buried. He believed it only fitting that he should be laid to rest in a mausoleum built like a classical Greek temple. It was carved with scenes of the Trojan War.

Three years after Schliemann's death, his assistant, Wilhelm Dorpfeld, revisited the site and began to excavate. He found high sloping walls, vast towers and massive gates dating back to the Bronze Age – the correct period for *The Iliad*. All the features matched Homer's story, which told how the warrior Patroclus managed to scale the city's walls because they sloped. Dorpfeld's discovery was proclaimed the real Troy.

Thus, what broke the hearts of genuine archaeologists long after Schliemann had finished at his Troy site was that the clumsy charlatan and his team had dug too far, missed the period of the siege and arrived at artefacts from around 2,500BC. The precious remains that he and his motley band of diggers had destroyed in getting to the bottom of the great mound had almost certainly been the Troy as described in Homer's epic work. Heinrich Schliemann had apparently unwittingly found the lost city of his dreams – only to ruin it.

Chapter 31

The Hunt for Non-Existent 'Jimmy'

It was such a poignant description that one could almost see the boy standing before them. 'Jimmy is eight years old and a third-generation heroin addict; a precocious little boy with sandy hair, velvety brown eyes and needle marks freckling the baby-smooth skin of his thin brown arms.' His one goal in life, he had plaintively said, was to be a heroin dealer when he was older.

The worst thing was that this sad little figure really existed. He was not just the touching figment of a writer's imagination. Jimmy's story struck at Washington's heart. The paper had no sooner reached the streets that Saturday than *The Washington Post* telephone switchboard lit up wildly. Readers were outraged. The story, written by journalist Janet Cooke, was described as racist and criminal. But the concern was for Jimmy.

By Monday, Washington Police Chief Burtell Jefferson had launched a mammoth citywide search. He had called on his youth division to get to work on Sunday. Mayor Marion Barry was incensed. All schools, social services and police contacts were to be asked for Jimmy's whereabouts. The word went out on the streets that big reward money was available. Assistant Chief Maurice Turner said the police were prepared to offer up to $10,000. The *Los Angeles Times-Washington Post* News Service moved the story out to 300 clients. 'Jimmy' was national, then international.

Police received letters from all over the country, including one signed by thirty students in a Richmond, Virginia, school, pleading that they find Jimmy. At one point, as *Washington Post* chiefs had predicted, police threatened to subpoena Janet Cooke in an effort to force her to reveal names and addresses.

But it was the ordinary folk of America who felt the most. Noone who read Cooke's heartbreaking story could believe, that even in today's times of tough-cookie kids left to fend for themselves, and with all the social problems that exist, there were little boys like Jimmy upon whom life had given up. He was at the heart of the thriving heroin trade that was devastating the low-income neighbourhoods of Washington DC.

Such a worthy story, written with such bite and grit, was certainly deserving of recognition. It was what fine journalism is all about: digging until you find a true victim of social injustice. And that is exactly what happened. Janet Cooke was awarded the prestigious Pulitzer Prize seven months after her article appeared.

But there was still the unresolved issue of Jimmy not being saved. It was obviously a controversial story, and demands continued that Cooke reveal where the boy lived so that he could be helped. Like a true professional, however, the twenty-seven-year-old journalist refused to reveal his location, claiming that she needed to protect her sources and that her life would be in danger from drug dealers if she failed to do so.

Meanwhile, headed by Mayor Marion Barry and other top officials, the city authority carried on its intensive search to find little victim Jimmy. All efforts proved unsuccessful. There were now whispers that the story was fraudulent – that no Jimmy existed. The situation became even more confusing when Mayor Barry said the boy was known to the city and was receiving treatment.

Despite such uncertainties, *The Washington Post* stood by its story, which had been nominated for the Pulitzer Prize by the paper's assistant editor, Robert Woodward – a name familiar to many. For it was he, with fellow *Post* investigative reporter Carl Bernstein, who brought down US President Richard Nixon in the infamous Watergate Scandal. Woodward has twice contributed to efforts that collectively earned his newspaper and its national reporting staff a Pulitzer Prize. So it was only natural that Woodward was eager to nominate the name of someone he saw as a star reporter who had uncovered a major human interest story reflecting social and political times. Janet Cooke was named winner of the prize on April 13, 1981.

But still little Jimmy could not be traced. Not because he had gone to ground... but because he was, in fact, not the product of a deprived background but the product of a journalist's imagination.

There were those who were not happy with Cooke's award for other reasons. When the editors of the *Toledo Blade*, where Cooke had previously worked, read her biographical notes, they noticed a number of discrepancies. Further investigation revealed that Cooke's credentials were false. Applying to – and being accepted on – the *Post*'s 'Weeklies' section staff under editor Vivian Aplin-Brownlee in 1980, Cooke said she had a degree from Vassar College, had studied at the Sorbonne University in France and was the recipient of an award at the *Toledo Blade*. Staff on the *Blade* challenged all this and made contact with *Post* editors. And under pressure from her superiors on the *Post*, Cooke confessed her guilt.

It was the end of a promising career. Janet Cooke had applied to *The Washington Post* executive editor, Ben Bradlee, eleven days before her twenty-fifth birthday. It was the kind of letter he received daily: 'Dear Mr Bradlee, I have been a full-time reporter for the *Toledo Blade* for slightly more than two years, and I believe I am now ready to tackle the challenge of working for a larger newspaper in a major city...'

Attached to the letter was a résumé and copies of six stories Cooke had written for the *Blade*. It was the reference to Vassar College that caught Bradlee's eye. When Cooke visited the *Post* two weeks later, every interviewer was impressed. She was a striking, smartly dressed, articulate black woman, precisely the kind of applicant editors welcome, given the pressures to hire minorities and women. Tom Wilkinson, assistant managing editor for personnel, recalled: 'Janet Cooke came in and saw everyone and was pretty high on everyone's list. What impressed me is that she had pretty well created her own beat. She seems to be a pretty good self-starter. I found her to be very smart.'

So impressed had the staff been with Cooke and her writing that the usual check of references was done in a cursory manner. Much later, Wilkinson vaguely remembered talking with someone at the *Blade*. Others couldn't remember any checks.

Two weeks after she was hired, Cooke's first byline appeared. It was a story about a black beauty contest. Other stories followed rapidly. On January 31 there were four. She was winning the confidence of her editor. Janet produced a lot of material; fifty-two of her stories were published before the ill-fated account of the non-existent Jimmy, her first major article appearing on Feb. 21. It was a dramatic story of Washington's drug-infested 'riot corridor', years after the 1968 disorders, and an hour-by-hour account of a police patrol along 14th Street.

'It was a fine piece of journalism, masterfully written', Vivian Aplin-Brownlee said. 'Janet had blind ambition. It was obvious, but it doesn't deny the talent. She was Gucci and Cardin and Yves St. Laurent. She went out on that 14th Street story in designer jeans and came back to tell me that somebody asked, "What kind of nigger are you?" She thought it was funny. She had to learn the street. She didn't know what was happening in the nitty-gritty. I was grooming her, training her. It was ironic that she became a reporter of the drug culture.'

Janet learned quickly about life in an urban slum. Her 14th Street story drew compliments not only from her colleagues; Bradlee and Richard Harwood, deputy managing editor, also congratulated her.

Janet's ambition was taking shape. She wanted to move to the daily Metro staff, which is responsible for seven-day coverage of local news. She also had her eye on a star prize. 'She set enormous goals for herself,' said Metro reporter Karlyn Barker. 'She wanted a Pulitzer Prize in three years, and she wanted to be on the national staff in three to five years. She had 'winner' written all over her. But though it was strange... every day she acted as though she was protecting her job. She was the last person who needed to do that.'

Once, when the 'Jimmy' saga was developing, Cooke told a friend: 'This story is my ticket off the Weekly.'

During background interviews on the story, Cooke failed to find the new type of heroin she been sent to track down, but she found out a lot about the use of heroin in Washington. Interviewing social workers and drug rehabilitation experts, Cooke amassed extensive notes and tape-recorded interviews, with intriguing leads. In all, there were two hours of taped interviews plus 145 pages of handwritten notes plus a collection of pamphlets and documents on drug abuse.

When Aplin-Brownlee saw what Cooke had collected, she immediately said: 'This is a story for the 'daily' – jargon for the Metro section. Cooke took her notebooks and her ideas to Milton Coleman. Aplin-Brownlee was not to see the story again until it appeared on the front page of *The Washington Post* of September 28 under the headline 'Jimmy's World'.

Two days after the prize had been awarded, *Washington Post* publisher Donald Graham held a press conference and admitted Cooke's story was made up. The Editorial in next day's paper offered a public apology. Robert Woodward stated: 'I believed it, we published it. Official questions had been raised but we stood by the story and her. Internal questions had been raised but ones about her other work. The reports were about the story not sounding right, being based on anonymous sources and primarily about purported lies (about) her personal life... (as told by three reporters) – two she had dated and one who felt in close competition with her. I think that the decision to nominate the story for a Pulitzer is of minimal consequence. It is a brilliant story – fake and fraud that it is. It would be absurd for me or any other editor to review the authenticity or accuracy of stories that are nominated for prizes.'

Woodward was later to admit: 'Janet had written a great piece. In a way, both she and the story were almost too good to be true. I had seen her go out on a complicated story and an hour later turn in a beautifully written piece. This story was so well-written and tied together so well that my alarm bells simply didn't go off. My skepticism left me. I was personally negligent.'

Cooke resigned and returned her prize. She appeared on America's *Phil Donahue Show* in January 1982 and said that it was the high-pressure environment of *The Washington Post* – still riding high from the Watergate story – that had corrupted her judgement. She said that her sources HAD hinted to her about the existence of a boy such as Jimmy but, unable to find him, she had eventually created a story about him in order to satisfy her editors.

Cooke was disgraced, however, and dropped out of the public eye for many years. She did stay in Washington, though, working as a sales clerk and went on to marry a city lawyer, but the marriage failed and Cooke moved to Kalamazoo, Michigan, where she took another job as a sales girl. She briefly emerged from her low-profile life in 1996 to tell her story to the magazine *GQ*. The film rights from that interview were subsequently sold for $1.5million, with the deal that Cooke got fifty-five per cent. But the movie about the journalist who turned in a fairy story has yet to be made.

Chapter 32

Adolf Hitler's Dodgy Diaries

It was an insight into the mind of one of the most evil dictators in history, the man who wanted to change the world, the man responsible for millions of deaths and whose name today still conjures up as much fear and loathing. The earth-shattering discovery was a collection of the private diaries of Adolf Hitler. They had never been seen before. And written between 1932 and 1945, they spanned a watershed in world history.

First to study these intimate revelations was the German news magazine *Stern* which, already envisaging a circulation rise to record figures, was fully prepared to pay the equivalent of £2.5million for the exclusive rights to the documents. Other prestigious publications were to follow: *Paris Match, Newsweek* and even Britain's august newspaper *The Sunday Times*. But in handing over small fortunes for Der Führer's diaries, they were paying the price of being too hungry and too hasty for a scoop. The diaries were fakes – and, as was later revealed, not even clever fakes. They were the work of a fraudster who succeeded in fooling hard-bitten newspaper executives and historical experts.

It was 1983 when *Stern* and *The Sunday Times* announced the existence of several volumes of Hitler's wartime jottings. No one had any reason to suspect they had been penned by a devious trickster who had teamed up with a chancer who was down on his luck. Front man in the scam was Gerd Heidemann, a fifty-three-year-old award-winning journalist employed by a reputable magazine – none other than *Stern*. The forger was Konrad 'Konni' Kujau, forty-six, erstwhile waiter and talented artist with a fertile imagination.

Kujau was born in 1938 in the Saxon town of Loebau which at

that time was enjoying the prosperity of Hitler's Third Reich. From 1946 to 1991, however, it became part of East Germany and Kujau fled to the West in 1957 to avoid arrest following petty theft whilst employed as a waiter. He settled in Stuttgart and changed his name to Peter Fischer, but this didn't stop him getting into more trouble, and further minor misdemeanours led to two prison sentences. He opened the Pelican Dance Bar in 1962, going into business with Edith Lieblang, a waitress and fellow refugee but when this failed, he returned to being a waiter. Kujau was evidently set in his criminal ways, however, and before long was in prison once more, this time for forging luncheon vouchers. Edith stuck by him and, after his release, Kujau persuaded her to put up the money for The Lieblang Cleaning Company. The business prospered and their happiness was marred only by another spell in jail when the authorities discovered 'Peter Fischer' was not who he said he was.

A visit back home to Loebau gave Kujau a money-making idea. It was now twenty-five years since Hitler's death but there was a growing market for Nazi memorabilia. Kujau got his family to place adverts in East German newspapers. They read: 'Wanted for research; old toys, helmets, jugs, pipes, dolls etc.' The response was great and although the East German government had banned the export of objects made before 1945, Kujau managed to smuggle many into West Germany. He now supplemented his living by selling these relics from a shop in Stuttgart's Aspergstrasse.

Kujau never missed a chance to pull a fast one on eager collectors, cashing in on their craving for historical material, and was not above manufacturing his own certificates of authenticity. For instance, a note authenticating a helmet as being worn by Adolf Hitler in 1917 was signed by Rudolf Hess. Kujau 'aged' documents by soaking them in tea – a technique well-learned, for it was to stand him in good stead when the great Hitler Diaries Hoax was conceived.

Kujau moved on to the art world, specialising in the supposedly original works of Adolf Hitler himself. This business venture was to lead to his relationship with another keen collector of Nazi memorabilia, Fritz Stiefel. A wealthy owner of a local engineering works, Stiefel was an avid collector of militaria. Over a period of six years, Stiefel spent large sums of money at Kujau's store, for the shopkeeper seemed to have a never-ending supply of prized Nazi items. There were 160 drawings, oil paintings and watercolours by Hitler himself, as well as poems, notes of speeches and letters. Their manufacture kept Kujau very busy. Poor Stiefel never suspected a thing.

Kujau decided that Stiefel deserved a real gem as a reward for his faithful custom. He would be offered a diary written in the Führer's own hand. It was now 1980 and news of the startling find soon reached the ears of *Stern* journalist Gerd Heidemann, who was also obsessed with the Third Reich. Indeed, his wife had left him when their apartment was taken over by Heidemann's collection of war games and toy soldiers. The purchase of Hermann Göering's old motor yacht, plus a string of love affairs, had left Heidemann heavily in debt, and he clearly saw the financial potential of Hitler's diaries.

Heidemann opened negotiations with Fritz Stiefel who, although refusing to name Kujau, was nevertheless happy to act as an intermediary. When he told Heidemann there could be as many as twenty-six volumes of the diaries, a deal was swiftly struck. Heidemann never doubted the authenticity of the new discovery, and his enthusiasm seems to have become infective. Thomas Walde, editor of the historical department at *Stern*, became involved in the negotiations. As any experienced reporter would do, he had embarked on background research and learned, to his great excitement, that on April 20, 1945, close to the end of the Second World War, a courier aircraft had crashed near the Czechoslovakian border. The plane had been carrying Hitler's personal papers to his retreat near Berchtesgaden. Heidemann concluded the diaries must have been among them.

Heidemann and Walde decided not to approach *Stern*'s editor Peter Koch with their incredible news, because Koch had repeatedly told Heidemann to drop his Nazi obsessions. The two men instead took the first of Hitler's diaries and their background information to senior executives of Gruner and Jahr, the owners of *Stern*. A total payment was agreed. It was to be made in instalments as and when the diaries were received.

Kujau began his work in earnest. He compiled the diaries

drawing on his huge reference library. They bore a red wax seal of a German eagle. Heidemann was the go-between and no one at Gruner and Jahr was aware that from every instalment of cash they gave him to pay to Kujau, Heidemann creamed off a cut for himself. The collation of the Hitler Diaries took two years. Crafty Kujau – still going under the alias Herr Fischer – insisted he could only pass on the books when they arrived in his hands from his contacts in East Germany. Kujau, of course, needed a fair amount of time between 'consignments' to write them from scratch.

Each time Herr Fischer insisted it was getting increasingly difficult to obtain the diaries, he was offered more and more money. It was no wonder that by 1983, the year of publication, *Stern* had paid £2.5million. Yet it seems incredible now that *Stern* and a host of eminent academics could have been taken in by the often childlike nature of the entries. Here are some of them:

> *Ten thousand Communists meet in Berlin Sports Palace, pledge will fight fascism to last breath. Demonstration, many arrests. By Jove, we must stamp out the reds.*

> *Meet all the leaders of the stormtroopers in Bavaria, give them medals. They pledge lifelong loyalty to the Fuhrer, with tears in their eyes. What a splendid body of men!*

Of the famous bomb plot against Hitler by the German generals, Kujau recorded gleefully:

> *Ha! Ha! Isn't it laughable? These people were bunglers. This scum, these loafers and good-for-nothings!*

Three experts who examined the handwriting before publication of the diaries agreed it was indeed that of Adolf Hitler. The verdict from a police expert that some of the paper in the diaries was not in use until after the war was somehow lost in the excitement as *Stern*'s momentous publication day drew near. Meanwhile, *The Sunday Times* offered $3.25million for the English-language rights. *Newsweek* offered $3million for American rights. As its big day, May 3,1993, came closer, *Stern* demanded $4.25million from both publications. But it had overplayed its hand. The asking price was too much and, sadly for *Stern*, *Newsweek* had already secured enough of Hitler's Diaries to go ahead and publish anyway. *Stern* retaliated by changing its publication date to April 25. It wooed *The Sunday Times* back into a deal by accepting $1.2million for the diaries, and it was planned that the great British newspaper would announce its scoop on April 24.

Stern, Newsweek, Paris Match and *The Sunday Times* had now all bought the rights in good faith and started to publish extracts. In their trusting diaries 'scoops', they explained that Heidemann had managed to obtain the historic material from East German contacts. The papers had been discovered in a hayloft where they had supposedly been hidden after the plane crash.

One correspondent was certainly fooled by what he read in *The Sunday Times*. In its fellow newspaper *The Times*, Frank Johnson wrote: 'At least when *The Sunday Times* published its first extract, your present correspondent, a lifelong amateur student of mid-twentieth-century European politics, had no doubt that the diaries were genuine; they were so boring. Hitler exerts his fascination with his deeds rather than his prose. On that Sunday, those of us familiar with *Mein Kampf,* the *Collected Speeches* and *Table Talk,* knew that this was the authentic voice.'

However, new forensic evidence was being produced that appeared to prove the diaries were fake. Experts at the Federal Archives in Koblenz were finally allowed to examine some of the writings – and declared them obvious fakes, produced on post-war paper. One detail that clinched the fact that the diaries were fraudulent was the result of Kujau's overconfidence. Although he had checked facts and dates about Hitler before creating the diaries, he had ended up making a ludicrous blunder. When he bought the Gothic letters in Hong Kong to stick on the diary covers, he mixed up the letters 'A' and 'F'. Adorning the volumes were the imitation metal initials 'FH' instead of 'AH'!

Kujau and Heidemann were arrested in May 1983 for forging the historical scoop. Heidemann, his record as a star writer ruined forever, was charged with defrauding the magazine of £2.5 million, paid in instalments between January 1981 and April 1983. He maintained throughout the eleven-month trial in Hamburg that he had believed the diaries to be genuine, and told the court that

Kujau had also offered him an unpublished volume of Hitler's autobiography *Mein Kampf*. He said: 'When I heard the diaries were fakes, I wondered whether to shoot myself then or later.'

The extent of Heidemann's obsession with Hitler was revealed after German police raided his home. They took photographs of objects which had once adorned Hitler's desk, including a swastika on a red background which Heidemann said was Hitler's 'martyr's flag'. Heidemann also had in his bizarre collection a pair of underpants that had once belonged to Idi Amin.

Kujau was charged with forgery. He pleaded guilty and appeared to bask in the attention he attracted during the court proceedings. In his defence, Kujau said he at first intended to write only three diaries in return for a uniform worn by Hermann Göering which Heidemann had shown him. 'I had to have it,' he told the court. He said he had forged one Hitler diary in 1978 because it annoyed him that the Fuhrer had apparently left no records of his life.

Kujau claimed Heidemann had first told him he wanted to discuss the diaries so that they could be sent to Martin Bormann, Hitler's former deputy, in South America. He told the court: 'Heidemann said the diaries would help to rehabilitate Bormann but I began to doubt the story. Then in January 1982, Heidemann told me Bormann was seriously ill and I should hurry my work.' Kujau, who admitted the forgeries had earned him £415,000, said he was sure Heidemann had rumbled his trickery after he had practised writing the word 'helmet' in Hitler's script on a piece of paper which the journalist had spotted. But an indication of Heidemann's gullibility came soon afterwards in Kujau's evidence. Court observers couldn't help but snigger when they heard that Kujau had once provided the obsessed journalist with fake ashes of Hitler, supplied by a friend who worked in a crematorium.

The prosecution's case against the forgers filled 4,000 pages and involved sixty-two witnesses and eight experts. Eminent historian Lord Dacre of Glanton (otherwise known as Hugh Trevor-Roper, author of *The Last Days of Hitler*) who had at first declared the diaries to be genuine, had the courage to admit his mistake. He expressed this doubt at a conference in Hamburg in April 1983, called by increasingly concerned executives of *Stern*. He also said he had tried to warn *The Sunday Times.*

As the trial dragged on, fascinating evidence was heard, producing material as riveting as the fake diaries themselves. A German professor, Eberhard Jaeckel, had published some of Kujau's earlier work before the big scandal broke – and said that experts had seen through them straight away. *Sunday Times* writer Gita Sereny said she had been dispatched to Germany after a tip-off about the diaries, but had not been allowed to consult Jaeckel because of the extra cost it would have involved. The court also heard that *Stern* executives had given a page of the diaries to experts to study, without explaining why. The experts they had engaged did not know what they were looking for and passed the copies as authentic. This meant the ink and tea-soaked paper used for the diaries had not been tested until it was too late.

On July 8, 1985, Heidemann and Kujau were both found guilty. Heidemann was jailed for four years and eight months. His friends said he had been used as a scapegoat by *Stern*, whose weekly circulation dropped by 100,000 when the deception was announced. Kujau was sent to jail for four years and six months. His faithful girlfriend, Edith Lieblang, who was accused of spending part of the ill-gotten gains, was given an eight-month suspended sentence. No one found out where all the money went.

Everyone else involved in the great Hitler Diary Hoax suffered some sorry fate. Poor Thomas Walde was humiliated in court for being so gullible. *Stern* editors Peter Koch and Felix Schmidt were fired, even though they had been kept in the dark about the diary dealings. Gruner and Jahr's managing director Gerd Schulte-Hillen, who had inherited the diaries from his predecessor but had backed Heidemann, was given a severe dressing down but was allowed to stay on at *Stern*. Frank Giles, editor of *The Sunday Times*, retired to become 'editor emeritus'.

In *Selling Hitler*, the *Story of the Hitler Diaries*, author Richard Harris tells how Rupert Murdoch, owner of *The Sunday Times*, justified Giles's new title: 'It's Latin. The 'e' means you're out and 'meritus' means you deserve it!' But perhaps Harris best sums up the whole scam with the following anecdote. Murdoch, who ordered *The Sunday Times* to continue printing even when told Lord Dacre was sounding the alarm, did so with the words: 'After all, we're in the entertainment business!'